JOURNAL OF COGNITIVE PSYCHOLOGY, 2012, 24 (1), 1–5

Information processing, affect, and psychopathology: A Festschrift for Michael W. Eysenck

Nazanin Derakshan[1] and Ernst H. W. Koster[2]

[1]Birkbeck University of London, UK
[2]Ghent University, Belgium

The past few decades has witnessed an explosion of research into the impact of emotions (both negative and positive) on cognition, with a special emphasis on the role of individual differences and personality factors that are now strongly believed to modulate this relationship. An accumulating wealth of evidence is suggesting that any explanation for such individual differences in emotional experience requires the integration of biological (genetic, neuropsychological, endocrine), personality, and cognitive and behavioural factors. This view makes perfect sense, and it owes much of its validity to the work of several pioneering researchers who, through their contributions, have unravelled the dynamics amongst these interrelated factors with increasing precision. Without question, the pioneering work of Professor Michael Eysenck has played a leading and most inspirational role in advancing the field of cognition and emotion in a number of important ways.

Keywords: Affect; Festschrift; Information processing; Michael W. Eysenck; Psychopathology.

Michael Eysenck's work covers many different facets of personality, cognition, and emotion. In his career, he has published outstanding research on the cognitive processes involved in anxiety. To celebrate Michael Eysenck's significant contributions to the study of cognition in psychopathology, and the importance of integrative work in this area, this Special Issue will highlight a number of contributions that centre around the cognitive, neuroscientific, and psychobiological approaches to emotional information processing in psychopathology. In line with Michael Eysenck's theoretical ideas, information processing and attentional control are dominant themes across a diversity of interesting specific studies and theoretical models. We start with a brief overview of Michael Eysenck's career and will then provide an outline of the Special Issue.

CAREER HIGHLIGHTS

Michael Eysenck was born in 1944 in London (UK), son of the famous British psychologist Hans Eysenck. In 1965, Michael Eysenck received his BA in psychology with first class honours from UCL to further pursue a career in cognitive psychology, and earned his PhD on the topic of "conditions modifying memory: The von Restdorff and the 'release' effect". He was appointed as lecturer at Birkbeck College University of London where he remained to earn the title of Reader in Psychology. In the late 1970s, Michael Eysenck published the first of many textbooks: *Human Memory: Theory, Research and Individual Differences*. His research in the 1970s played a critical role in advancing major theories on memory in relation to individual differences in

Correspondence should be addressed to Nazanin Derakshan, Department of Psychological Sciences, Birkbeck University of London, Malet Street, London WC1E 7HX, UK. E-mail: n.derakhshan@bbk.ac.uk extraversion (Eysenck, 1976) and also in relation to arousal (Eysenck, 1977); such theories which are still influential to this day (see Baddeley, Eysenck, & Anderson, 2009). It is important to note that at this time it was clear that Michael Eysenck's research was not bound to singular phenomena and perspectives. Instead his research was a reflection of his remarkable talent in explaining and relating psychological phenomena with remarkable eloquence and insight. The breadth of these phenomena ensured that many of the ideas he postulated were applied in a number of different disciplines within psychology.

In the 1980s new major achievements followed. Just to name a few, the monograph on attention and arousal published in 1982 had a major impact on the relation between anxiety and performance. Moreover, his handbook of cognitive psychology (first–sixth editions, 1984–2011) became an important key textbook for anyone (including undergraduate as well as graduate students and academics alike) studying cognitive psychology. In the 1980s, Michael Eysenck also published a series of articles on the influence of (trait) anxiety on cognitive functioning. This work ultimately led to two research monographs (*Anxiety: A Cognitive Perspective*, 1992; and *Anxiety and Cognition: A Unified Theory*, 1997) outlining a cognitive perspective on anxiety and its disorders that are to this day considered hallmark cognitive theories on anxiety. In 1987, Michael Eysenck moved to Royal Holloway University of London to take up a full professorship; he remained there for the rest of his research career.

In subsequent years, Michael Eysenck continued to inspire the field of anxiety and cognition by applying his knowledge of cognitive psychology to further delineate many of the cognitive processing characteristics of anxiety, which originated at the level of memory and attention but also now included inferences and interpretations due to innovative and careful studies. One important feature of his studies was that they did not just provide new empirical data to better understand the detrimental effects of anxiety on cognition. Instead, the empirical work was embedded in a clear theory-driven and systematic approach to understand cognitive processes across a range of personality features where the empirical data often gave rise to new and most influential theoretical insights. One of the major theoretical achievements, published in 1992, was represented in an article coauthored by Manuel Calvo on "Anxiety and Cognitive Performance: The

Processing Efficiency Theory". This theory proposed that it makes sense to differentiate between cognitive effectiveness and cognitive efficiency, as these processes could be differentially affected by personality traits and/or certain conditions. This distinction had a major impact on the field and lay the foundations for the more recently published Attentional Control Theory (Eysenck, Derakshan, Santos, & Calvo, 2007), a major development of Processing Efficiency Theory, that provided a more detailed account of anxiety-related influences on working memory functions and cognitive performance. Indeed, this theory has seen a substantial increasing level of support from recent cognitive neuroscience work. Both of these theoretical papers are of profound influence in the current literature on anxiety and cognition and are highly cited.

Next to these influential papers, Michael Eysenck has shown a strong dedication to translating emerging findings from the cognitive psychology literature into both undergraduate as well as graduate textbooks. To this day Michael Eysenck has either sole-authored or coauthored 42 textbooks, many of which have been translated into different languages. These textbooks have been very successful due to Michael Eysenck's ability to explain sophisticated material in an accessible and engaging manner without reverting to simplification. The elegance and clarity of his writing has undoubtedly impressed anyone who has read his books, chapters, or articles.

In addition to his scientific writings, Michael Eysenck has also generously contributed to the advancement of cognitive psychology in numerous ways. He was one of the founding members of the European Society of Cognitive Psychology and has served as president for the International Society for Stress and Anxiety Research. He also carried several editorial duties. He served as founding editor for the *European Journal of Cognitive Psychology* (now the *Journal of Cognitive Psychology*), and has served on editorial boards of several major journals in the field of cognitive-experimental psychology. He was an often-invited speaker at many major international conferences and has supervised numerous students to successfully complete their PhD.

As of 2009 he is Professor Emeritus at Royal Holloway, University of London and he currently also holds a position as Professorial Fellow at Roehampton University.

THE SPECIAL ISSUE

The special issue consists of a collection of empirical papers as well as a number of reviews on cognition, emotion, and psychopathology. These papers have been written by a number of eminent scholars who helped transform the field of cognition and emotion in their own right, including, but not restricted to collaborators and former students of Michael Eysenck. The Special Issue provides a state-of-the-art update on current thinking about information processing in relation to emotion and psychopathology. Each contribution can be related directly to the work initiated by Michael Eysenck and in this way underscores the legacy of this eminent scholar.

The papers are on the broad topic of information processing of emotional information in relation to individual differences in anxiety and depression. This area of research has witnessed a tremendous growth in the past 40 years. Where this area arose during the cognitive revolution in the 1960s, it took more than a decade before researchers began systematically investigating the role of emotional factors, such as valence and arousal on information processing and considered the role of individual differences. Currently, this is one of the most exciting areas in experimental psychopathology research.

The Special Issue can be divided into three main sections, each of which has profited from the seminal studies of Michael Eysenck: (1) memory processes, (2) attentional processes, and (3) interpretation bias.

The section on memory is comprised of a paper on the role of working memory and affect authored by Baddeley, Banse, Huang, and Page (this issue, 2012). This paper presents two experiments aimed at examining a suitable methodology to test some of the core predictions of the influence of mood on working memory processes involved in hedonic judgements as proposed by Baddeley (2007). The authors advocate the use of a task requiring affective judgements of "neutral" stimuli as a way to examine the influence of negative and positive mood on working memory. The authors observed that negative mood compared with positive mood influenced subsequent hedonic judgements.

In the section on attentional processes, a first paper by Öhman, Soares, Juth, Lindstrom, and Esteves (2012) provides a review on the mechanisms underlying attentive processing of threat within an evolutionary framework. Their data suggests that attentive processing is shaped by the demands that adaptive responding requires for certain classes of stimuli. This paper builds on their influential idea that cognitive processing of threat is a hard-wired mechanism that has evolved through evolutionary influences related to the adaptive value of prompt detection and responding to threat (Öhman & Mineka, 2001). As recent years have seen several arguments against the idea that threat processing is automatic and encapsulated from higher order cognitive influences (e.g., Pessoa & Adolphs, 2010), the new paper by Öhman et al. is likely to revitalise this debate.

A second paper in this section represents another interesting advancement in the area of attentional bias for emotional information and individual differences. The extensive literature in this area typically only focuses on attentional bias for emotional information in relation to negative affect (e.g., anxiety and depression). Grafton, Watkins, and MacLeod (2012) examine the influence of both negative and positive affectivity on an interesting new modification of the attentional probe task that allows the separation of cognitive processes related to attentional engagement and disengagement. They find that anxiety-related negative affectivity is characterised by an increase in attentional preference for negative relative to positive information both at the level of facilitated attentional engagement with, and impaired attentional disengagement from, such information. Attenuated depression-related positive affectivity instead is characterised by reduced attentional preference for negative information relative to positive information, and this bias is due to enhanced attentional disengagement from such information. This dissociation between the attentional characteristics of negative and positive affect helps to explain the pattern of attentional bias in anxiety and depression.

Two papers have complemented the use of cognitive–experimental attentional tasks with eye-movement methodology to obtain a more complete picture of the time course of threat processing. Both studies have examined the processing of emotional facial expressions in relation to anxiety vulnerability. A first study by Reinholt-Dunne et al. (2012) used the antisaccade task which is an increasingly popular task to examine the inhibition of reflexive saccades to appearing peripheral cues (see Derakshan & Eysenck, 2009). This study found that high anxious individuals had more difficulty to shift gaze away from threatening compared with neutral facial expressions. The study by Berggren, Koster, and Derakshan (2012) also examined behavioural responding as well as eye movements. They investigated whether processing of emotional facial expressions was dependent on cognitive load using a visual search paradigm, which provides a test of the theoretical idea that threat is processed in an "automatic" way. They found that manual responding indicated emotional information captured attention more strongly than neutral information on trials where the crowd had a different emotional valence than the targets. The eye movement data showed that this effect was caused by delayed target processing efficiency in such trials. Additionally, trait anxiety did not influence threat processing, but costs were observed under cognitive load that were not present for nonanxious participants. These results suggest that cognitive load mainly interfered with task performance but not with emotion processing. Finally, this section ends with a paper by Calvo, Gutiérrez, and Fernández-Martín (2012), who investigated several features of threat processing. They examined whether interference of threatening words differed as a function of foveal versus parafoveal presentation of these words in relation to anxiety levels in two experiments. Their results suggest that anxious individuals do not show enhanced preattentive processing of threatening words but that they have reduced inhibitory control over threat processing when threat is attended.

The section on interpretive processing in psychopathology starts with a review paper by Mathews (2012) who describes how the field of interpretive bias research has evolved from the initial groundbreaking studies of Michael Eysenck to the more recent work that examines whether interpretive bias plays a causal role in anxiety vulnerability. This review paper describes in depth the different ways to investigate and modify interpretive bias. Moreover, a clear overview is provided about both the theoretical and clinical application of such innovative procedures.

Recent work on genetic vulnerability to anxiety and depression has linked genes that are thought to be related to these disorders to emotion-specific biases in information processing. Particularly, it has been shown that the "serotonin transporter gene" (5-HTT gene) plays an important role in the susceptibility for social signals

(Homberg & Lesch, 2011). In a groundbreaking paper, Fox and Standage (2012) show that a negative interpretive bias is related to variations in this serotonin transporter gene. This study contributes to a growing literature that helps to explain the ways in which genes heighten susceptibility to anxiety and depression.

Collectively, these papers showcase the exciting developments in the field of information processing, affect, and psychopathology. Clearly, this field will continue to profit from the seminal work of Michael Eysenck, who was among the first to link the study of cognitive processes to individual differences, affect, and psychopathology.

REFERENCES

Baddeley, A. D. (2007). *Working memory, thought and action.* Oxford, UK: Oxford University Press.

Baddeley, A. D., Banse, R., Huang, Y, & Page, M. (2012). Working memory and emotion: Detecting the hedonic detector. *Journal of Cognitive Psychology, 24*(1), 6–16.

Baddeley, A. D., Eysenck, M. W., & Anderson, M. C. (2009). *Memory.* Hove, UK: Psychology Press.

Berggren, N., Koster, E. H. W., & Derakshan, N. (2012). The effect of cognitive load in emotional attention and trait anxiety: An eye-movement study. *Journal of Cognitive Psychology, 24*(1), 79–91.

Calvo, M. G., Gutiérrez, A., & Fernández-Martín, A. (2012). Anxiety and deficient inhibition of threat distractors: Spatial attention span and time course. *Journal of Cognitive Psychology, 24*(1), 66–78.

Derakshan, N., & Eysenck, M. W. (2009). Anxiety, processing efficiency, and cognitive performance: New developments from Attentional Control Theory. *European Psychologist, 14*, 168–176.

Eysenck, M. W. (1976). Extraversion, verbal learning, and memory. *Psychological Bulletin, 83*, 75–90.

Eysenck, M. W. (1977). Arousal, learning, and memory. *Psychological Bulletin, 83*, 389–404.

Eysenck, M. W., Derakshan, N., Santos, R., & Calvo, M. G. (2007). Anxiety and cognitive performance: Attentional control theory. *Emotion, 7*, 336–353.

Fox, E., & Standage, H. (2012). Variation on the serotonin transporter gene and bias in the interpretation of ambiguity. *Journal of Cognitive Psychology, 24*(1), 106–114.

Grafton, B., Watkins, E., & MacLeod, C. (2012). The ups and downs of cognitive bias: Dissociating the attentional characteristics of positive and negative affectivity. *Journal of Cognitive Psychology, 24*(1), 33–53.

Homberg, J. R., & Lesch, K.-P. (2011). Looking at the bright side of serotonin transporter gene variation. *Biological Psychiatry, 69*, 510–512.

Mathews, A. (2012). Effects of modifying the interpretation of emotional ambiguity. *Journal of Cognitive Psychology, 24*(1), 92–105.

Öhman, A., & Mineka, S. (2001). Fears, phobias, and preparedness: Toward an evolved module of fear and fear learning. *Psychological Review, 108*, 483–522.

Öhman, A., Soares, S. C., Juth, P., Lindstrom, B. R., & Esteves, F. (2012). Evolutionary derived modulations of attention to two common fear stimuli: Serpents and hostile humans. *Journal of Cognitive Psychology, 24*(1), 17–32.

Pessoa, L., & Adolphs, R. (2010). Emotion processing and the amygdala: From a "low road" to "many roads" of evaluating biological significance. *Nature Reviews Neuroscience, 11*, 773–783.

Reinholdt-Dunne, M. L., Mogg, K., Benson, V., Bradley, B. P., Hardin, M. G., Liversedge, S. P., et al. (2012). Anxiety and selective attention to angry faces: An antisaccade study. *Journal of Cognitive Psychology, 24*(1), 54–65.

JOURNAL OF COGNITIVE PSYCHOLOGY, 2012, 24 (1), 6–16

Working memory and emotion: Detecting the hedonic detector

Alan Baddeley[1], Rainer Banse[2], Yang-Ming Huang[3], and Mike Page[4]

[1]Department of Psychology, University of York, UK
[2]Department of Psychology, University of Bonn, Germany
[3]Department of Psychology, Fu Jen Catholic University, Taipe, Taiwan
[4]School of Psychology, University of Hertfordshire, UK

In an attempt to account for the impact of emotion on cognition, Baddeley (2007) proposed the existence of a hedonic detection system. Malfunctioning of this system was assumed to play a crucial role in depression. Exploring this hypothesis requires a simple and rapid way of assessing the neutral point of proposed hedonic detector. We describe two experiments that aim to develop such a method of investigating this system. Both are based on the assumption that the hedonic judgement of simple stimuli will be influenced by the valence of an induced mood. Experiment 1 showed that a negative mood leads to the more negative evaluation of words than the positive mood. Experiment 2 also includes a neutral condition and the evaluation of words, pictures, and faces. In each case the negative mood led to lower hedonic ratings, whereas no difference was found between neutral and positive moods. Implications for further investigating the hypothetical hedonic detector are discussed.

Keywords: Depression; Emotion; Hedonic detector; Mood; Working memory.

Michael Eysenck and the first author (AB) share a long-standing interest in the impact of emotion on cognition, in Michael's case, theoretically driven and based on extensive evidence, in AB's case sporadic and often divorced from theory, beginning as it did with an attempt to study a quite different issue, the impact of nitrogen narcosis on the capacity of divers to function at depth.

The study in question was an attempt to extend a US Navy experiment showing a modest decline in manual dexterity when divers in a dry chamber were exposed to pressures equivalent to a depth of 30 metres of water (Kiessling & Maag, 1962). The study in question (Baddeley, 1966) simply carried out the same experiment, with the exception that it was conducted both in the open Mediterranean, and in a dry pressure chamber. A substantial interaction occurred, with the 8% decrement shown at pressure under dry conditions increasing to a decrement of 49% underwater. Later studies replicated this broad finding when nonprofessional divers were operating under open sea conditions, but not when diving from the shore, suggesting an important role for anxiety (Baddeley, de Figueredo, Hawkswell-Curtis, & Williams, 1968; Baddeley & Flemming, 1967). The importance of anxiety to this result was further established under shore-based but comparatively threatening conditions off the coast of Scotland (Davis, Osborne, Baddeley, & Graham, 1972).

Correspondence should be addressed to A. Baddeley, Department of Psychology, University of York, Heslington, York YO10 5DD, UK. E-mail: ab50@york.ac.uk

We are grateful to Hannah Anstey, Gemma Knight, Nicola Pilkington, and Laura Snaith for their enthusiastic contribution to running Experiment 1, and to Barry Hannon for his help on Experiment 2.

This led to a series of studies investigating the role of anxiety in rather dryer conditions, including skydiving and preparing to give a talk at the MRC Applied Psychology Unit in Cambridge, events that, perhaps surprisingly, seemed to be equally anxiety-provoking (Idzikowski & Baddeley, 1983, 1987). We observed effects of anxiety, but they tended to be small. Given the logistic difficulty of collecting data in such environments (frequent disruption by weather in one case, and the limited number of speakers in the other), it proved difficult to carry out the kind of sustained programme necessary to develop a theoretical understanding of the underlying processes.

Michael Eysenck, however, avoided these limitations by capitalising on the individual differences in susceptibility to anxiety found within a normal population of undergraduate students, gradually building up an understanding of the probable mechanism whereby anxiety interferes with performance, together with the strategies that people adopt to counter these limitations. He showed that people are certainly susceptible to the impact of anxiety, but for many and for much of the time, it is possible to withstand these effects, using a range of strategies to resist the potential attentional disruption from threatening stimuli (Derekshan & Eysenck, 1998; Eysenck & Calvo, 1992).

Another approach to the study of anxiety is to focus on people who consistently fail to make such adaptations, resulting in the kind of emotional disorder that is the province of clinical psychology. This approach was taken by a group of experienced clinicians with an interest in cognitive psychology at the MRC Applied Psychology Unit in Cambridge, a group that focused on studies of anxiety and depression with considerable success, reflected by setting up a new journal, *Cognition and Emotion*, and producing two highly influential editions of a book applying cognitive psychology to emotional disorders (Williams, Watts, MacLeod, & Mathews, 1988, 1997).

This in turn led to a belated attempt by AB to incorporate such developments within the multi-component working memory model (Baddeley, 2007).

The initial working memory model had three components, an attentionally limited control system, the *central executive*, aided by two subsystems, the *phonological loop* and the *visuospatial sketchpad*. The loop was capable of storing and manipulating verbal and potentially other audi-tory material, and the sketchpad performed a similar service for material processed visually or spatially. Michael Eysenck's work had provided strong evidence for what he termed the *processing efficiency hypothesis* (Eysenck & Calvo, 1992). Evolution has provided us with a mechanism whereby threatening stimuli break through normal attentional control to serve as a timely warning. Heightened level of anxiety increases the potency of such stimuli, a mechanism that is valuable if the anxiety is prompted by genuine increase in level of danger, but which can be disruptive in chronically anxious individuals, for whom the threshold of threat is set at an unreasonably low level, allowing constant disruption of normal cognitive processing, and reduced processing efficiency.

A broadly similar model has been developed in the study of patients with anxiety disorder, by Williams et al. (1997), and by Mogg and Bradley (1998). Patients with anxiety disorders are assumed to have a particularly low threshold for the detection of threat, leading both to excessive anxiety feelings and potentially to disruption of cognitive processing.

Disruption of cognition by anxiety fits relatively easily within the initial model of working memory if one assumes some kind of attentional filter that protects the central executive from unnecessary disruption. As Derakshan and Eysenck (1998) demonstrate, anxious people are sometimes able to adopt strategies such as subvocalisation (reflecting the phonological loop) or regressive eye movements (reflecting visuospatial sketchpad) that are able to help protect executive processes from disruption.

Baddeley (2007) initially hoped to apply a similar model to the effects of depression on cognition. However, this proved surprisingly difficult. Even though anxiety and depression often co-occur, there are a number of major differences between the nature of cognitive disruption shown by the two, as illustrated in Table 1.

As already described, anxiety has its major effect by disrupting attentional control, something that can occur, even for stimuli that are below the level of conscious awareness, whereas there is little evidence for this in the case of depression. Both can disrupt the capacity to learn, but for different reasons. Anxiety may disrupt attentional focus, whereas depression appears to lead to apathy and lack of initiative which in turn limits the development and use of optimal strategies. Depression may have a marked effect on

TABLE 1
A comparison between the affects on cognition of anxiety and depression

Fear and anxiety	Depression
Major preattentional and attentional disruption of cognition	Weaker purely postattentional effects
Effect on learning principally due to distraction	Disruption of learning attributable to lack of initiative
Little evidence of mood-congruent disruption of retrieval	Major mood-congruency
Evolutionary context clear	Evolutionary context controversial

retrieval, via mood-dependency, with depressed patients tending to recall negative memories, whereas no equivalent effect occurs for anxiety. Finally, the evolutionary value of anxiety is obvious; it is potentially highly valuable to have a system that interrupts when a major threat occurs. On the other hand, it is far from simple to know in what way depression might be useful, although there are many speculations on the issue (see Baddeley, 2007, Chap. 15, for further discussion).

In an attempt to account for these differences within a broad working memory framework, Baddeley (2007) proposed the following: Whereas anxiety reflects a malfunctioning of an alerting system responsible for detecting danger, depression reflects the malfunction of a motivational/choice system. The working memory framework, and indeed cognitive psychology in general, is principally concerned with the question of how behaviour is controlled. It neglects the question of "why" we act; why do we do anything? An answer to this very basic question was offered by Hume (1739/1978), who proposed that reason is controlled by "the passions", by which he did not mean the sort of extreme emotional response that today we think of as reflecting passion, but also "certain calm desires, more known by their effects than by their immediate feelings or sensation" (p. 407). We thus steer ourselves through the world by maximising the positive and minimising the negative consequences of our actions.

This view has elements in common with Damasio's (1998) *somatic marker hypothesis*. This assumes the capacity to use positive and negative features of the environment as positive "beacons of incentive" or negative "alarm bells". Damasio was led to this conclusion by studying patients with damage to certain areas of the frontal lobes who did not appear to be cognitively impaired, and yet lived chaotic lives because of their incapacity to make wise decisions. Such decisions are assumed by Damasio to be based on the capacity to sense the positive and negative nature of potential outcomes. Damasio assumes that such markers are physiologically based, but are reflected as feelings through the operation of working memory, although the exact nature of this link is not discussed.

In an attempt provide such a link, Baddeley (2007) suggested the need to assume some form of hedonic detection system, capable of assessing stimuli so as to allow optimum actions to be chosen. It was suggested that this system would require both temporary storage and the capacity to manipulate such stored hedonic information, which in turn implies the involvement of working memory. It was suggested that the system would need the following characteristics.

1. The hedonic detection system would have a neutral point, with readings above that point reflecting a positive and below it a negative valence.
2. Its sensitivity and stability would be important if there were to be consistency of action over time.
3. If it is to be used in complex situations, then it may need to average across a number of features of each potential action, and this turn will require some form of memory storage.
4. The system must be able to discriminate between the averaged hedonic value of two or more such potential actions.
5. Such manipulation and judgement of hedonic information seems likely to depend on working memory in general and the central executive in particular.

It was suggested that depression might reflect an inappropriate setting of the neutral point of the hedonic detection system, with the result that previously neutral stimuli appear negative, and negative options become even more negative (Baddeley, 2007). It was further suggested that a number of factors are capable of influencing this neutral point. These include genetic factors such as temperament, gloomy versus happy-go-lucky, and it seems likely that the neutral point may also be influenced pharmacologically, by means of antidepressants. It is also assumed that the neutral point can be influenced by events, either acutely or when for example your favourite football team loses a game, or chronically, for instance following a family bereavement. A long-term negative change in the hedonic neutral point could explain the tendency for depressed patients to view the world negatively and to retrieve evermore negative memories, hence deepening the depression. An important component of the cognitive treatment of depression does of course involve helping the patient to break out of this cycle. This hypothesis has a final advantage in that it provides an explanation of why evolutionary pressures have not removed the susceptibility to depression. If it is indeed a malfunction of an essential decision-making mechanism, the system's removal would have drastic consequences for survival.

Even if one accepts this view as a plausible hypothesis, however, the question arises as to how to take it further. One of the assumptions underpinning the hedonic detector hypothesis is that emotional tone or mood will influence the neutral point, with the result that a negative mood will result in a previously neutral event being perceived as negative. For example, Isen, Shalker, Clark, and Karp (1978) found that giving customers a small gift led to their giving a more positive subsequent rating of unrelated goods. Krosnick, Betz, Jussin, and Lynn (1992) required participants to make hedonic judgements about people performing neutral activities; they found that negative emotional primes led to lower hedonic ratings of the activities, even when the priming stimuli were masked. Similar effects have also been found when judging words (Fazio, 1986). Such effects are found even when the priming stimuli comprised meaningless items such as nonwords and irregular shapes that had previously been rated as positive or negative, with negative items facilitating an avoidance response whereas pleasant items facilitated approach responses (Duckwork, Bargh, Garcia, & Chaiken, 2002).

This study aimed to build on the work by developing a simple method that would allow multiple observations within a single session. We might for example wish to test the durability of an induced emotion or mood as a function of elapsed time or potential interference, or to explore the interaction of induced mood with executive processing. It seemed possible that a very simple task such as judging the pleasantness of a series of relatively neutral stimuli might provide such a measure. In order to investigate the potential sensitivity we designed two studies using well-established methods of mood induction. In each case we used a mood rating scale to determine whether the method had been successful. This has the disadvantage that participants may have responded to the demand characteristics of the situation. Without self-report, however, a negative result would be hard to interpret. More implicit mood induction techniques such as giving an unexpected present (Isen, 1970), relying on weather conditions (Schwarz & Clore, 1983), or inducing a positive mood by presenting easy tasks (Estrada, Isen, & Young, 1994) do not readily allow the observations of both positive and negative moods within the same session we thought would be necessary to adequately test our proposed task. Masked primes (Krosnik et al., 1992) was another possibility, but this introduces additional methodological complexity in setting an appropriate masking threshold. We decided therefore to use a range of well-established methods of mood-induction, leaving until later the further refinement of method, should our simple judgement task prove sensitive. We return to this issue in the Discussion.

Our experiments therefore aimed to treat the hypothetical hedonic detector as if it were a perceptual system by simply asking our participants to make judgements under positive or negative induced moods. In order to ensure generality, we used two different methods of mood induction, in each case followed by the presentation of a series of words whose pleasantness must be judged. By using mildly positive, neutral, and mildly negative words we are able to judge whether any effects observed operate only on neutral items, or whether items across a somewhat broader range of hedonic valences are influenced.

EXPERIMENT 1

Method

Participants

A total of 80 undergraduate students (mean age 20.58 years) were tested. Fifty of these were female. On entering the study, each participant was required to complete the Beck Depression Inventory (Beck, Ward, Mendelson, Mock, & Erbaugh, 1961). For ethical reasons, three further participants who had scored above 16, indicating mild mood disturbance, were exposed only to positive mood induction, and were excluded from the study.

Evaluation words

These comprised 60 words selected from the Affective Norms for English Words (ANEW database) which rates words from 1 ("negative") to 9 ("positive"). The mildly negative words were rated between 4.02 and 5.08, (e.g., *skull*, *dirt*), the neutral between 5.14 and 5.34 (*kettle*, *finger*), and the mildly positive ranged from 5.61 to 6.57 (*jelly*, *whistle*). We chose to avoid extremely negative or positive words because of the observation that less extreme stimuli are more likely to be influenced by mood (Isen & Shalker, 1982).

Mood induction

Participants were explicitly informed that the study involved a comparison between methods that aimed to induce different moods and that these would be followed by questionnaires. They were informed that they could withdraw at any time and signed a consent form.

Two methods of inducing mood were included, with half the participants using each. They were:

The Velten Mood Induction Procedure (MIP). We used a total of 60 statements, of which half were positive and half were negative, which participants were required to read and then repeat in an empathic way. Positive mood was induced by requiring statements such as "I feel cheerful and lively", whereas a typical negative statement might be "People annoy me; I wish I could be by myself". Half the participants started with the positive statements and half with the negative (Velten, 1968).

Induction by Music and Pictures (MAP). This combined two methods that had previously been used for mood induction, music and pictures. We selected two pieces of music that had been successfully used by Etzel, Johnsen, Dickerson, Tranel, and Adolphs (2006), who found that the music induced physiological effects consistent with the two emotions, and Johnsen (2004) produced evidence confirming that they induced appropriate subjective experiences of happiness or sadness. The pieces in question were "Mammy", involving a quick rhythm and melody,

and a sad piece from "Brothers", which involved a slower tempo. The music was combined with emotionally toned pictures from the International Affective Picture System (IAPS) database (Lang, Bradley, & Cuthbert, 2005). This set of pictures was rated on a number of dimensions by Mikels et al. (2005). This allowed us to exclude for ethical reasons any pictures that were included in the top 50 when rated for disgust. We also excluded any items that showed pronounced sex differences or that appeared to have a cultural basis, for example piles of dollar bills. In order to match the rate of presentation to the slower tempo of sad music we elected to show negative images for 8 s each, and positive for 5 s.

Music and pictures were combined to provide two happy and two sad presentation sets. In each of the sad sets, 11 different pictures were displayed for 8 s each, and then repeated in a random order. The tempo of the happy sets was faster with 18 pictures each being shown for 5 s, and then repeated. Both the happy and sad sets therefore lasted approximately 3 min.

Mood checklist

Participants rated their current mood on a scale between 0 ("not at all") and 6 ("very much"), on each of 10 mood adjectives. Three were positive, namely happy, content, and hopeful; three were negative, namely depressed, gloomy, and sad; and the remaining four were filler items relating to more mixed emotions of which two were negative, namely guilty and angry, and two were positive, namely lively and cheerful. The mood checklist was administered on arrival and was used throughout the experiment to monitor the effectiveness of the induction procedures. The three positive and three negative ratings were combined by subtracting mean negative from mean positive scores. Hence, a positive overall rating would reflect an overall positive mood.

Word evaluation task

This involved the presentation of each word for 1 s, after which participants had to evaluate that word on a scale ranging between 1 ("very negative") and 8 ("very positive"), responding by pressing the numbers on the top of the computer keyboard. The range was selected so as to avoid a mid point, and a possible strategy of pressing the neutral point when in doubt.

Procedure

After completing a consent form and the Beck Depression Inventory, participants completed the initial mood adjective checklist to assess their mood on entering the study. Participants were then practiced on the evaluation task, judging six words, using the 8-point scale displayed at the bottom of the computer screen.

This was then followed by the first mood induction procedure, with half of the group randomly assigned to the Velten and half to the music and pictures (MAP) procedures. In each case, half began with negative and half with positive induction. Immediately after mood induction, participants filled out a second mood checklist, before proceeding to the initial word evaluation, after which a third assessment of mood was made using the checklist, thereby completing the first half of the experiment.

Before proceeding to the second mood induction, participants were given a filler task involving completion of a series of six mazes selected from an online database at yahoo.com. These had been found to be sufficiently difficult to keep participants occupied for 2 min, during which it was hoped that the previously induced mood would tend to dissipate. The filler task was then followed by the second mood induction procedure, which always involved the opposite mood to that induced in the first part. The efficacy of this second induction was then evaluated, again using the adjective checklist, before requiring evaluation of the next 30 words, followed by a fifth mood checklist, included to assess any change in mood during the word evaluation task.

Results

Mood induction

Data were analysed using a mixed ANOVA. Between-subject variables were method of mood induction (Velten or MAP) and test order (positive first or negative first). Within-subject factors were evaluation valence (positive or negative) and time of evaluation (before or after mood induction).

The order of presentation of positive and negative mood induction did not influence ratings, either as a main effect or an interaction, and hence the two orders were combined for further analysis. As Figure 1 suggests, there was a main effect of induction valence, $F(1, 76) = 150.34$, $p < .001$, with mean ratings of 1.36, $SE = 0.22$ after negative, and of 3.46, $SE = 0.15$ after positive induction, and a significant interaction between induction valence and subsequent mood rating, $F(1, 76) = 69.70$, $p < .001$. There was a main effect of type of induction, $F(1, 76) = 7.89$, $p < .001$, with the MAP condition leading to lower levels of negative mood than did the Velten technique. As Figure 1 suggests, there is also an effect of mood check position with the induced mood effect tending to be less marked following the word evaluation task, $F(1, 76) = 24.27$ $p < .001$.

To summarise, we appear to have been successful in manipulating mood, with effects being particularly marked in the case of the MAP procedure and negative mood.

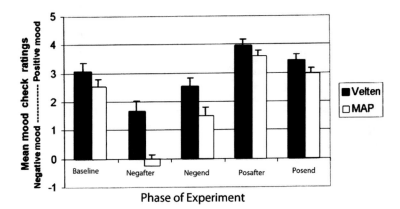

Figure 1.   Mean mood checklist ratings across the phases of Experiment 1.

Word evaluation

There was no significant effect of order of presentation either as a main effect or an interaction, hence both orders were combined. The results are shown in Figure 2. Unlike the mood induction procedure there was no effect of method of induction, $F(1, 76) = 1.24$, $p > .05$. There was, as expected, a substantial effect of word type, with ratings of negative words significantly lower than neutral, $F(1, 76) = 264.86$, $p < .001$, whereas positive words were given significantly higher ratings, $F(1, 76) = 280.68$, $p < .001$. This result of course simply reflects the fact that the words were selected appropriately. A crucial prediction of our hypothesis is that mood evaluation should influence the ratings of the words, and this was indeed the case, $F(1, 76) = 8.29$, $p < .01$, with words rated significantly more positively after positive than negative mood induction.

Discussion

Both of our mood induction procedures were effective in inducing reliably different moods, with the negative induction having a particularly marked effect when compared to the relatively positive pretest mood of our participants. There is also a clear tendency, particularly for the negative mood, to persist, although somewhat weakened, during the word evaluation session, suggesting that it is reasonable to include evaluations for the whole of the sequence of words judged.

Our word evaluation scale was clearly effective in separating out the words rated as positive from those rated as neutral or negative, even though these did not reflect items from the extreme end of the scale. Crucially, our mood induction procedures were able to significantly influence the ratings of words at all three levels, indicating an influence that operated throughout the range sampled, and was not limited to relatively neutral items. Although reliable, the mood induction effects are small compared to the magnitude of difference between the positive and negatively selected items, raising the question of its reliability. The obvious test of this issue is by replication.

Although Experiment 1 showed a clear effect of induced mood on subsequent word judgement, it has a major limitation. We detected a difference between a positive and negative mood, but in the absence of a neutral baseline we are unable to detect whether this is principally a result of the negative mood, of the positive mood or of both. The second experiment aimed to control for this by including a third, neutral condition. This presented a problem in the case of induction by music, since it is suggested that music is never emotionally neutral (Krumhansl, 1997). We therefore chose to use the Velten method of mood induction. In order to further increase the generality of our results, we extended the judgement process to three types of material: words as in Experiment 1, together with pictures and faces. In order to reduce complexity, in each case we chose test items that were rated as neutral. Hence, the design was equivalent to Experiment 1, except that only one method of mood induction was used, and combined with three types of stimulus material, rather than with three levels of rated emotionality.

EXPERIMENT 2

Method

Participants

Eighteen participants (14 female) participated in this study. All participants were students at the University of York.

Design

This experiment used a 3×3 repeated measures design. The first within-subject factor was the mood induced (positive, neutral, and or negative). The order of mood induction was counterbalanced between participants. The

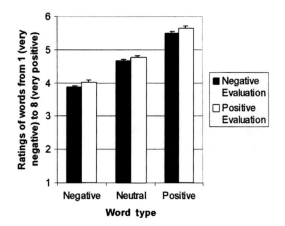

Figure 2. Mean hedonic ratings of negative, neutral, and positive words following negative or positive mood induction. Both mood induction methods are combined.

second within-subject factor was the type of stimulus evaluated (word, picture, or face). The participants evaluated all three types of stimuli during different evaluation blocks with the order counterbalanced between participants.

Procedure

The participants filled out the Beck Depression Inventory followed by 18 practice trials on the pleasantness evaluation task. The item to be evaluated was presented at the centre of the screen for 1000 ms. Participants were asked to evaluate the pleasantness of the item on a 1–8 scale. Their response was following by a 500 ms interval before the next item was presented. Participants then filled out the mood check questionnaire before the first mood induction procedure, using the Velten mood induction technique (Velten, 1968). After the first mood induction session, participants rated their current mood states followed by the first pleasantness evaluation block. There were 18 items in each evaluation block composed of 10 neutral, four slightly positive and four slightly negative filler items. The item to be evaluated could be a word, a picture, or a face depending on the counter-balanced order.

After the pleasantness evaluation task, participants were given a boost in the induced mood state by reading 20 further sentences from the Velten induction material from the same mood category. This was followed by the second hedonic evaluation block. Another boost in the mood state was given after the participants finished this block, followed by the third block of the hedonic evaluation task. Participants were asked to rate their mood state again after completing this third block. This was then followed by a break. Participants then performed a word generation task for 2 min, requiring them to produce as many words as possible from one of two target town names, Constantinople and Weston-Super-Mare, so as to neutralise the mood previously induced before the next mood induction session started. The entire procedure was then repeated with each of the other moods to complete the counter-balanced design.

Material

The mood checklist was that used in Experiment 1, as was the Velten mood induction technique, except that the sentences were presented on a computer screen rather than on cards.

Rating items. The words used were again taken from the ANEW (Bradley & Lang, 1999). Thirty neutral words comprised the target set (mean valence = 5.24, $SD = 0.05$; the smaller the value the more negative the stimulus; mean arousal = 3.74, $SD = 0.36$, the smaller the value, the less arousing the stimulus). To broaden the range, a further 12 positive and 12 negative words served as fillers that were included but not scored. Another six words (two from each valence category) were selected to be used during the practice session.

The pictures used were taken from the International Affective Picture System (IAPS; Lang et al., 2005). Thirty neutral pictures (mean valence = 4.41, $SD = 0.46$; (mean arousal = 3.93, $SD = 0.89$), formed the target set, with 12 positive and 12 negative filler pictures. Another six pictures (two from each valence category) were selected to be used during the practice session.

The faces used were taken from the AR Face Database (Martinez & Benavente, 1998). All 44 faces chosen were those categorised as neutral. However, we selected 12 of the faces that we judged as posing a slightly positive expression as positive fillers and 12 of the faces that posed a slightly negative expression as negative fillers. Within each valence category, half were female and half were male faces.

Results

Mood check

As Figure 3 indicates, the mood induction procedure was successful; a one-way analysis of variance (ANOVA) was conducted with the valence of mood induction as the factor (negative, neutral, or positive). The data to be analysed were the mood index after the first mood induction in each mood condition.

The effect of the valence of mood induction reached statistical significance, $F(2, 34) = 14.463$, $p < .001$. Tukey's post hoc analysis revealed that participants rated themselves as less positive after negative mood induction compared to their mood after neutral or positive induction. No difference between the ratings after neutral and positive mood induction was observed.

Evaluation task

Only the data for the neutral items were analysed. Our principal measure involved the

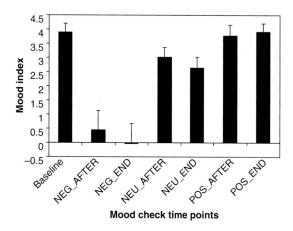

Figure 3. Mean mood ratings across the various phases of Experiment 2.

TABLE 2
Data from Experiment 2. The mean pleasantness ratings for different types of stimuli under different moods (standard deviation are shown in parentheses)

Type of mood	Type of stimulus		
	Faces	Pictures	Words
Negative	3.31 (0.88)	4.19 (0.72)	4.46 (0.60)
Neutral	3.73 (0.91)	4.59 (0.85)	4.89 (0.64)
Positive	3.72 (0.75)	4.53 (1.00)	4.82 (0.76)

mean pleasantness ratings for different types of items under different mood manipulations. The data are shown in Table 2. Data were analysed using ANOVA, with the mood state (negative, neutral, or positive) and type of stimuli (face, picture, or word) entered as separate within-subject factors.

The effect of different mood states was significant, $F(2, \ 34) = 8.237$, $p < .001$, $\eta_G^2 = .055$. Tukey's post hoc analysis revealed that participants evaluated the items as less pleasant when induced into a negative mood compared to when induced into neutral or positive mood. However, no difference was observed whether participants were induced into neutral or positive mood. The effect of the type of stimulus (words, faces, or pictures) also reached statistical significance, $F(2, 34) = 30.717$, $p < .001$. Tukey's post hoc analysis revealed that participants evaluated the faces as less pleasant than the pictures or the words. No difference in pleasantness evaluation was observed between pictures and words. The interaction between the two factors did not reach statistical significance, $F < 1$.

Discussion

Experiment 2 replicated the difference between positive and negative induced mood on subsequent hedonic judgements, an effect that was found not only for words as in Experiment 1, but also with faces and neutral IAPS pictures. Our inclusion of a neutral mood induction condition suggested that our previous findings were probably attributable principally to the presence of negative mood, since we found no suggestion of

an effect of positive mood. However, the lack of a positive mood effect should be viewed with caution, given that the baseline mood of our participants was already high, and that the difference between the mood induced by neutral and positive stimuli was not as powerful as the negative mood induction, with only nine of the 18 subjects showing higher mood following positive then neutral induction. It would clearly be advisable to repeat this study with less cheerful participants.

GENERAL DISCUSSION

Our two experiments both suggest that an emotionally toned mood is capable of influencing a subsequent hedonic judgement. The effect was found to occur with two different methods of mood induction, the Velten technique and a combination of pictures and music. The negative mood effect was found for judgements of words, pictures, and faces, and in the case of words was found to operate across different levels of stimulus valence. Although the effect was clearly demonstrated in the case of negative mood, we do not have strong evidence of an equivalent positive mood effect. This could be due to fundamental difference in the way in which positive and negative moods operate. Ashby, Isen, and Turken (1999) argue strongly for a distinction between the basic systems responsible for positive and negative affect, citing for example a study of the influence of affect on two problem-solving tasks. Positive affect enhanced performance, which was not influenced by either increased arousal through exercise or the induction of negative mood by a depressing film clip (Isen, Daubman, & Nowicki, 1987). It would, however, be premature to reject the possibility of a positive effect on judgement, given the fact that the baseline mood of our participants was high, making it difficult to produce a substantial elevation in mood.

One possible criticism of both studies is that our participants were simply responding to the demand characteristics of the experimental situation, behaving in a way that was consistent with the perceived expectations of the experimenter, with a negative mood encouraging a negative subsequent hedonic judgement. If this were the case, however, we would expect the positive condition to be just as effective as the negative inducement, whereas we found no difference. This could not be attributed to a ceiling effect, since the three types of item in Experiment 2 were all emotionally relatively neutral, whereas in Experiment 1 the effect occurred for words of low medium and high affective value. However, it is clearly important as a next step, to establish the validity of the task in a less artificial and more ecologically valid context, using depressive patients, for example.

A second issue relates to the magnitude of the change detected. Is a small effect, however reliable, of potential importance? We suggest that it is, for two reasons; first, because small but reliable deviations can provide extremely valuable indicators of major underlying phenomena, as for example in the case of human body temperature, where a change of a few degrees may mark the difference between health and illness. It is worth noting that the level of mood change induced by either of our methods is probably quite minor compared for example to the chronic difference in mood between a healthy person and a patient suffering from a major depression; a greater deviation in mood could well result in more substantial changes in judgement.

Finally, although our study was prompted by an attempt to extend the multicomponent working memory model to the study of emotion, we do not wish to claim that our results favour the hypothesis of a hedonic detector over other approaches to the study of emotion. Our aim was methodological, to provide a tool that might potentially allow us to develop what is currently a theoretical speculation into an empirically fruitful model. The task proposed is simple, rapid to perform and produces reliable effects even with relatively small participant groups. We hope to use it to explore the mechanism underlying the proposed hedonic evaluation system, testing assumptions about its resting point in different chronic mood states, its sensitivity to change, its capacity to average across hedonically complex situation and to maintain and manipulate such information in working memory. If a coherent concept of a hedonic detection system were to emerge, it would then be important to relate it to the more developed existing models of the interaction of cognition and emotion.

REFERENCES

Baddeley, A. D. (1966). Influence of depth on the manual dexterity of free divers: A comparison between open sea and pressure chamber testing. *Journal of Applied Psychology, 50*, 81–85. doi:10.1037/h0022822

Baddeley, A. D. (2007). *Working memory, thought and action*. Oxford, UK: Oxford University Press.

Baddeley, A. D., de Figueredo, J. W., Hawkswell Curtis, J. W., & Williams, A. N. (1968). Nitrogen narcosis and performance underwater. *Ergonomics, 11*, 157–164. doi:10.1080/00140136808930952

Baddeley, A. D., & Flemming, N. C. (1967). The efficiency of divers breathing oxy-helium. *Ergonomics, 10*, 311–319. doi:10.1080/0014013670 8930873

Bargh, J. A., & Ferguson, M. J. (2000). Beyond behaviorism: On the automaticity of higher mental processes. *Psychological Bulletin, 126*(6), 925–945. doi:10.1037//0033-2909.126.6.925

Beck, A. T., Ward, C. H., Mendelson, M., Mock, J., & Erbaugh, J. (1961). An inventory for measuring depression *Archives of General Psychiatry, 4*, 561–571.

Damasio, A. R. (1998). The somatic marker hypothesis and the possible functions of prefrontal cortex. In A. C. Roberts, T. W. Robbins, & L. Weiskrantz (Eds.), *The prefrontal cortex* (pp. 36–50). New York, NY: Oxford University Press.

Davis, F. M., Osborne, J. P., Baddeley, A. D., & Graham, I. M. F. (1972). Diver performance: Nitrogen narcosis and anxiety. *Aerospace Medicine, 43*, 1079–1082.

Derakshan, N., & Eysenck, M. W. (1998). Working memory capacity in high trait-anxious and repressor groups. *Cognition and Emotion, 12*, 697–713. doi:10.1080/026999398379501

Duckworth, K. L., Bargh, J. A., Garcia, M., & Chaiken, S. (2002). The automatic evaluation of novel stimuli. *Psychological Science, 13*, 513–519. doi:10.1111/1467-9280.00490

Estrada, C. A., Isen, A. M., & Young, M. J. (1994). Positive affect influences creative problem solving and reported source of practice satisfaction in physicians. *Motivation and Emotion, 18*, 285–299.

Etzel, J. A., Johnsen, E. L., Dickerson, J., Tranel, D., & Adolphs, R. (2006). Cardiovascular and respiratory responses during musical emotion induction. *International Journal of Psychophysiology, 61*, 57–69. doi:10.1016/j.ijpsycho.2005.10.025

Eysenck, M. W., & Calvo, M. G. (1992). Anxiety and performance—the processing efficiency theory. *Cognition and Emotion, 6*(6), 409–434. doi:10.1080/02699939208409696

Fazio, R. H. (1986). How do attitudes guide behavior? In Sorrentino & Higgins (Eds.) *Handbook of motivation and cognition* (Vol. 1, pp. 204–243).

Hinson, J. M., Jameson, T. J., & Whitney, P. (2002). Somatic markers, working memory, and decision making. *Cognitive, Affective and Behavioural Neuroscience, 2*, 341–353. doi:10.3758/CABN.2.4.341

Hume, D. (1978). *A treatise of human nature.* Oxford, UK: Oxford University Press. (Original work published 1739).

Idzikowski, C., & Baddeley, A. D. (1983). Waiting in the wings: Apprehension, public speaking and performance. *Ergonomics, 26*, 575–583.

Idzikowski, C., & Baddeley, A. D. (1987). Fear and performance in novice parachutists. *Ergonomics, 30*, 1463–1474. doi:10.1080/00140138708966039

Isen, A. M. (1970). Success, failure, attention, and reactions to others: The warm glow of success. *Journal of Personality and Social Psychology, 15*, 294–301.

Isen, A. M., Daubman, K. A., & Nowicki, G. P. (1987). Positive affect facilitates creative problem solving. *Journal of Personality and Social Psychology, 52*, 1122–1131.

Isen, A. M., & Shalker, T. E. (1982). The effect of feeling state on the evaluation of positive, neutral, and negative stimuli: When you "accentuate the positive", do you eliminate the "negative"? *Social Psychology Quarterly, 45*, 58–63.

Isen, A. M., Shalker, T. E., Clark, M., & Karp, L. (1978). Affect, accessibility of material in memory, and behevior: A cognitive loop? *Journal of Personality and Social Psychology, 36*, 1–12. doi:10.1037//0022-3514.36.1.1

Johnsen, E. L. (2004). *Neuroanatomical correlates of emotional experiences from music.* Iowa City, IA: University of Iowa.

Kiessling, R. J., & Maag, C. H. (1962). Performance impairment as a function of nitrogen narcosis. *Journal of Applied Psychology, 46*, 91–95. doi:10.1037/h0039500

Krosnick, J. A., Betz, A. L., Jussin, L. J., & Lynn, A. R. (1992). Subliminal conditioning of attitudes. *Personality and Social Psychology Bulletin, 18*, 152–162. doi:10.1177/0146167292182006

Krumhansl, C. L. (1997). An exploratory study of musical emotions and psychophysiology. *Canadian Journal of Experimental Psychology, 51*, 336–352. doi:10.1037/1196-1961.51.4.336

Lang, P. J., Bradley, M. M., & Cuthbert, B. N. (2005). *International Affective Picture System (IAPS): Digitized photographs, instruction manual, and affective ratings* (Tech. Rep. No. A-6). Gainesville, FL: University of Florida, Center for Research in Psychophysiology.

Martinez, A. M., & Benavente, R. (1998, June). *The AR Face Database* (CVC Tech. Rep. No. 24).

Mikels, J. A., Fredrickson, B. L., Larkin, G. R., Lindberg, C. M., Maglio, S. J., & Reuter-Lorenz, P. A. (2005). Emotional category data on images from the International Affective Picture System. *Behaviour Research Methods, 37*, 626–630.

Mogg, K., & Bradley, B. P. (1998). A cognitive-motivational analysis of anxiety. *Behaviour Research and Therapy, 36*, 809–848. doi:10.1016/S0005-7967(98)00063-1

Schwarz, N., & Clore, G. L. (1983). Mood, misattribution, and judgements of well-being: Informative and directive functions of affective states. *Journal of Personality and Social Psychology, 45*, 513–523.

Velten, E. (1968). A laboratory task for induction of mood states. *Behavioral Research and Therapy, 6*, 473–482. doi:10.1016/0005-7967(68)90028-4

Williams, J. M. G., Watts, F. N., MacLeod, C., & Mathews, A. (1988). *Cognitive psychology and emotional disorders.* New York, NY: Wiley.

Williams, J. M. G., Watts, F. N., MacLeod, C., & Mathews, A. (1997). *Cognitive psychology and emotional disorders* (2nd ed). Chichester, UK: Wiley.

JOURNAL OF COGNITIVE PSYCHOLOGY, 2012, 24 (1), 17–32

Evolutionary derived modulations of attention to two common fear stimuli: Serpents and hostile humans

Arne Öhman[1], Sandra C. Soares[2], Pernilla Juth[1], Björn Lindström[1], and Francisco Esteves[3]

[1]Department of Clinical Neuroscience, Karolinska Institutet, Stockholm, Sweden
[2]Department of Education, University of Aveiro, Portugal
[3]Center for Psychological Research and Intervention, ISCTE/Lisbon University Institute, Lisbon, Portugal

In this paper we present an evolutionary analysis of attention to stimuli that are threatening from an evolutionary perspective, such as angry faces and snakes. We review data showing that angry, photographically depicted angry faces are more rapidly detected than happy faces in a visual search setting provided that they are male and that distractors are redundant in the sense that they are drawn from a small set of faces. Following Isbell's (2009) novel Snake Detection Theory, we predicted that snakes, as the prototypical predators, should be more rapidly detected than spiders, given that spiders have provided less of a predatory threat for primates. We review a series of experiments from our laboratory showing that snakes indeed are more rapidly detected than spiders provided that the target stimuli are presented in a demanding visual context, such as many distractor stimuli, or in peripheral vision. Furthermore, they are more distracting than spiders on the performance of a primary attention task. Because snakes were not affected by perceptual load, whereas spiders followed the usual rule of better detection with low perceptual load, we concluded that attending to snakes might constitute an evolutionary adaptation.

Keywords: Attention; Emotional stimuli; Evolution; Faces; Snake Detection Theory; Snakes.

Curiously enough, the products of biological evolution, the changes in gene distribution, are often understood as alternative, independent causal agents to those summarised as residing in the environment. Yet, the effect of the basic mechanism of evolution, natural selection, is to subordinate genes to specific environmental conditions. As evolution has proceeded, these conditions have become more and more specific, from those shared by all living creature, such as availability of oxygen, water and some form of nutritious substance, to parents as attachment figures, conspecifics to affiliate with or fear, and specific predators to avoid and escape. In terms of statistical analyses, this means that genes seldom exert main effects, i.e., effects that cut across contexts. Rather they are likely to operate as modulatory factors in relation to other causal agents (inside and outside the organism) that are revealed as statistical interactions, albeit at a highly complex level with many genes and many environmental conditions simultaneously involved. This general

Correspondence should be addressed to Arne Öhman, Section of Psychology, Department of Clinical Neuroscience, Karolinska institutet, SE-171 77 Stockholm, Sweden. E-mail: arne.ohman@ki.se

The writing of this paper and the research that is reviewed were supported by grants to the first author from the Swedish Science Research Council and the US National Institute of Mental Health (P50 MH 72850) to the Center for Research on Emotion and Attention, University of Florida, Gainesville, FL, USA. Arne Öhman is also affiliated with the Stockholm Brain Institute.

perspective suggests a research strategy that encourages psychologists to look for boundary conditions (e.g., environmental factors that block gene effects, and genetic effects that modulate environmental influences), that is, potentially interacting factors both among genes and environmental factors. In this paper we will use this general evolutionary perspective to look for interaction between two ubiquitous psychological phenomena, attention and emotion, both of which involve many potentially interacting psychological and genetic processes.

In an evolutionary perspective, emotions are vehicles for regulating behaviour in relation to agendas set by biological evolution. This evolutionarily defined agenda deals with the adaptive problems that organisms have to solve in order for their genes to become represented in coming generations. A basic assumption is that evolutionary analyses help to delineate causal factors that in interactions with environmental factors produce adaptive behaviour that we recognise as related to emotion and attention.

In general terms, emotion puts value on events in- and outside of the organism by making them relevant for more or less urgent action, given the currently active goals (e.g., Dolan, 2002; Lazarus, 2004). Emotion, therefore, recruits attention by giving signal value to emotionally relevant stimuli, thereby securing their privileged cognitive processing, and in the next step, adaptive behaviour.

This formulation implies that emotion-evoking stimuli should be effective attention-attractors, and that different emotional states should sensitise organisms to particular classes of stimuli. These general hypotheses have been developed and tested particularly in the emotional context of fear and anxiety, where they, for example, played a central part in cognitive theories of anxiety disorders (Beck, Emery, & Greenberg, 1985; Eysenck, 1992; MacLeod & Mathews, 1987; Mathews & MacLeod, 1994).

The present paper focuses on the theoretical and empirical analysis of two sources of fear in humans: other humans and animals. For both types of fear we present evolutionary scenarios as well as relevant empirical data. The latter focus particularly on a series of studies that address the relationships between the related emotional phenomena of fear and anxiety, on the one hand, and attention, on the other. For both types of, the empirical data originate in experiments on visual search, and therefore we start with a short description of this methodology.

THE VISUAL SEARCH METHODOLOGY

The visual search paradigm (e.g., Wolfe, 1998) is one of the standard experimental designs for studying attention. It is modelled on a frequently encountered situation in real life in which we look for a target stimulus among several distractor stimuli. For example, at the grocery store we may look for the ripest tomato in a box of tomatoes, or a particular brand of cereal among stacks of different brands. Or, to take a somewhat more psychologically interesting example, we may look for a particular person when encountering a group of friends. Thus, in more general terms, a visual search experiment requires participants to look for a target stimulus that differs in more or less well-defined dimensions (ripeness of tomatoes, trademarks of cereal, or an opposite-sex face that makes one's heart beat faster) from a set of distractor stimuli. The participants provide speeded responses by pressing different buttons depending on whether a target is present or absent in a display defining a single trial in an experiment that may involve hundreds of trials. Reaction time (RT) for hitting the button defining the presence of the target in a display is the primary measure of attending to the target. Accuracy of target detection is another often used measure. Typically the number of distractors is varied across trials under the assumption that efficient deployment of attention results in only small increases with each added distractor. This is measured by the slope coefficient of a least-square fitted line estimated from plots of RTs across number of distractors (see Wolfe, 1998).

AN EVOLUTIONARY ANALYSIS OF HUMAN SOCIAL FEARS

Inspired by a distinction proposed by the great evolutionary biologist Ernst Mayr (1974), Öhman, Dimberg, and Öst (1985) classified fear behaviour in terms of what those that concerned other humans ("intraspecific fears"), and those that concerned animals ("interspecific fears"). They noted that this categorisation coincides with two important classes of human phobias (American Psychological Association, 1994), namely, social phobia (fear of, e.g., high-status persons, meeting unknown people, being stared at by others), and animal phobias (fear of, e.g., snakes, spiders, birds, dogs, cats). They proceeded to suggest that these two classes of fear of living creatures have their origin in two evolved behavioural systems, a social submissiveness and a predatory defence system built around human faces and snakes as central stimuli. Thus, pictures of human faces and snakes are the emotionally stimuli whose effect on attention (as defined in visual search paradigms) and emotion will be covered in this paper.

Fear and the social submissiveness system

The place of faces in primate social life. Social rank is a ubiquitous feature of primate social life. It is defined by the position of individuals in the dominance hierarchies that provide the key to the social organisation of primate groups (e.g., de Waal, 2005). Evolutionary speaking, these hierarchies serve as vehicles for distributing resources (e.g., sexual partners, food) within the group. They are established on the basis of the ability to manage social conflicts by means of power motivation, smartness, strength, and social skills in forming coalitions, all of which may serve as proxies for the genetic potential to breed successful offspring.

Different individuals are differentially prepared to use one or the other of these strategies, partly because of genetic differences and partly because of prior experience of status conflicts. A substantial part of the signalling actions centres on the faces of the combatants taking measures of their relative strength. As recognised by Darwin (1872), the design of the primate face suggests that it has evolved as a means of communication. The facial muscles are unique in their function by primarily moving dermal tissue rather than body limbs, thus producing coordinated changes in the visual appearance of the face (Fridlund, 1994). The basic human facial displays are similar to those of other primates, but the human face has a more complex musculature than that of other primates, with a more versatile neural innervation, allowing a more advanced communication than that of our closest primate relatives (Dimberg & Öhman 1996; Fridlund, 1994; Öhman, 2002).

Strategies for handling dominance conflicts. Status conflicts are staged as a struggle about who will successfully be able to use a dominant strategy, which is defined by a stereotyped set of powerful behaviours emanating from a "Social Dominance System" (Öhman et al., 1985). The choice of a dominant strategy is announced by an erect posture and signs of physiological arousal such as widening pupils and—in monkeys and apes—a general piloerection that makes the individual look larger, enhancing the threat of an imminent, potentially devastating attack. The face has a tightly closed mouth conveying decisiveness, and staring eyes under frowned eyebrows, with the gaze intensely focused on the opponent, the forward thrust of the forehead reinforcing the perceived threat of an imminent attack (see, e.g., Hinde, 1975)

The losers of the struggle acknowledge their defeat by another set of stereotyped submissive behaviours constituting a "Social Submissiveness System", the function of which is to limit potential serious physical damage in an active fight (Öhman et al., 1985). Following Darwin's (1872) "principle of antithesis", its bodily expression is opposite to that of dominance. The posture tends towards crouching with lowered head, the eyes wide opened but tending to avoid gaze contacts, and the readiness pertaining to flight rather than attack.

The anger superiority effect. Hansen and Hansen (1988) were pioneers in deducing from these mainly ethological findings that facial expressions suggesting dominance and submission would be differentially effective in capturing attention. They tested this hypothesis in a visual search paradigm and reported that subjects were faster to locate a deviant threatening (angry) face in a background crowd of friendly (happy) faces than vice versa. The validity of the anger superiority effect, however, has turned out to be controversial (e.g., Byrne & Eysenck, 1995; Calvo & Nummenmaa, 2008; Juth, Lundqvist, Karlsson, & Öhman, 2006; Purcell, Stewart, & Skov, 1996).

The anger superiority effect—i.e., faster detection of angry than happy faces in visual search—is unanimously supported by data from studies using *schematic faces* (see Figure 1) in a visual search setting (e.g., Calvo, Avero, & Lundqvist, 2006; Fox et al., 2000; Juth et al., 2005, Exp. 5; Lundqvist & Öhman, 2005; Mather & Knight, 2005; Öhman, Lundqvist, & Esteves, 2001; See Öhman, Juth, & Lundqvist, 2010, for further

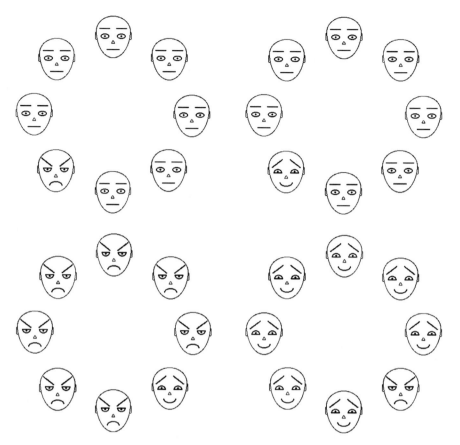

Figure 1. Visual search for schematic emotional faces. In the two upper panels the emotional face targets (angry and happy) are presented among neutral distractor faces, and in the two lower displays the emotional targets are presented among emotional distractors. In both cases, angry targets are found faster than happy targets.

references) but the results from studies that like Hansen and Hansen (1988) used *photographically depicted real faces* (e.g., Figure 2) are highly inconsistent. For example, Juth et al. (2005) failed consistently to obtain an angry (or fear advantage) with real faces across four experiments with real stimulus faces. Instead, they consistently reported faster detection of happy than angry faces. However, in a final experiment with schematic faces, a highly reliably angry advantage was demonstrated. Happy advantages were also demonstrated by Byrne and Eysenck (1995) and Calvo and Nummenmaa (2008). Further contributing to the elusiveness of angry advantages with real faces, some studies (Purcell et al., 1996; Williams, Moss, Bradshaw, & Mattingly, 2005)

Homogeneous display   Heterogeneous

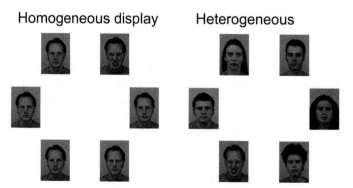

Figure 2. Participants searched for a discrepant emotional face among neutral distractors faces. In the display to the left both the target and the distractor faces were posed by the same individual (homogeneous display). In the display to the right, on the other hand, all faces came from different individuals (heterogeneous display).

have failed to find difference between happy and angry targets, and some have reported the expected shorter detection latency to angry than happy target faces among neutral distractor faces (e.g., Fox & Damjanovic, 2006; Gilboa-Schechtman, Foa, & Amir, 1999; Horstman & Bauland, 2006; Pinkman, Griffin, Baron, Sasson, & Gur, 2010; Williams & Mattingley, 2006). To further understand the role of facial expression in guiding attention, it appears highly fruitful to delineate which factors determine whether angry or happy targets in a set of photographed faces will guide attention most efficiently. This has defined an important research agenda for several years in our laboratory.

Schematic and real faces: A theoretical analysis. The contrasting results of studies using schematic and real faces might provide a point of departure for defining factors that determine whether angry or happy advantages will be observed. An obvious difference between these two classes of stimuli is that schematic faces lack the variation in identity and gender that are conspicuous features of real faces. Indeed, studies with real faces reporting anger advantages have minimised individual variability by using displays in which the faces in a given display were posed by the same individual as both distractors and target (Fox & Damjanovic, 2006; Horstmann & Bauland, 2006). Studies reporting a happy advantage (Byrne & Eysenck, 1995; Calvo & Nummenmaa, 2008; Juth et al., 2005, Exps. 1–3), on the other hand, like Juth et al. (2005), used sets of distractors composed of many individual stimulus persons. Thus, a critical factor may be the number of individuals constituting the total set of stimulus faces that participants are exposed to in an experiment.

The concept of distractor redundancy. The variability of the *total set of individuals in an experiment*—the "implicit stimulus set size" to distinguish it from the (explicit) "set size" *of a particular display* in a visual search experiment—can be subsumed under the concept of *distractor redundancy*, which was proposed by Rauschenberger and Yantis (2006) as a central determinant of visual search performance. A set of distractors composed by repetition of the same individual (i.e., a "homogeneous display") is highly redundant because it is completely specified by one of its members ("if you have seen one, you have seen them all"). However, when all faces in a display show different individuals (a "heterogeneous display"), complete specification of a

display is more demanding, because it requires analysis of all its members. This gives minimal redundancy, because knowledge of one of the set members has limited generalisability to other members of the set. Thus, distractor redundancy can be (inversely) defined in relation to an *implicit set of associated stimuli* a given distractor can be mistaken for (Rauschenberger & Yantis, 2006). This definition implies that the size of the implicit stimulus set (i.e., the total number of stimulus individuals shown in an experiment) is a central parameter of redundancy. Thus, if the same set of homogeneous distractors (e.g., identical faces posed by the same actor) are used on all trials in an experiment, the distractor set size = 1. However, even if the distractors on each trial are homogeneous, all trials may show different individuals, which results in a distractor set size that equals the number of trials. From this discussion it follows that schematic faces, because they lack identity and gender information (have a set size = 1), is a much more redundant stimulus set than any set of real faces.

The role of target face gender. Because redundant distractor faces are more easily encoded than nonredundant ones, they require less perceptual processing resources to be excluded as targets. Hence, redundant distractors facilitate target search (Duncan & Humphreys, 1989; Rauschenberger & Yantis, 2006). Following Lavie (1995, 2005), it could be hypothesised that the diminished perceptual load of redundant distractors allows deeper processing of the target stimulus. The fact that happy faces are more quickly recognised than angry faces when presented alone (e.g., Juth et al., 2005, Exp. 4; Leppänen & Hietanen, 2003, 2007), and indeed appear to be automatically identified by a unique, diagnostic feature (Calvo & Nummenmaa, 2008), suggests that they need less perceptual resources to be identified than do angry faces. As a consequence, redundant distractors may benefit angry target faces more than happy ones, because angry faces need resources for configural processing rather than the simpler feature processing required by happy faces (Calvo & Nummenmaa, 2008). These effects, furthermore, may be modulated by target gender because anger is more quickly and accurately recognised in male than in female faces, and the reverse is true for happiness, which was interpreted as an evolutionarily derived coupling between males and hostility and females and friendliness (Becker, Kenrick, Neuberg,

Blackwell, & Smith, 2007). Thus, even though there may be ceiling effects, the general happy advantage reported by Calvo and Nummenmaa (2008) could be potentiated for female targets. Moreover, the benefit of distractor redundancy for angry target faces would be enhanced if they were male. From this analysis it could be hypothesised that redundant distractors (one identity drawn from a small set/display) would result in an anger advantage, particularly for male target faces.

Testing the theory. This theory was tested in an experiment where the effects of target emotion, target gender, distractor redundancy, and distractor homogeneity were assessed (Öhman et al., 2010). Sixty-four participants (32 females) were exposed to displays showing six faces (see Figure 2). In half of the trials participants were exposed to displays in which all faces showed a neutral expression, and in the other half, an angry or a happy target face replaced one of the neutral faces. The task was to press different buttons depending on whether a target was present or not in the display. Participants were randomly allocated to four sex-balanced groups. The stimulus display always showed six faces (see Figure 2). However, for half of the participants the faces shown in a given display were sampled from a large implicit stimulus set (little redundancy;

32 male and 32 female stimulus individuals), whereas for the other half they were sampled from a small stimulus set (large redundancy; six male and six female stimulus individuals). The other between-subject factor concerned whether the displays were homogeneous (the same individual posing all faces in a display) or heterogeneous (six different individuals posing the six faces shown on a display; see Figure 2).

The results showed no effect of participant sex, but there was a strong interaction between target emotion and target gender reflecting a large happy advantage when the targets were females compared to no effect of target emotion when they males. This interaction between the emotion and the gender of the target faces was a central component in several other significant interactions. Most important for our hypothesis predicting that redundancy would determine whether happy or angry advantages would emerge, the three-way interactions between target gender, stimulus set size, and emotion (see Figure 3, upper panels), and between target gender, homogeneity, and emotion (see Figure 3, lower panels), were both significant. For male targets there was a highly significant interaction between emotion and stimulus set size (Figure 3, left upper panel), directly addressing our main hypothesis that a small stimulus set would favour an angry

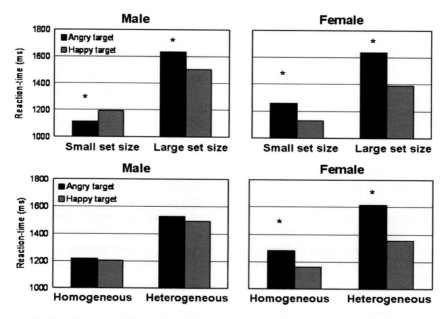

Figure 3. Upper panels: Reaction-time (RT) data (in milliseconds, ms) for participants searching for emotional (happy or angry) male (left panel) and female target (right panel) faces among neutral distractor faces as a function of target emotion and implicit stimulus set size. Lower panels: Target trial RT data for male (left panel) and female (right panel) target faces as a function of target emotion and homogeneous versus heterogeneous distractors. *Significant difference (Tukey follow-up tests on significant interactions between angry and happy target faces.

advantage, particularly for male targets, whereas a large stimulus set would promote a happy advantage. Thus, male targets were more quickly detected when they were angry than when they were happy, provided that the implicit stimulus set was small. In contrast, with a large implicit stimulus set, male happy targets were more quickly detected than angry targets. Somewhat surprisingly, the crossover interaction between target emotion and set size shown for males in the upper left panel of Figure 3 was not present when redundancy was assessed by homogeneous versus heterogeneous displays, which suggests that implicit set sizes is more important for these effects than is the homogeneous versus heterogeneous factor.

For female targets, the weaker albeit significant interactions of target emotion with implicit set size (Figure 2, upper right panel), and display homogeneity (Figure 2, lower right panel), showed that the happy advantage was larger with heterogeneous displays and large stimulus sets, but there was never any crossover to angry advantage as it was for male targets and implicit stimulus set size (Figure 3, left upper panel).

Discussion

These data suggest two interacting conditions for obtaining an angry advantage both in male and female observers: (1) the target stimuli should be male rather than female, and (2) the faces in a display should be redundant in the sense that they were drawn from a small stimulus set. Thus, in agreement with the common assumption of a threat advantage in detecting emotional faces, we demonstrated an angry advantage, but only provided that these quite narrowly defined conditions were met. In contrast, when the displayed faces were drawn from a large set of stimulus individuals, male happy faces were more quickly detected than male angry faces, particularly in the second trial block. With female target faces, on the other hand, there was a very strong overall happy advantage across all the conditions we studied (Figure 3, right panels).

It is noteworthy that we did not observe any effect of participant sex. In contrast, Williams and Mattingley (2006) compared large groups of males and females ($N = 78$ for both) in detecting emotional target faces among neutral distractors and reported that males showed specifically shorter RTs than females for angry male, but not for angry female target faces. Because males are more concerned with power struggles than females among other primates (e.g., de Waal, 2005), this is an evolutionary meaningful result. Yet subsequent replications of the paradigm used by (Öhman et al., 2010) in our laboratory have also failed to find effects of participant sex in participant groups of similar size. Given the much larger Ns in Williams and Mattingley's study, the discrepancy between our and their studies may be attributable to larger power in their study.

Our findings provide avenues for understanding some of the inconsistencies in the literature. Thus, the important role of distractor redundancy that we uncovered accounts for the discrepant findings between studies with real faces using homogeneous displays with small stimulus sets and reporting an anger advantages (e.g., Gilboa-Schechtman et al., 1999; Horstman & Bauland, 2006), on the one hand, and studies with heterogeneous displays and larger stimulus sets, which obtained happy advantages (e.g., Byrne & Eysenck, 1995; Juth et al., 2005), on the other. Similarly, because schematic faces give vastly more redundant distractor sets than real faces (cf. Figures 1 and 2), our findings suggest an explanation for the consistent reports of anger advantages with schematic stimuli (e.g., Fox et al., 2000; Öhman et al., 2001; Tipples et al., 2002), which contrasts with the inconsistent data for real faces (e.g., Byrne & Eysenck, 1995; Purcell et al., 1996).

AN EVOLUTIONARY ANALYSIS OF ANIMAL FEARS

Snake fears: The predatory defence system

Predator–prey arms races. Predators and prey are mutually tied in competitive interactions called evolutionary arms races (Dawkins & Krebs, 1979), which are considered important pacemakers of evolution. For example, improved hunting skills in predators provide selective pressure on members of prey species for improved defence, which in turn put pressures on predators to catch ever more attentive, faster, and more unpredictably moving prey, and so on.

The prototypical predator on primates. Isbell (2006, 2009) presents a persuasive argument that snakes as predators played a central role in shaping evolving mammalian and primate brains. First, constrictor snakes were critical predators on the first, small ancestors of modern placental mammals (about 100 million years ago), and because competing predators (e.g., raptors and felines) first emerged about 20–50 million years later, snakes played an important role in establishing the primate order via their effects on the visual sense. Second, the evolutionary invention of effective venom by snakes about 60 million years ago constituted a decisive step introducing a new powerful weapon in the arsenal of snakes as predators in the predator–prey arms race with primates. Indeed, being bitten by venomous snakes is still potentially disastrous (Warell, 2011, even for primates that are now too large to serve as prey. For example, envenoming by snakebites accounts for an estimated worldwide human death rate of close to 100,000/year (Kasturiratne et al., 2008). Effective defence to venomous snakes is visually demanding because they are often cryptically concealed in vegetation on the ground or in trees, thus providing strong evolutionary pressure on primates for developing astute perceptual mechanisms for their detection.

The Snake Detection Theory. Isbell (2009) argued that the response to this evolutionary pressure by the emerging, most advanced primates was a series of coordinated changes in their visual system, resulting not only in superior vision, but also in the integration of defence and sensory systems through direct thalamic links to the amygdala, as well as through extensive efferent connections between different parts of the amygdala and the visual system (LeDoux, 1996; Öhman, Carlsson, Lundqvist, & Ingvar, 2007; Tamietto & de Gelder, 2010). These anatomical connections are consistent with behavioural, lesion, and neuroimaging data suggesting that the amygdala tunes visual brain areas for effective perception of fear-related stimuli (e.g., Phelps, Ling, & Carrasco, 2006; Vuilleumier, Richardson, Armony, Driver, & Dolan, 2004).

The arms races between snakes, and primates took mainly place in Gondwanaland, the southern supercontinent that incorporated the current South America, Africa, Madagascar, India, Australia, and Antarctica, which was home to constrictors, the pythons and boas. By the time venomous snakes appeared, Gondwanaland was well split apart, and India had begun sharing its flora and fauna with Asia, as part of the northern

supercontinent of Laurasia. In the intervening millennia since then, venomous snakes spread from Asia, their likely place of origin, to Africa, North and Central America, and finally South America. They are still not in Madagascar. Consistent with Isbell's theory, African and Asian anthropoid primates (the Old World anthropoids), which, of all the primates, have been most enduringly exposed to venomous snakes, uniformly show fear of snakes, whereas the only primates in Madagascar, the lemurs, are much less responsive. Furthermore, when anthropoid primates arrived in South America from Africa, they were given a roughly 25-million-year reprieve from venomous snakes until the snakes arrived in South America from North America, perhaps as late as about three million years ago, when the Panamanian land bridge formed. Accordingly, because they evaded the evolutionary pressure from venomous snakes until relatively recently, New World monkeys not only are more variable than Old World monkeys and apes in their responses to snakes, but also have more variable visual systems than the Old World monkeys.

Isbell's "Snake Detection Theory" (SDT) has obvious implication for human attention mechanisms. Earlier work from our group (Öhman, Flykt, & Esteves, 2001) has shown that participants in visual search experiments detect pictures of snakes or spiders presented among neutral pictures (flowers, mushrooms) faster than they detect mushrooms or flowers among snakes or spiders. However, because the fear relevant stimuli (snakes and spiders) were collapsed in the data analysis, and the number of participants in the separate animal groups was too low to give adequate power for direct comparison of snakes and spiders, no data on this difference were presented. A more recent study with adequate power (Soares, Esteves, Lundqvist, & Öhman, 2009), suggested that snakes were more efficiently detected than spiders. This result is expected from the SDT, which postulates that snake has been a prototypical predator on primates. Spiders in the other hand have hardly provided any serious survival threat to primates. We therefore followed up our preliminary finding of more efficient detection of snakes than spiders in a series of experiment in which we systematically evaluated hypotheses derived from the SDT.

Snakes, and particularly venomous snakes, provide a lethal danger to primates only when they are close by, but their detection is complicated by their tendency to be camouflaged in vegetation and foliage. Failed detection, furthermore, might result in a deadly injection of poison. Isbell's (2009) argument suggest that the powerful selective pressure exerted by venomous snakes supported evolution of coordinated early detection and rapid defence activation to potential targets of attack through a direct brainstemthalamic route to the amygdala (LeDoux, 1996; Öhman et al., 2007). The integration of evolutionary, neural, and behaviour levels in the SDT (Isbell, 2009) allows empirical tests at each of these different levels. To illustrate the empirical fruitfulness of the SDT for behavioural experiments, we will review some behavioural studies that examined a few general hypotheses from the theory.

Stimulus material. Pictures of snakes were central to the experiments and they were compared to two categories of control stimuli, both of which showing pictures of a distinct central object against similar backgrounds to those of the snakes. The first control category was selected as an emotionally neutral control stimulus (mushrooms), and the second control category—spiders—matched that of snakes in emotional impact as assessed from ratings of valence, arousal, and dominance (Lang, Bradley, & Cuthbert, 2005). Furthermore, spiders are frequent objects of phobias (American Psychological Association, 2000), and they are rated as very frightening in the general population (Agras, Sylvester, & Oliveau, 1969). Importantly, it is questionable whether spiders ever have provided a serious predatory threat to primates, because very few have potentially deadly venoms, and they appear primarily specialised on insects as prey. Thus, spiders are similar to snakes in emotional impact but the case for an evolutionary origin of this fear is considerably more tenuous than that we have reviewed for snakes (e.g., Davey, 1994). Thus, dissociations between snakes and spiders in the fear-related behaviours they evoke are expected from their different evolutionary origins.

Testing the SDT: Detection in peripheral vision. The first experiment examined if detection of snakes was less degraded than that of spiders and mushrooms in peripheral vision. Because venomous snakes are dangerous particularly when they are close, the enlarged visual field that follows from better peripheral vision may promote detection of a nearby snake outside the restricted field of foveal vision, which may result

in a saccade that brings the threat into foveal visions and activates active defence.

We used a visual search paradigm in which pictures of snakes, spiders, or mushrooms served as discrepant targets that were searched among different numbers (3, 6, 8, 12, or 18) of distractor stimuli (fruits). The spatial distribution of the distractors across the screen was randomised across an imaginary 6 × 6 matrix of rectangles that covered the screen, with nonoccupied slots being empty. Thus, the displays changed from trial to trial not only in number but also in spatial locations of the pictures. The spatial location of the target was systematically varied between foveal ($<1.2°$), parafoveal ($3.4°$), and peripheral ($5.7°$) locations.

Consistent with our hypothesis, the data for the most direct measure of attentional efficiency, the slope of RTs on distractor set size (see Wolfe, 1998) showed a strongly significant interaction between targets and eccentricity (Figure 4), As predicted, this effect vindicated that search efficiency remained stable across eccentricities for snakes, but deteriorated at the peripheral target location for spiders and even more so for mushrooms (Figure 4). However, contributing to this interaction, spiders unexpectedly showed more shallow slopes than snakes at foveally presented targets, suggesting that they were more efficiently detected than snakes at this location. The results for the slope measure were, with one exception

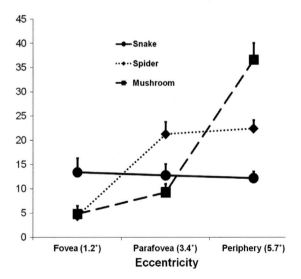

Figure 4. Results relating slopes across different explicit set sizes (3, 6, 12, 18) (expressed as the mean search time [in milliseconds]/searched item) for locating the target picture (a snake, a spider, or a mushroom) as a function of eccentricity (foveal, parafoveal, or peripheral presentation of the target). Error bars represent Standard Error of Measurement (SEM).

(see later) fully confirmed when the analyses were based directly on RTs, i.e., there was a strongly significant three-way interaction between stimulus category, eccentricity of the stimulus, and the number of distractors.

Closely similar findings were revealed in accuracy of target detection (Figure 5), with a reliable interaction between target and eccentricity, reflecting that the differences between the three target conditions was significant only at the peripheral target location. It is noteworthy that neither accuracy nor direct RT analyses confirmed the reliably better detection performance with spider than snakes for foveally presented targets observed in the slope measure.

The results from this experiment showed that snakes were more efficiently detected than both a related class of fear-relevant stimuli (spiders) and fear-irrelevant control stimuli (mushrooms). Consistent with our hypothesis that snakes have provided a more deadly threat than spiders for evolving primates, the advantage for snake detection relative to spiders and mushrooms was primarily obtained when the target stimulus was presented in the peripheral visual field and with cluttered visual displays.

Distracting effects of nontarget stimuli. The strong modulatory effects of set size observed in the previous experiments accords with the hypothesis that detection of snakes should not deteriorate under demanding visual conditions,

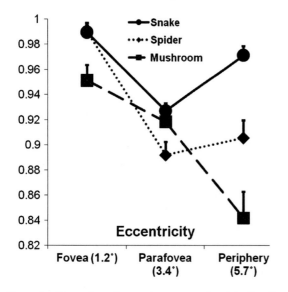

Figure 5. Proportion of accurate responses for detecting the different target stimuli as a function of eccentricity (foveal, parafoveal, or peripheral location of the target). Error bars represent standard errors of measurement (SEM).

for example as provided by dense vegetation, and modelled in the laboratory by set size. However, this support is somewhat limited by the fact that it was obtained with top-down controlled attention in which participants actively looked for targets that deviated from the background distractors. An evolutionarily more relevant situation is provided by the need to detect snakes that lurk unannounced in the background while active attention is focused on something else in the visual environment. For example, one could think of a hunter-gatherer woman, who—some hundred thousand years ago—picks berries from a bush, with her children around her. Not only would she risk touching a snake hidden in the bush, but the evolutionary logic would also require that she protected her genes carried in her offspring by efficient detection of lurking snakes. The objective of the next experiment was to model this situation by using a search arrangement in which snakes, spiders, and mushrooms were presented as occasional unexpected, task-irrelevant distracting stimuli, while the subjects were searching for a different target (a bird) among fruit distractors. The pictures were presented on the periphery of an imaginary circle. Participants were instructed to concentrate their attention on finding the birds, but they were also informed that on some trials (one out of five) one of the distractors would be exchanged with another picture that was completely irrelevant for their task of detecting birds, and which therefore should be neglected. These novel distractor stimuli were snakes, spiders, or mushrooms. We predicted that snakes should retain their attention priority and thus that RTs for finding the target should be more slowed when the snake rather than spiders or mushrooms served as the novel distractor. Furthermore, this effect should most obvious with six rather than four standard distractors (fruits).

This hypothesis is most directly tested by the interaction between type of distractor and set size, which was highly significant. With the larger stimulus set (six items), snakes produced clearly more interference than spiders, and mushrooms (Figure 6), and were the only task-irrelevant distractor stimulus that produced a significant interference effect, as shown by a reliable slowing of RTs compared to the basic condition with only the standard set of distractors (Figure 6). In contrast, decisively contributing to the stimulus time set size interaction, with the four-item stimulus set, spider distractors produced increased interference compared to snakes, and

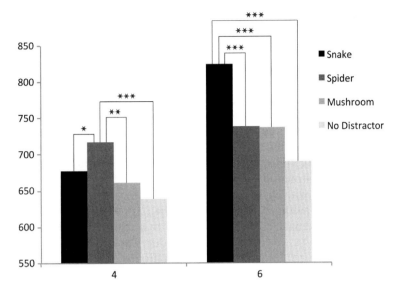

Figure 6. Effects of set size (4, 6) and type of task-irrelevant distractors (snake, spider, or mushroom) when participants searched for bird target pictures among pictures of birds. The task-irrelevant distractors replaced one of the standard bird distractors on 20% of the trials); also shown are RTs for finding birds on trials with only fruits as distractors [80% of the trials]. *Significant differences in follow-up Tukey tests.

mushroom distractors, and displays with no task-irrelevant distractor stimulus (Figure 6).

Thus, in agreement with our hypothesis, the results showed that snakes were the only distractors to produce reliable interference with target detection when the perceptual load was high (set size = 6). In addition, with the large set size, snakes produced significantly more interference than spiders and mushrooms (none of which produced reliable interference). In contrast, with the smaller set size (4) only the spiders provided any evidence of interference. Thus, similar pattern of results were obtained in previous and present experiments in the sense that different conditions (peripheral stimulus presentation and six distractors, respectively) favoured snake detection and the detection of spiders (foveal presentation and four distractors, respectively).

This pattern of results imply that the better detection of snakes than other stimuli is restricted to perceptually demanding contexts, whereas spiders were detected faster than snakes in perceptually less demanding context. Thus, the critical boundary variables for both the snake and the spider detection advantage could be subsumed under Lavie's (1995, 2005) concept of perceptual load, which refers to the "amount of perceptual work", "perceptual effort", or colloquially speaking, "the perceived difficulty" of a perceptual task. In neural terms, it has been identified with the effort needed to bias the competition for neural representation between stimuli for further visual processing (Beck & Kastner, 2009; Torralbo & Beck, 2008). Specifically, then, our data suggest that spider detection shows the commonly observed deteriorating performance with increasing perceptual load, whereas in clear contrast, snake detection actually improves with rising perceptual load.

The concept of perceptual load. The previous experiments show that snakes recruit attention more efficiently than spiders (and mushrooms) only in what could be characterised as visually demanding contexts: peripheral presentation, and displays cluttered by many distractors. These effects, furthermore, seem to be produced regardless of whether the attention control mode is primarily top-down or bottom-up. The central tenet of the Perceptual Load Theory is that potential objects for perception compete for limited resources to become further analysed and eventually consciously represented (cf. Desimone & Duncan, 1995). If the task at hand recruits all available resources, little is left for processing of task-irrelevant, potentially distracting stimuli. Conversely, "leftover" perceptual resources will allow more or less complete perceptual analyses of stimuli that are not task relevant, which might show up as distraction in the central task. Consequently, in conditions with high perceptual load, which fully occupy attentional resources, no attention is available to "spill over" to task-irrelevant stimuli. High perceptual load is known to completely prevent the processing of information unrelated to the task, both in behavioural and brain imaging terms. For example, RT during low perceptual load are affected by additional characters placed outside the relevant search area (e.g., Lavie, 1995, 2005, 2010), or stimuli known to preferentially engage attention, such as human faces with fearful or hostile expressions (Bishop, Jenkins, & Lawrence, 2006; Pessoa, Padmala, & Morland, 2005). However, at high perceptual load, such distraction effects diminish or disappear, along with associated activation in brain regions such as the amygdala (e.g., Bishop et al., 2006; Lim, Padmala, & Pessoa, 2008; Pessoa et al., 2005).

Testing the independence of snake detection and perceptual load. In our final experiment we tested the perceptual load hypothesis more formally by using an experimental task developed by Lavie and colleagues (e.g., Forster & Lavie, 2008; Lavie, 1995, 2005, 2010) for stringent tests of task-independent distraction effects. Thus, we presented snake, spider, flowers, and mushroom distractor pictures—in greyscale equalised on low level features such as luminance and contrast and displayed against uniform white background—completely independent of the central task. They appeared outside (9.5° from the fixation point) the foveal area in which the very demanding perceptual task performed by the participant was presented. It consisted of a two-choice reaction time task that required the identification of designated target letters (X or N) in letter strings. During low perceptual load, the relevant target letter was presented in isolation at the centre of the display, whereas at high load, five nontarget characters surrounded the target letter. The letter display as well as the distractor stimuli were presented for only 50 ms.

Rather than the colour slides used in the previous experiments, we used carefully matched greyscale pictures of snakes, spiders and mushrooms. Finally, whereas the previous experiments had a strong gender bias with too few males for allowing a meaningful statistical evaluation of sex differences. Thus, so far we can only conclude that the reported results are valid for females, but that we do not know about males. Given the double genetic gain for food-gathering females by protecting both themselves and their children when detecting lurking snakes, there is good evolutionary reason to expect that females surpass males in this ability. Therefore in the final experiment, in order to address the question of sex differences, we incorporated close to an equal number of females and males in a reasonably large sample of participants ($N = 49$).

In support of our hypothesis, and on the basis of only preliminary data analyses, snakes were the only distractor type to cause significant interference during high perceptual load, expressed as increased mean RT relative to the no-distractor baseline. In contrast to the often reported perceptual load interaction effect (i.e., distraction during low but not high load, e.g., Forster & Lavie, 2008; Lavie, 1995), snake distraction gave rise to a main effect. However, when participant gender was included in the analysis, the interpretation of this simple effect was modified by a three-way interaction between perceptual load, snake distractors, and gender, indicating that the distraction effect was driven by the detrimental influence of snake distractors on the performance of female, but not male participants at high perceptual load. This effect cannot be attributed to larger fear of snakes among females than males, because statistically control for the effect of self-reported snake fear did not eliminate the gender difference in snake distraction effect. It should be noted that spiders did not produce reliable distraction on perceptual load level, even though the degree of spider and snake fear was comparable in the sample. Thus, in summary, task-irrelevant snakes caused a unique effect on performance, where particularly the performance of females suffered by peripherally presented snakes.

GENERAL DISCUSSION

The data that we have reviewed in this paper prompts an interesting but often neglected insight: It is most often futile to look for main effects when examining evolutionary hypotheses about behaviour. Evolutionary adaptations reflect cumulative effects of natural selections over eons of time. This implies that the adaptation in question has been ground to fit the ecological niche in which the organism has evolved. Because adaptations are coded in the genome of the organism, it also means that the genetically mediated effects that constitute behavioural adaptations are designed to be sensitive to environmental constraints. In effect, genes can be viewed as a record of the habitats in which a species has evolved. This, in turn, undermines the all too common tendency to pit genes against the environment in explaining behaviour, that is, even highly genetically loaded behaviour typically need environmental support to be activated. To put it more boldly, when it comes to the control of behaviour, it is meaningless to talk about gene effects without specifying the environmental support that is needed for its expression in behaviour.

Even though we found some main effects in the experiments we have reviewed, the most interesting aspects of our findings are the interactions that they uncovered. Two of them are related to sex. First, for faces, we found that threatening male faces had attentional priority to male friendly faces, but only when presented in a context of familiar faces. For female faces, on the other hand, there was always a detection advantage to those looking friendly. The confluence of an angry male sex and a familiar group as requirements for attentional priority is suggestive. Speculatively, a hypothesis could be ventured that this reflects that male violence all too often is acted out within the family (Garcia-Moreno, Jansen, Ellsberg, Heise, & Watts, 2007).

The critical effect of male sex for the angry face advantage was not moderated by the sex of the observer. This variable, however, was important in the detection of snakes. As shown in our last experiment with snakes and spiders, which was the only one to include a test of the effect of participant sex, only females showed the critical interaction between perceptual load and attention capture by task-irrelevant snakes. As we have already noted, this makes evolutionary sense. Assuming that the distribution of labour between the sexes among our distant forefathers included female responsibility for taking care of young offspring and food gathering, whereas males were primarily hunters, then it is reasonable to assume that females not only were at larger risk for snake encounters themselves, but also that this increased risk also included their children.

The most surprising and interesting aspect of our findings is that snakes, but not spiders, nor angry faces, turned out to be quite independent of perceptual load. Male angry faces captured attention only when the distractors were redundant and thus left spillovers of perceptual resources that could be allocated for deeper analyses of the target face. With nonredundant distractors consuming much of the available perceptual resources for their analysis, little was left to allow the deeper processing necessary to identify an angry face. Happy faces, however, which can be identified by shallow processing of salient stimuli (Calvo & Nummenmaa, 2008), do not need the extra resources that are available because of redundant distractors.

Not only does the independence of snakes fail to conform to the Lavie Perceptual Load theory (Lavie, 1995, 2005), but is also contrary to a large body of research that concurs in concluding that the number of distractors is a major (inverse) determinant of efficient visual search performance (e.g., Wolfe, 1998). Against this background it is quite remarkable that snakes do not respect this established relationship, and furthermore, that in contrast to another frequently feared animal, spiders, did so by showing best detection during high perceptual load. It is particularly important that the insensitivity of snake targets to peripheral target presentation, increased number of distractors, and the competition for perceptual load by a demanding task, makes eminent biological sense. Throughout evolutionary history, snakes have been (Isbell, 2009) and still are (Kasturiratne et al., 2008) a deadly threat to primates, primarily in close encounters. In this perspective, primate ability to detect snakes in perceptually very demanding contexts (foliage, vegetation, peripheral vision) appears to be an important adaptation of evolutionary origin. The clear contrast in detection efficiency between snakes, on the one hand, and spiders and "normal" neutral stimuli, on the other, is telling. A pattern of behaviour that appears to answer an important adaptive question posed by evolution, and that is opposite to the received wisdom concerning parametrical relationships, indeed, could be taken as fulfilling a key characteristic of an evolutionary adaptation.

Snakes and threatening faces, which both have been postulated as engaging evolutionarily shaped behaviour systems, are similar to each other in terms of showing more persistent conditioned fear responding than do evolutionary neutral stimuli (Öhman et al., 1985; Öhman & Mineka, 2001). Furthermore, stimuli from both these categories can elicit psychophysiological responses even when masked by other, neutral stimuli (e.g., Dimberg & Öhman, 1996; Öhman & Soares, 1994). Finally, as demonstrated in this paper, both snakes and threatening faces showed attention priority in a visual search task in which they were presented among several distractor stimuli, albeit under different boundary conditions. Whereas threatening faces appears to conform to the general rule of improved detection with decreased perceptual load, snakes, as we have seen, showed quite the opposite with increasing superiority to spider and mushrooms with increasing perceptual load. Thus, it appears that snakes and threatening faces depend on different mediating mechanisms for their fast response to danger. However, given the likely origin of these behaviour systems in different evolutionary stages, this difference is not so surprising. The impact of snakes on primates, as we have seen, is evolutionary old, going back 50–100 million years, whereas the impact of a social life that favours facial communication is considerably later. Accordingly, the response to snakes is reflexive and automatic and presumably generates immediate defence behaviour by an automatic link to the amygdala, via the superior colliculi in the brain stem and the pulvinar nucleus of the thalamus (e.g., Isbell, 2009; Morris, Dolan, & Öhman, 1999). Responses to faces, on the other hand, are more strategic and tactical, requiring deeper, cortical processing of the situation, which depend on the availability of perceptual resources before a response can be selected. Nonetheless, this does not exclude a role for fast automatic emotive activation fuelling response generation, even though they must be restrained from their full expression by cortical areas monitoring the relationship between the selected behaviour and the goal defined by the strategy. Thus, remnants of systems that were incorporated into primitive mammalian brains at a very early stage could still be operative in the advanced brains of African apes (including humans), producing overlaps between attention performance in threatening situations related to snakes and threatening faces.

REFERENCES

Agras, W. S., Sylvester, D., & Oliveau, D. (1969). The epidemiology of common fear and phobia. *Comprehensive Psychiatry*, 10, 151–156. doi:10.1016/0010-440X(69)90022-4

American Psychological Association. (2000). *Diagnostic and statistical manual of mental disorders* (4th ed., Text rev.). Washington, DC: Author.

Beck, A. T., Emery, G., & Greenberg, R. L. (1985). *Anxiety disorders and phobias: A cognitive perspective*. New York, NY: Basic Books.

Beck, D. M., & Kastner, S. (2009). Top-down and bottom-up mechanisms in biasing competition in the human brain. *Vision Research*, 49, 1154–1165. doi:10.1016/j.visres.2008.07.012

Becker, D. V., Kenrick, D. T., Neuberg, S. L., Blackwell, K. C., & Smith, D. M. (2007). The confounded nature of angry men and happy women. *Journal of Personality and Social Psychology*, 92(2), 179–190. doi:10.1037/0022-3514.92.2.179

Bishop, S. J., Jenkins, R., & Lawrence, A. (2007). The neural processing of task-irrelevant fearful faces: Effects of perceptual load and individual differences in trait and state anxiety. *Cerebral Cortex*, 17, 1595–603.

Byrne, A., & Eysenck, M. W. (1995). Trait anxiety, anxious mood, and threat detection. *Cognition and Emotion*, 9, 544–562. doi:10.1080/02699939508408982

Calvo, M. G., Avero, P., & Lundqvist, D. (2006). Facilitated detection of angry faces: Initial orienting and processing efficiency. *Cognition and Emotion*, 20, 785–811. doi:10.1080/02699930500465224.

Calvo, M. G., & Nummenmaa, L. (2008). Detection of emotional faces: Salient physical features guide effective visual search. *Journal of Experimental Psychology: General*, 137(3), 471–494. doi:10.1037/a0012771

Darwin, C. (1872). *The expression of the emotions in man and animals*. London, UK: John Murray.

Davey, G. C. L. (1994). The "disgusting spider": The role of disease and illness in the perpetuation of fear of spiders. *Society and Animals*, 2(1), 17–24. doi:10.1163/156853094X00045

Dawkins, R., & Krebs, J. R. (1979). Arms races between and within species. *Proceedings of the Royal Society London: Biological Sciences*, 205B(1161), 489–511. doi:10.1098/rspb.1979.0081

De Waal, F. B. M. (2005). A century of getting to know the chimpanzee. *Nature*, 437, 56–59. doi:10.1038/nature03999

Dimberg, U., & Öhman, A. (1996). Behold the wrath: Psychophysiological responses to facial stimuli. *Motivation and Emotion*, 20, 149–182.

Duncan, J., & Humphreys, G. W. (1989). Visual search and stimulus similarity. *Psychological Review*, 96, 433–458.

Eysenck, M. W. (1992). *Anxiety: The cognitive perspective*. Hove, UK: Lawrence Erlbaum Associates Ltd.

Eysenck, M.W., Derakshan, N., Santos, R., & Calvo, M. G. (2007). Anxiety and cognitive performance: Attentional control theory. *Emotion*, 7, 336–353.

Eysenck, M. W., MacLeod, C., & Mathews, A. (1987). Cognitive functioning and anxiety. *Psychological Research*, 49(2–3), 189–195.

Farah, M. I., Tanaka, J. N., & Drain, M. (1995). What causes the face inversion effect? *Journal of Experimental Psychology: Human Perception and Performance*, 21, 628–634.

Forster, S., & Lavie, N. (2008). Failures to ignore entirely irrelevant distractors: The role of load. *Journal of Experimental Psychology: Applied*, 14, 73–83.

Fox, E., & Damjanovic, L. (2006). The eyes are sufficient to produce a threat superiority effect. *Emotion*, 6, 534–539. doi:10.1037/1528-3542.6.3.534

Fox, E., Lester, V., Russo, R., Bowles, R. J., Pichler, A., & Dutton, K. (2000). Facial expressions of emotion:

Are angry faces detected more efficiently? *Cognition and Emotion, 14*, 61–92. doi:10.1234/12345678

Garcia-Moreno, C. G., Jansen, H., Ellsberg, M., Heise, L., & Watts, C. H. (2006). On behalf of the WHO Multi-country Study on Women's Health and Domestic Violence against Women Study Team. Prevalence of intimate partner violence: Findings from the WHO multi-country study on women's health and domestic violence. *The Lancet, 368*(9543), 1260–1269. doi:10.1016/S0140-6736(06)69523-8

Gilboa-Schectman, E., Foa, E. B., & Amir, N. (1999). Attentional biases for facial expression in social phobia. *Cognition and Emotion, 13*, 305–318. doi:10.1080/026999399379294

Hansen, C. H., & Hansen, R. D. (1988). Finding the face in the crowd: An anger superiority effect. *Journal of Personality and Social Psychology, 54*, 917–924. doi:10.1037//0022-3514.54.6.917

Horstmann, G., & Bauland, A. (2006). Search asymmetries with real faces: Testing the anger superiority effect. *Emotion, 6*, 193–207. doi:10.1037/1528-3542.6.2.193

Isbell, L. A. (2006). Snakes as agents of evolutionary change in primate brain. *Journal of Human Evolution, 51*(1), 1–35. doi:10.1016/j.jhevol.2005.12.012

Isbell, L. A. (2009). *The fruit, the tree, and the serpent.* Cambridge, MA: Harvard University Press.

Juth, P., Lundqvist, D., Karlsson, A., & Öhman, A. (2005). Looking for foes and friends: Perceptual and emotional factors when finding a face in the crowd. *Emotion, 5*, 379–395. doi:10.1037/1528-3542.5.4.379

Kasturiratne, A., Wickremasingh, A. R., de Silva, N., Gunawardena, N. K., Pathmeswaran, A., Premaratna, R. et al. (2008). The global burden of snakebite: A literature analysis and modeling based on regional estimates of envenoming and deaths. *PLoS Medicine, 5*, 1591–1604. doi:10.1371/journal.pmed.0050218

Lang, P. J., Bradley, M. M., & Cuthbert, B. N. (2005). *International Affective Picture System (IAPS): Instruction manual and affective ratings* (Tech. Rep. No. A-6). Gainsville, FL: Center for Research in Psychophysiology, University of Florida.

Lavie, N. (1995). Perceptual load as a necessary condition for selective attention. *Journal of Experimental Psychology: Human Perception and Performance, 21*, 451–468. doi:10.1234/12345678

Lavie, N (2005). Distracted and confused? Selective attention under load. *Trends in Cognitive Sciences, 9*, 75–82.

Lavie, N. (2010). Attention, distraction, and cognitive control under load. *Current Directions in Psychological Science, 19*, 143–148. doi: 10.1177/0963721410370295

Lavie, N., & Cox, S. (1997). On the efficiency of visual selective attention: Efficient visual search leads to inefficient distractor rejection. *Psychological Science, 8*, 395–398. doi:10.1111/j.1467-9280.1997.tb00432.x

Lazarus, R. E. (1991). *Emotion and adaptation.* New York, NY: Oxford University Press.

LeDoux, J. (1996). *The emotional brain: The mysterious underpinnings of emotional life.* Hemel Hempstead, UK: Simon & Schuster.

Leppänen, J. L., & Hietanen, J. K. (2003). Affect and face perception: Odors modulate the recognition advantage of happy faces. *Emotion, 3*, 315–326. doi:10.1037/1528-3542.3.4.315

Leppänen, J. L., & Hietanen, J. K. (2007). Is there more to a happy face than just a big smile? *Visual Cognition, 15*, 468–490. doi:10.1080/13506280600765333

Lim, S.-L., Padmala, S., & Pessoa, L. (2008). Affective learning modulates spatial competition during low-load conditions. *Neuropsychologia, 46*, 1267–1278.

Lundqvist, D., & Öhman, A. (2005). Emotion regulates attention: The relations between facial configurations, facial emotions, and visual attention. *Visual Cognition, 12*, 51–84. doi:10.1080/13506280444000085

Mather, M., & Knight, M. (2005). Goal-directed memory: The role of cognitive control in older adults' emotional memory. *Psychology and Aging, 20*, 554–570. doi:10.1037/0882-7974.20.4.554

Mathews, A., & MacLeod, C. (1994). Cognitive approaches to emotion and emotional disorders. *Annual Review of Psychology, 45*, 25–50. doi:10.1146/annurev.ps.45.020194.000325

Mayr, E. (1974). Behavior programs and evolutionary strategies. *The American Scientist, 62*, 650–659.

Morris, J. S., Öhman, A., & Dolan, R. J. (1999). A subcortical pathway to the right amygdala mediating "unseen" fear. *Proceedings of the National Academy of Science, 96*, 1680–1685.

Öhman, A. (1993). Fear and anxiety as emotional phenomena: Clinical phenomenology, evolutionary perspectives, and information-processing mechanisms. In M. Lewis & J. M. Haviland (Eds.), *Handbook of emotions* (pp. 511–536). New York, NY: Guilford Press.

Öhman, A. (2002). Automaticity and the amygdala: Nonconscious responses to emotional faces. *Current Directions in Psychological Science, 11*(2), 62–66. doi:10.1111/1467-8721.00169

Öhman, A. (2008). Fear and anxiety: Overlaps and dissociations. In M. Lewis, J. M. Haviland-Jones, & L. F. Barret (Eds.), *Handbook of emotions* (3rd ed., pp. 709–729). New York, NY: Guilford Press.

Öhman, A., Carlsson, K., Lundqvist, D., & Ingvar, M. (2007). On the unconscious subcortical origin of human fear. *Physiology and Behavior, 92*(1–2), 180–185. doi:10.1016/j.physbeh.2007.05.057

Öhman, A., Dimberg, U., & Öst, L.-G. (1985). Animal and social phobias: Biological constraints on learned fear responses. In S. Reiss & R. R. Bootzin (Eds.), *Theoretical issues in behavior therapy* (pp. 123–178). Orlando, FL: Academic Press.

Öhman, A., Flykt, A., & Esteves, F. (2001). Emotion drives attention: Detecting the snake in the grass. *Journal of Experimental Psychology: General, 130*, 466–478. doi:10.1037/0096-3445.130.3.466

Öhman, A., Juth, P., & Lundqvist, D. (2010). Finding the face in a crowd: Relationships between distractor redundancy, target emotion, and target gender. *Cognition and Emotion, 24*(7), 1216–1228.

Öhman, A., Lundqvist, D., & Esteves, F. (2001). The face in the crowd revisited: A threat advantage with schematic stimuli. *Journal of Personality and Social Psychology, 80*, 381–396.

Öhman, A., & Mineka, S. (2001). Fears, phobias, and preparedness: Toward and Evolved module of fear and fear learning. *Journal of Personality and Social Psychology, 80*, 381–396. doi:10.1234/12345678

Öhman, A., & Soares, J. J. F. (1994). "Unconscious anxiety": Phobic responses to masked stimuli. *Journal of Abnormal Psychology, 103*, 231–240.

Pessoa, L., Padmala, S., & Morland, T. (2005). Face of unattended fearful faces in the amygdala is determined by both attentional resources and cognitive modulation. *NeuroImage, 28*, 249–255.

Phelps, E. A., Ling, S., & Carrasco, M. (2006). Emotion facilitates perception and potentiates the perceptual benefits of attention. *Psychological Science, 17*, 292–299. doi:10.1111/j.1467-9280.2006.01701.x

Purcell, D. G., Stewart, A. L., & Skov, R. B. (1996). It takes a confounded face to pop out of a crowd. *Perception, 25*, 1091–1108. doi:10.1068/p251091

Rauschenberger, R., & Yantis, S. (2006). Perceptual encoding efficiency in visual search. *Journal of Experimental Psychology: General, 135*, 116–131. doi:10.1037/0096-3445.135.1.116

Soares, S. C. (2010). *Fear commands attention: Snakes as the archetypal fear stimulus?* (Doctoral thesis). Stockholm, Sweden: Karolinska Institutet.

Soares, S. C., Esteves, F., Lundqvist, D., & Öhman, A. (2009). Some animal specific fears are more specific than others: Evidence from attention and emotion measures. *Behaviour Research and Therapy, 47*, 1032–1042. doi:10.1016/j.brat.2009.07.022

Tammietto, M., & de Gelder, B. (2010). Neural bases of the non-conscious perception of emotional signals. *Nature Reviews Neuroscience, 10*, 697–709.

Torralbo, A., & Beck, D. M. (2008). Perceptual-load-induced selection as a result of local competitive interactions in visual cortex. *Psychological Science, 19*(10), 1045–1050. doi:10.1111/j.1467-9280.2008.02197.x

Vuilleumier, P., Armony, J. L., Clarke, K., Husain, M., Driver, J., & Dolan, R. J. (2002). Neural response to emotional faces with and without awareness: Event-related fMRI in a parietal patient with visual extinction and spatial neglect. *Neuropsychologia, 40*(12), 2156–2166. doi:10.1016/S0028-3932(02)00045-3

Vuilleumier, P., Richardson, M., Armony, J., Driver, J., & Dolan, R. J. (2004). Distant influences of amygdala lesion on visual cortical activation during emotional face processing. *Nature Neuroscience, 7*, 1271–1278. doi:10.1038/nn1341

Warrell, D. A. (2010). Snake bite. *The Lancet, 375*, 77–88.

Williams, D., Gutiérrez, J. M., Harrison, R., et al. (2010). The Global Snake Bite Initiative: An antidote for snake bite. *The Lancet, 375*, 89–91.

Williams, M. A., & Mattingley, J. B. (2006). Do angry men get noticed? *Current Biology, 16*, D402–D404.

Williams, M. A., Moss, S. A., Bradshaw, J. L., & Mattingley, J. B. (2005). Look at me, I'm smiling: Visual search for threatening and non-threatening facial expressions. *Visual Cognition, 12*, 29–50. doi:10.1080/13506280444000193

Wolfe, J. M. (1998). Visual search. In H. Pashler (Ed.), *Attention* (pp. 13–73). Hove, UK: Psychology Press.

JOURNAL OF COGNITIVE PSYCHOLOGY, 2012, 24 (1), 33–53

The ups and downs of cognitive bias: Dissociating the attentional characteristics of positive and negative affectivity

Ben Grafton[1], Ed Watkins[2], and Colin MacLeod[1]

[1]University of Western Australia, Crawley, WA, Australia
[2]University of Exeter, Exeter, UK

Despite considerable past interest in distinguishing the patterns of attentional bias that characterise vulnerability to anxiety and to depression, little research has yet sought to delineate the attentional correlates of two affective dimensions that differentially contribute to these alternative forms of emotional vulnerability—negative and positive affectivity. In the present study, we employ a novel variant of the attentional probe task to examine selective attentional engagement with, and disengagement from, negative words, in participants whose heightened emotional vulnerability reflects either elevated negative affectivity, or attenuated positive affectivity. Elevated negative affectivity was found to be associated with both increased attentional engagement with, and impaired attentional disengagement from, negative information, especially when this was anxiety relevant. In contrast, attenuated positive affectivity was associated with facilitated attentional disengagement from negative information, especially when this was depression relevant. We discuss how this new insight into the attentional characteristics of negative and positive affectivity may serve to illuminate the basis of previously observed discrepancies between the patterns of attentional selectivity observed in anxious and in depressed participants.

Keywords: Affectivity; Anxiety; Attentional bias; Depression; Disengagement bias; Engagement bias.

Although anxiety and depression are different emotions, there is much evidence that they share a close relationship. Measures of anxiety and depression typically correlate strongly (Watson et al., 2007), individual differences in the disposition to experience anxiety and depression are predicted by the same personality constructs (Watson & Naragon-Gainey, 2009), and clinical depression often is comorbid with clinical anxiety (Kessler, Gruber, Hettema, Hwang, & Sampson, 2010). Therefore, efforts to better understand individual differences in anxiety and depression must focus on illuminating both the similarities, and the differences, between these emotions.

Particularly helpful in this regard has been the distinction drawn, by Watson and Tellegen (1985), between individual differences in negative and in positive affectivity. It now is widely accepted that elevated negative affectivity, reflecting the heightened tendency to experience negative emotion, is a shared characteristic of dispositional anxiety and depression, whereas attenuated positive affectivity, reflecting the reduced tendency to experience positive emotion, is a distinctive characteristic of depressive disposition (Lee, Watson, & Mineka, 1994). Consequently, it seems plausible that some similarities between anxiety and depression may reflect the characteristics of

Correspondence should be addressed to Ben Grafton, School of Psychology, University of Western Australia, 35 Stirling Highway, Crawley, WA 6009, Australia. E-mail: benjamin.grafton@uwa.edu.au

This work was partly supported by Australian Research Council Grant No. DP0879589.

their shared negative affectivity, whereas some differences between anxiety and depression may reflect the characteristics of the attenuated positive affectivity that is peculiar to the latter emotion.

There has been a steady growth of interest in the patterns of selective information processing that underpin vulnerability to anxiety and depression, largely inspired by the work of M. W. Eysenck, whose profound influence on the cognitive study of emotion has been sustained throughout a long and distinguished career (e.g., Eysenck, 1979, 1985, 1997, 2010; Eysenck & Derakshan, 2011; Eysenck, Derakshan, Santos, & Calvo, 2007). Cognitive psychologists investigating the patterns of attentional selectivity associated with emotional vulnerability have been interested in both the similarities of, and the differences between the selectivity associated with vulnerability to anxiety and with vulnerability to depression. Individuals who report heightened levels of emotional vulnerability, or who suffer from emotional dysfunction, commonly demonstrate an attentional bias towards emotionally negative information (cf. Cisler, Bacon, & Williams, 2009; Mathews & MacLeod, 2005). Many theorists contend that this attentional bias causally contributes to emotional vulnerability, and so plays a functional role in the aetiology and maintenance of emotional pathology (Beck & Clark, 1997; Mathews & Mackintosh, 1998; Williams, Watts, MacLeod, & Mathews, 1988, 1997). However, it does not appear that attentional preference for negative information is equally characteristic of heightened vulnerability to depression, and heightened vulnerability to anxiety. Individuals who score high on measures of trait anxiety, or who suffer from anxiety pathology, reliably demonstrate an attentional bias towards negative information (cf. Cisler & Koster, 2010; MacLeod & Rutherford, 2004). This bias often has been demonstrated using the dot probe task which, in its original form, involves exposing participants to word pairs for 500 ms on a computer screen, and requiring them to discriminate small probe stimuli that appear in the locus of either word. High trait anxious participants, and people suffering from anxiety disorders, display speeded processing of probes that appear in the locus of more negative words, indicating that they selectively shift their attention towards such negative stimuli (MacLeod, Mathews, & Tata, 1986; Mogg, Bradley, & Williams, 1995; Frewen, Dozois, Joanisse, & Neufeld, 2008). Indeed, this

finding has been so robust that, in a recent meta-analysis of the experimental literature on anxiety-linked attentional bias, Bar-Haim, Lamy, Pergamin, Bakermans-Kranenburg, and van IJzendoorn (2007) noted that it would require consistently null results across a series of 11,339 further studies of this type before the effect would be reduced to nonsignificance.

In contrast, evidence has been more mixed concerning the possibility that vulnerability to depression also may be characterised by an attentional preference for negative information (cf. Gotlib & Joorman, 2010). Some studies employing the original version of the probe task, which exposes word pairs for 500 ms, have produced evidence for such an effect (Mathews, Ridgeway, & Williamson, 1996). However, also using this stimulus exposure duration, other studies have revealed no evidence of attention bias in depressed participants (MacLeod et al., 1986). Several researchers, motivated by the idea that reliable evidence of depression-linked attentional bias may require longer stimulus presentations, have modified the probe approach by exposing the stimuli for 1000 ms before the probe appears. In studies employing this 1000 ms exposure condition, there has better evidence of a depression-linked attentional preference for negative information (Donaldson, Lam, & Mathews, 2007; Gotlib, Krasnoperova, Yue, & Joormann, 2004; Joorman & Gotlib, 2007), though again there have been failures to find such an effect (Bradley, Mogg, & Lee, 1997). Another suggestion has been that depression-linked attentional bias may be observed only when negative stimuli are specifically related to depressogenic concerns (Mathews & MacLeod, 1994; Taghavi, Neshat-Doost, Moradi, Yule, & Dalgleish, 1999). Again, whereas some studies reporting evidence of depression-linked attentional bias have employed negative stimuli with particular relevance to depression (Bradley et al., 1997; Joorman & Gotlib, 2007), other studies using similar stimuli have found no such effects (Mogg, Bradley, Williams, & Mathews, 1993; Neshat-Doost, Moradi, Taghavi, Yule, & Dalgleish, 2000). Thus, individuals with high vulnerability to anxiety, and those with high vulnerability to depression, are similar in that both sometimes display heightened attentional preference for negative information. However, they differ in that this attentional bias is reliably demonstrated by the former individuals, but is a more fragile and inconsistent effect in the latter (cf. Mogg &

Bradley, 2005; Wilson, MacLeod, & Campbell, 2006).

It seems possible that the attentional similarities and differences between anxious and depressed participants may be amenable to hypothetical explanation in terms of the potentially discrepant patterns of attentional selectivity that characterise heightened negative affectivity and attenuated positive affectivity. If heightened negative affectivity is associated with a robust and pervasive attentional preference for negative information, whereas attenuated positive affectivity instead is associated with attentional avoidance of negative information under certain circumstances, then the observed pattern of findings would be anticipated. Given that it involves elevated negative affectivity, but not attenuated positive affectivity, heightened anxiety would be characterised by a reliable attentional preference for negative information. However, because it combines elevated negative affectivity with attenuated positive affectivity, heightened depression would less consistently be characterised by this pattern of attentional selectivity. Specifically, to the extent that an attentional assessment task taps the attentional avoidance of negative information associated with their attenuated positive affectivity, so depressed participants would be unlikely to display the attentional preference for negative information associated with their elevated negative affectivity.

This idea, that the specific dimension of emotional vulnerability which differentiates depression from anxiety may be characterised by attentional avoidance of negative information, also can explain Bradley, Mogg, Millar, and White's (1995) findings concerning the patterns of attentional selectivity shown by participants whose generalised anxiety disorder (GAD) either was, or was not, comorbid with major depression. Whereas participants suffering from GAD alone demonstrated an attentional preference for negative words on the dot probe task, those whose GAD was accompanied by major depression did not. As noted by Bradley and colleagues, this suggests that the emotional attributes that distinguish dysfunctional depression from anxiety must be associated with a pattern of attentional selectivity that negates the attentional preference for negative information characteristic of anxiety alone. Bradley et al.'s position is compatible with our proposal that attenuated positive affectivity may, under certain circumstances, be associated with attentional avoidance of negative

information, whereas heightened negative affectivity instead is associated with a robust attentional preference for negative information.

Clearly, if attenuated positive affectivity were always characterised by attentional avoidance of negative information, then depressed participants would never display the attentional preference for negative information that they sometimes do. Therefore, it is necessary to suppose that this pattern of attentional avoidance, hypothesised to characterise attenuated positive affectivity, sometimes does not occur, perhaps depending upon the precise facet of attentional selectivity tapped by any given implementation of the dot probe task. A recent conceptual distinction that has appeared in the literature, between biases in attentional engagement with negative information and biases in attentional disengagement from negative information, provides a framework that could potentially accommodate this inconsistency. An attentional preference for negative information may reflect enhanced attentional engagement with such information. Operationally, such an attentional engagement bias can be defined as greater attentional capture by negative stimuli, relative to nonnegative stimuli, when such stimuli appear distally from initial attentional focus. Alternatively, an attentional preference for negative information may reflect impaired attentional disengagement from negative information. Operationally, such an attentional disengagement bias can be defined as greater continued attention to negative stimuli, relative to nonnegative stimuli, when these stimuli have initially been attended to.

Early research into emotionally linked attentional bias was motivated by models predicting that, in emotionally vulnerable individuals, attention would selectively favour the processing of negative information presented outside initial attentional focus (Beck, Emery, & Greenberg, 1985; Bower, 1981; Williams et al., 1988). Thus, the consistent theoretical view was that such vulnerability would be characterised by enhanced attentional engagement with negative information. In contrast, more recent interest in the patterns of attentional selectivity that operate subsequent to initial attentional focus on emotional information has been marked by theoretical conflict. One influential position, put forward by Mogg and Bradley (1998), is that initial attention to negative information is followed by subsequent avoidance of this information in emotionally vulnerable individuals. According to this "approach-avoidance" account, heightened emotional vulnerability should be characterised by *facilitated* attentional disengagement from negative information. An alternative but equally influential position, put forward by Fox, Russo, Bowles, and Dutton (2001), and by Yiend and Mathews (2001), instead maintains that heightened emotional vulnerability should be characterised by *impaired* attentional disengagement from negative information. Empirical evidence has failed to convincingly resolve this issue, because experimental support has been claimed both for the former position (Carlson & Reinke, 2008) and the latter position (Amir, Elias, Klumpp, & Przeworski, 2003; Salemink, van den Hout, & Kindt, 2007). Such mixed findings invite speculation that some aspects of emotional vulnerability may be characterised by enhanced attentional disengagement from negative information, whereas other aspects of emotional vulnerability instead may be characterised by impaired attentional disengagement from negative information.

We suggest that increased attentional engagement with negative information may be a ubiquitous feature of heightened emotional vulnerability, representing a characteristic of both elevated negative affectivity and attenuated positive affectivity, but that these two types of emotional vulnerability may differ in terms of their characteristic patterns of selective attentional disengagement from negative information. Specifically, we suggest that heightened negative affectivity may be associated with impaired attentional disengagement from negative information, whereas attenuated positive affectivity may instead be associated with facilitated attentional disengagement from such information. If this were the case then high levels of anxiety vulnerability, being characterised primarily by elevated negative affectivity, would be associated with a robust and pervasive attentional preference for negative information, regardless of whether an assessment procedure tapped selective engagement with or disengagement from such information. In contrast, because heightened vulnerability to depression involves both elevated negative affectivity, and attenuated positive affectivity, observed patterns of selectivity would be more variable. To the extent that an assessment procedure specifically tapped selective attentional engagement, so the more depressed individuals should show attentional preference for negative information. However, if an assessment procedure were simultaneously influenced both by

patterns of selective attentional engagement and disengagement, then there should be less consistent findings with depressed participants. In some cases, the increased attentional engagement with negative information associated with their heightened negative affectivity may dominate, leading to an overall attentional preference for negative information. However, it might be expected that this attentional preference effect would be attenuated, and perhaps often eliminated, by the facilitated attentional disengagement from negative information associated with their attenuated positive affectivity. It is generally accepted that the attentional bias measures yielded by the conventional form of the dot probe task will reflect the combined influence of any bias in attentional engagement and in attentional disengagement (Cisler & Koster, 2010). Therefore, our hypothesis explains why an anxiety-linked attentional preference for negative information has been more reliably observed, on this task, than has a depression-linked attentional preference for negative information.

The objective of the present study was to directly test this hypothesis, by examining the patterns of selective attentional engagement with, and disengagement from, negative information, demonstrated by participants whose elevated emotional vulnerability reflected either heightened negative affectivity or attenuated positive affectivity. This required an attentional probe procedure capable of cleanly dissociating these two forms of attentional selectivity. In recent years, some investigators have attempted to do this using a single stimulus variant of the original probe task. This variant first requires participants to fixate a central screen location, then delivers only a single negative or nonnegative stimulus in either of two adjacent screen locations for a brief duration, followed by a probe stimulus in either of these two loci (Fox et al., 2001; Koster, Leyman, de Raedt, & Crombez, 2006). The pattern of latencies to discriminate probes in the locus of the initial stimuli is used to infer differential attentional engagement with these stimuli, whereas the pattern of latencies to discriminate probes in the opposite screen location is used to infer differential attentional disengagement from them. On this type of task, it has been found that emotionally vulnerable participants are not speeded to process probes in the locus of the single negative stimuli, compared to those in the locus of single neutral stimuli, which has led researchers to claim that they do not display facilitated attentional engagement with negative information. Rather, emotionally vulnerable participants are slowed to process probes in the opposite location from the single negative stimuli, compared to those in the opposite location from single neutral stimuli, which has led researchers to claim that they display impaired attentional disengagement from negative information. However, the single stimulus probe task has two significant limitations, which seriously compromise its capacity to differentiate selective attentional engagement with, and disengagement from, emotional stimuli (Clarke, MacLeod, & Guastella, 2011; Mogg, Holmes, Garner, & Bradley, 2008; Yiend, 2010). We will comment on each limitation in turn, and also will indicate the steps needed to overcome each problem.

The first limitation is that, before the patterns of discrimination latencies observed on probes distal to initial emotional stimuli can be used to infer differential attentional disengagement from these stimuli, it is necessary that attention must always have been initially focused on these emotional stimuli, to an equivalent degree regardless of their valence or the participant group. Otherwise, relative slowing to discriminate probes presented distally to one type of initial stimulus may not reflect impaired attentional disengagement from this initial stimulus, but rather may result from a greater degree of prior attentional engagement with this type of initial stimulus. In previous versions of the single stimulus probe task, differential attentional engagement with the single stimulus has been permitted. Hence, the measure of individual difference in attentional disengagement from any given type of emotional stimuli will be systematically contaminated by individual differences in attentional engagement with this type of emotional stimuli. To prevent this confound, an experimental approach is required that reliably secures initial attention in a predetermined locus, either proximal to or distal from differentially valenced stimuli, then assesses subsequent attention, to independently index individual differences in attentional engagement with the initially distal emotional information, and individual differences in attentional disengagement from the initially proximal emotional information.

The second limitation of the single stimulus probe task employed by previous researchers, such as Fox et al. (2001) and Koster et al. (2006), is that it fails to take account of the possibility that emotionally vulnerable individuals may display generic slowing of response latencies in the presence of negative information. As Yiend (2010) points out, if emotionally vulnerable participants display such an effect, then this could explain their slowing to probes appearing opposite negative stimuli, without the need to suppose impaired attentional disengagement from these stimuli. This general slowing also would be overlaid upon, and hence may obscure, the relative speeding to probes in the locus of negative stimuli that otherwise would result from facilitated attentional engagement with them. The severity of this potential methodological limitation depends upon whether emotionally vulnerable individuals do demonstrate generic slowing in the presence of negative information, independent of their attentional response to this information. Mogg et al. (2008) directly addressed this issue, when recently carrying out a single stimulus probe task. They found that their emotionally vulnerable participants did indeed display general response slowing when negative, rather than neutral stimuli, were presented, under conditions that precluded differential attention to these two categories of stimuli. When attentional selectivity was assessed in a manner that controlled for this general slowing effect, these participants showed evidence of selective attentional engagement with negative information, which otherwise would have gone undetected. Therefore, in order to sensitively assess selective attentional engagement with, and disengagement from, emotional information, it is necessary to appropriately control for possible individual differences in general response slowing incurred by the presence of negative information.

Consequently, we developed a novel attentional probe variant to differentiate these two facets of attentional selectivity, in a manner that circumvents both of these previous methodological limitations. On each trial, the participant first is informed, by a central arrow display, whether to initially attend to an upper or lower screen location. A cue stimulus then flashes up briefly at this location, before a pair of letter strings appear, one string at each of the two screen loci. One of these strings is a word, related either to anxiety of depression, which can be either negative or positive in emotional valence, while the other string is a meaningless nonword. Thus, the participant begins each trial either with attention already focused on an emotional word, or with attention focused distally to an emotional word (i.e. focussed on the nonword). After either a

500 ms or 1000 ms exposure, the letter strings then disappear, and a final probe stimulus appears in either screen location, which either does or does not match the identity of the cue stimulus. Participants must quickly decide whether the cue and probe match in identity. Accurate responding on this task is possible only if the participant starts the trial with attention on the briefly exposed cue, and finishes with attention on the probe. Thus, the task fulfils the need for attention to initially be secured in a predetermined locus, either proximal to or distal from differentially valenced stimuli (by the need to process the cue), before attention is then subsequently assessed 500 or 1000 ms later, by contrasting the speed to process probes in each locus. The resulting pattern of response latencies will independently index individual differences in selective attentional engagement with emotional information distal from initial attentional focus, and individual differences in selective attentional disengagement from emotional information proximal to initial attentional focus. Furthermore, because the measures used to infer attentional selectivity in this task reflect *relative* speed to process probes in differing screen loci, when a given valence of information is present, they control for possible individual differences in general response slowing in the presence of negative information. Thus, variation in degree of response slowing elicited by the mere presence of negative information would not compromise the assessment of selective attentional engagement with, and disengagement from, such information.

Given previous research interest in contrasting the patterns of attentional selectivity observed on emotional information specifically related to anxiety, or specifically related to depression, we included both types of stimulus materials in the task. Using this task we compared attentional preference for negative information, revealed by the engagement bias measure and the disengagement bias measure, in student participants reporting high and low levels of emotional vulnerability, subdivided into two types. For half of these participants, high and low emotional vulnerability reflected elevated and attenuated levels of negative affectivity, respectively, and these participants did not differ in terms of positive affectivity. For the remaining participants, high and low emotional vulnerability reflected attenuated or elevated positive affectivity, respectively,

and these participants did not differ in terms of negative affectivity.

Our hypothesis predicts that the high emotional vulnerability participants selected on the basis of elevated negative affectivity will show greater attentional preference for negative words than their low emotional vulnerability counterparts, on both the attentional engagement and disengagement measures. In contrast, the hypothesis predicts that the high emotional vulnerability participants selected on the basis of attenuated positive affectivity will display discrepant patterns of selectivity on the engagement and disengagement bias measure. On the disengagement bias measure alone, they will show reduced attentional preference for negative words, relative to their low emotional vulnerability counterparts.

METHOD

Participants

Approximately 800 first-year students at the University of Western Australia were screened on the trait version of the Positive and Negative Affect Schedule (PANAS; Watson, Clark, & Tellegen, 1988), which yields separate scores representing the disposition to experience positive and negative affect. Forty participants were selected on the basis of differing in emotional vulnerability in terms of negative affectivity, but not positive affectivity. Twenty of these participants scored in the top third of the negative affectivity distribution, and so were considered high in emotional vulnerability, 20 scored in the bottom third of this distribution, and so were considered low in emotional vulnerability, and all 40 scored in the middle third of the positive affectivity distribution. A further 40 participants were selected on the basis of differing in emotional vulnerability in terms of positive affectivity, but not negative affectivity. Twenty of these participants scored in the bottom third of the positive affectivity distribution, and so were considered high in emotional vulnerability, 20 scored in the top third of this distribution, and so were considered low in emotional vulnerability, and all 40 scored in the middle third of the negative affectivity distribution.

These four subgroups of participants gave rise to two nested between-group factors, emotional vulnerability level (high emotional vulnerability vs. low emotional vulnerability), and vulnerability type (discrepant negative affectivity vs. discrepant positive affectivity). Participant characteristics are shown in Table 1. Separate 2×2 ANOVAs carried out on age, and on gender ratio, revealed no significant effects of either emotional vulnerability level, vulnerability subtype, or their interaction, confirming that the groups did not differ on these dimensions. However, when such an ANOVA was carried out on negative affectivity scores, it revealed a significant main effect of emotional vulnerability level, $F(1, 76) = 108.67$, $p < .001$, $\eta^2 = .59$, modified as expected by vulnerability type, $F(1, 76) = 105.38$, $p < .001$, $\eta^2 = .58$. As required, this two-way interaction resulted from the fact that the simple main effect of emotional vulnerability level was significant for participants selected on the basis of discrepant negative affectivity, $F(1, 38) = 125.65$, $p < .001$, $\eta^2 = .77$, but not for participants selected on the basis of discrepant positive affectivity, $F < 1$. An equivalent ANOVA carried out on positive affectivity scores also revealed a significant main effect of emotional vulnerability level, $F(1, 76) = 121.13$, $p < .05$, $\eta^2 = .61$, and once more confirmed that this was modified by vulnerability type, $F(1, 76) = 100.11$, $p < .001$, $\eta^2 = .57$. Again as required, this two-way interaction now resulted from the fact that the simple main effect of emotional vulnerability level was significant for participants selected on the basis of discrepant positive affectivity, $F(1, 38) = 122.76$, $p < .001$, $\eta^2 = .76$, but not for participants selected on the basis of discrepant negative affectivity, $F(1, 38) = 2.48$, ns, $\eta^2 = .06$.

Positive and Negative Affect Schedule

The Positive and Negative Affect Schedule (PANAS; Watson et al., 1988) comprises two 10-item mood scales, one assessing positive affect and the other negative affect. Depending upon the manner of its delivery, it can be employed as either a state measure (to assess current affect), or as a trait measure (to assess dispositional affectivity). In the state version of the questionnaire, participants are directed to rate "to what extent you feel this way right now; that is, at the present moment". In the trait version, participants are instead instructed to rate "to what extent you generally feel this way; that is, how you feel on average". The PANAS has been found to have good reliability and validity (Crawford & Henry, 2004).

Apparatus

A Hewlett-Packard Compaq dc7800 with a 22-inch colour monitor, and a standard two button mouse, were used to present stimuli and to record participant responses.

Stimuli

Experimental stimuli comprised 64 emotional words, each paired with a length matched non-word. The words were selected on the basis of an initial rating procedure, which involved six clinical psychologists rating 400 candidate words on two dimensions. One rating concerned the emotional valence of the word, which was judged on a 7-point scale ranging from –3 (extremely negative) to +3 (extremely positive), where the midpoint of zero was identified as emotionally neutral. Half of the experimental words (32 words) were chosen on the basis of receiving highly negative ratings, and half were chosen because, although their ratings deviated from

TABLE 1
Participant characteristics (*SD*s in parentheses)

Emotional vulnerability level and subtype	Measure			
	Trait positive affectivity score	*Trait negative affectivity score*	*Age*	*Gender (% of females)*
High				
Discrepant positive affectivity	27.45 (2.86)	19.20 (1.47)	18.30 (1.38)	80
Discrepant negative affectivity	33.10 (1.02)	26.85 (4.23)	17.85 (1.09)	90
Low				
Discrepant positive affectivity	39.00 (3.68)	19.1 (1.59)	18.35 (1.84)	75
Discrepant negative affectivity	33.65 (1.18)	13.85 (1.90)	18.75 (1.83)	70

zero by an equivalent amount, these words had received highly positive ratings. This gave rise to a stimulus valence factor (negative words vs. positive words).

The raters also assessed the degree to which the candidate words were related either to the emotional dimension associated with variations in anxiety (ranging from anxious to relaxed experiences), or to the emotional dimension associated with variations in depression (ranging from sad to happy experiences). Half of the negative words and half of the positive words in the final stimulus set were selected because they had been rated more closely related to the former emotional dimension, and half were selected because they had been rated more closely related to the latter emotional dimension. This gave rise to a stimulus domain factor (anxious/relaxed words vs. sad/happy words), nested within the stimulus valence factor.

The full set of experimental words is provided in Table 2. A two-way ANOVA carried out on the valence ratings confirmed a significant main effect of stimulus valence, $F(1, 60) = 3357.61$, $p < .05$, $\eta^2 = .98$, while providing reassurance that neither the main effect of stimulus domain, $F(1, 60) = 1.88$, ns, $\eta^2 = .03$, nor the interaction between the two factors, $F(1, 60) = 1.60$, ns, $\eta^2 = .03$, was significant. Thus, stimulus emotionality differed as required, and was not confounded with the domain distinction. Additional ANOVAs carried out on word frequency (according to Kucera & Francis, 1967) and on word

TABLE 2
Experimental stimulus words

Anxious/relaxed		Sad/happy	
Negative word	Positive word	Negative word	Positive word
intimidated	brave	sluggish	happier
fretting	ease	disappointed	enjoy
fearful	relaxed	aimless	pleased
tense	composed	unhappy	brightness
dangerous	heroic	emptiness	energetic
worried	confident	lonely	lively
neurotic	serene	dreary	satisfaction
agitation	calm	forlorn	buoyant
frightened	restful	dismal	merry
nervous	tranquil	defeat	passionate
suffocating	assertive	brooding	euphoric
attack	courageous	hopeless	zeal
panicky	peaceful	gloomy	excited
uneasy	secure	failure	eager
restless	safe	upset	fulfilled
alarmed	fearless	discouraged	fun

length (expressed in terms of letters) revealed no significant effects, indicating that the stimulus distinctions were not confounded with either word length or frequency.

Attentional assessment task

Each trial commenced with the appearance of an upper and lower string of asterisks, centralised horizontally on the computer screen and separated vertically by a distance of 3 cm. These asterisk strings demarcated the two critical screen regions, and between them was an arrow display pointing either towards the upper or the lower region, with equal frequency. Participants were required to direct their attention to the screen region indicated by the arrow display. One second later, the screen was cleared, and a cue stimulus was briefly exposed (150 ms) in this attended region. The cue stimulus was a small (2 mm) red line, sloping upwards 45 degrees to either the left or to the right, with equal frequency. Immediately thereafter, a word/nonword stimulus pair was presented, one member appearing in each of the two critical screen regions. Thus, the word either appeared where the participant was already attending, or else it appeared in the distal screen region, with equal frequency. This lexical display was exposed for either 500 ms, or 1000 ms, with equal frequency, representing the same two stimulus exposure durations employed in the previous dot probe variants reviewed within the introduction. A probe stimulus then appeared in either of the two critical screen regions, with equal frequency. Again this was a small (2 mm) red line, sloping upwards 45 degrees to either the left or to the right. Participants were required to quickly indicate whether the slope direction of the probe stimulus matched that of the cue stimulus, which was the case on 50% of trials. They registered their response by pressing either the right or left mouse button, to respectively indicate either that the slopes did or did not match. Response latency to make this probe discrimination decision was recorded, as was its accuracy.

Using these probe discrimination latencies, selective attention to the word members, relative to the nonword members, of the stimulus pairs will be revealed by relative speeding to discriminate probes in the loci of the words relative to probes in the opposing loci, where the nonwords appeared. Therefore, attentional preference for negative words, relative to positive words, can be indexed by the degree to which this speeding to probes in the loci of words (relative to probes in their opposing loci) is greater when these words are negative, compared to when they are positive. Greater attention preference for the negative words relative to the positive words will be revealed higher scores on this Attentional Preference for Negativity index, which can be expressed as follows:

Attentional Preference for Negativity index

= (RT for probes opposite negative word loci

    − RT for probes in negative word loci)

    − (RT for probes opposite positive word loci

    − RT for probes in positive word loci)

Importantly, this task enabled us to compute attentional preference for negativity under two conditions, to discriminate selective attentional engagement with, and disengagement from, the negative words. It can be computed to index attentional response to emotional words presented distally to initial attentional focus, by using the RT data from those trials on which the initial cue appeared in the nonword locus. This provided our Attentional Preference for Negativity: Engagement Bias Index (APN:EBI). A high score of this index will reflect facilitated attentional engagement negative words, relative to positive words. Attentional preference for negativity also can be computed to index attentional response to emotional words presented within the initial focus of attention, by using the RT data from those trials on which the initial cue appeared in the word locus. This provided our Attentional Preference for Negativity: Disengagement Bias Index (APN:DBI). A high score of this index will reflect impaired attentional disengagement from negative words, relative to positive words.

Across the attentional assessment task, each of the 64 lexical string pairs was presented a total of four times, twice with the word in the locus of initial attention and twice with the word distal to the focus of initial attention, and in each case with the probe appearing once in the locus of initial attention and once in the opposing screen location. Order of presentation was randomised.

Procedure

Participants were tested individually. The test session commenced with completion of the state version of the PANAS. The participant then was seated approximately 60 cm from the computer screen, and the requirements of the cue–probe matching task were described. Instructions emphasised the need for accuracy, but stressed that the response should be made as quickly as possible without compromising accuracy. A short practice was then given, comprising 20 trials that employed only neutral stimuli. Following this, the participants completed the attentional assessment task, before being thanked and debriefed.

RESULTS

Participant characteristics at test time

To confirm that required between group differences in negative and positive affect remained evident at test time, state negative and positive affect scores collected during the experimental test session were examined. These scores are shown in Table 3. They were subjected to two-way between-group ANOVAs, which considered the factors of emotional vulnerability level (high emotional vulnerability vs. low emotional vulnerability), and vulnerability type (discrepant negative affectivity vs. discrepant positive affectivity).

The ANOVA carried out on state negative affect scores revealed a significant main effect of emotional vulnerability level, $F(1, 76) = 12.07$, $p < .001$, $\eta^2 = .14$, modified as anticipated by vulnerability type, $F(1, 76) = 6.65$, $p < .05$,

TABLE 3
PANAS state affect scores at test time (*SDs* in parentheses)

Emotional vulnerability level and subtype	Measure	
	State positive affect score	*State negative affect score*
High		
Discrepant positive affectivity	23.44 (5.15)	14.65 (4.45)
Discrepant negative affectivity	27.20 (6.86)	19.00 (8.52)
Low		
Discrepant positive affectivity	30.85 (7.88)	13.60 (3.36)
Discrepant negative affectivity	28.50 (5.10)	11.90 (2.51)

$\eta^2 = .08$. As expected, this two-way interaction arose because a significant simple main effect of emotional vulnerability level was observed on the negative affect scores for participants selected on the basis of discrepant negative affectivity, $F(1, 38) = 12.78$, $p < .01$, $\eta^2 = .25$, but not for those selected on the basis of discrepant positive affectivity, $F < 1$.

Analysis of state positive affect scores also revealed a significant main effect of emotional vulnerability level, $F(1, 76) = 9.15$, $p < .01$, $\eta^2 = .11$, again modified by vulnerability type, $F(1, 76) = 4.45$, $p < .05$, $\eta^2 = .06$. Also as expected, the two-way interaction now was due to the fact that a significant simple main effect of emotional vulnerability level was observed on the positive affect scores for participants selected on the basis of discrepant positive affectivity, $F(1, 38) = 12.04$, $p < .01$, $\eta^2 = .24$, but not for those selected on the basis of discrepant negative affectivity, $F < 1$.

Probe task measures of attentional selectivity

Participants displayed a high level of accuracy on the cue–probe matching task, averaging less than 9% errors. Such accuracy indicates that they complied with the requirement to initially attend to the locus of the cue, and subsequently attend to the locus of the probe. For each participant, mean latencies for accurate responses were computed under each experimental condition, after eliminating RT outliers using a 95% confidence interval.[1] Using the full set of participants, SPSS (ver. 19) was employed to run a boxplot analysis, as recommended by Howell (2002), to determine if any participants were extreme outliers in terms of overall mean RT, and so should be excluded.[2] No participants prove to be extreme outliers in terms of mean RT. The mean probe discrimination latencies obtained in every experimental condition, by each group of participants, are shown in Table 4. There was no significant difference

between the mean probe discrimination latencies shown by high emotional vulnerability participants and low emotional vulnerability participants, either overall (1080.35 ms vs. 1047.73 ms), $F < 1$, or for the subsets of participants whose discrepant emotional vulnerability reflected either differential positive affectivity (1103.33 ms vs. 1075.07 ms), $F < 1$, or differential negative affectivity (1085.64 ms vs. 992.13 ms), $F(1, 38) = 1.45$, ns, $\eta^2 = .04$.

From these raw response latencies, two attentional bias scores were calculated for each participant as described in the Method section; the Attentional Preference for Negativity: Engagement Bias Index (APN:EBI), and the Attentional Preference for Negativity: Disengagement Bias Index (APN:DBI). A boxplot analysis again was carried out on the full participant set, using SPSS (ver. 19), this time to determine if any participants were extreme outliers in terms of their attentional preference for negativity scores (see Footnote 2). This revealed one participant, from the high positive affectivity group, to be an extreme outlier in terms of attentional preference for negativity scores. Consequently, this participant was excluded from further analysis. The attentional preference for negativity scores for the remaining participants, respectively indexing the degree to such attentional preference was evident when the task assessed attentional engagement with initially distal negative words, and when it assessed attentional disengagement from initially proximal negative words, are shown in Table 5. In all cases, higher scores reflect greater attentional preference for negative words.

These attentional preference for negativity scores were subjected to a mixed-design ANOVA, that considered two between-group factors and three within-group factors. The between-group factors were emotional vulnerability level (high emotional vulnerability vs. low emotional vulnerability) and vulnerability type (discrepant negative affectivity vs. discrepant positive affectivity).[3] The within-group factors were attentional bias

---

[1]Specifically, for each participant and in each condition, any RT falling more than 1.96 SD from that participant's mean RT for that condition was classified as an outlier and excluded. This resulted in exclusion of 4.6% of latencies.

[2]In this approach, SPSS defines as an extreme outlier any score that falls more than three times the magnitude of the interquartile range above, or below, the 75th and 25th percentile of the score distribution, respectively (Weinberg & Abramowitz, 2008).

[3]We could instead have run two independent ANOVAs that separately contrasted participants high and low in each type of emotional vulnerability. However, this would have prevented us from statistically determining whether the patterns of attentional selectivity associated with the two types of emotional vulnerability differed significantly. Given that our hypothesis predicts differences between the attentional concomitants of these two types of emotional vulnerability, it can best be tested using the chosen ANOVA design, which statistically tests for these predicted differences.

TABLE 4

Mean probe discrimination latencies, in milliseconds, under each experimental condition (SDs in parentheses)

Emotional vulnerability level and subtype	Anxious/relaxed								Sad/happy							
	Engagement condition				Disengagement condition				Engagement condition				Disengagement condition			
	Positive		Negative		Positive		Negative		Positive		Negative		Positive		Negative	
	Nonword	Word	Nonword	Word	Word	Nonword	Word	Nonword	Nonword	Word	Nonword	Word	Word	Nonword	Word	Nonword
500 ms exposure duration																
High																
Discrepant positive affectivity	1156.04 (486.90)	1101.26 (366.50)	1085.79 (488.89)	1089.12 (317.16)	1022.14 (257.73)	1071.48 (318.16)	1044.29 (282.87)	1067.72 (253.74)	1020.79 (194.57)	1057.23 (235.79)	1100.74 (363.45)	1052.70 (242.68)	982.68 (202.41)	1108.40 (446.22)	1141.70 (425.18)	1103.42 (429.65)
Discrepant negative affectivity	1003.71 (217.74)	1122.58 (299.24)	1125.36 (370.05)	1118.19 (304.06)	1040.87 (278.71)	1101.33 (316.30)	1062.12 (310.43)	1226.92 (697.19)	1070.40 (323.13)	1058.02 (329.87)	1004.94 (236.31)	1146.38 (463.86)	983.69 (198.88)	1090.54 (306.62)	1067.21 (307.62)	1111.84 (349.11)
Low																
Discrepant positive affectivity	1090.34 (294.88)	1072.10 (196.66)	1075.74 (230.41)	1171.39 (260.01)	1048.57 (216.74)	1143.80 (354.15)	1055.96 (194.28)	1144.21 (316.90)	1064.15 (289.32)	1104.39 (256.34)	1049.27 (224.40)	1131.56 (253.85)	1138.45 (328.46)	1024.38 (265.90)	1086.25 (360.55)	1069.24 (181.93)
Discrepant negative affectivity	1021.03 (289.27)	960.26 (196.12)	966.74 (210.87)	1035.84 (281.06)	972.42 (277.74)	1020.03 (303.20)	981.45 (163.02)	956.78 (197.10)	967.29 (233.24)	989.98 (228.71)	1021.08 (258.49)	991.07 (226.46)	932.69 (120.74)	988.79 (194.54)	1030.26 (367.41)	985.13 (204.00)
1000 ms exposure duration																
High																
Discrepant positive affectivity	1035.58 (268.82)	1088.11 (355.67)	1129.54 (313.84)	1055.63 (232.65)	1013.08 (261.48)	1092.47 (301.38)	1039.30 (276.99)	1053.40 (276.84)	1064.69 (364.16)	1123.58 (396.50)	1062.83 (305.67)	1145.62 (369.62)	1068.99 (512.89)	1112.48 (307.81)	1027.97 (287.60)	1083.33 (338.61)
Discrepant negative affectivity	1048.82 (244.19)	1109.30 (274.33)	1069.81 (300.63)	1073.41 (299.35)	997.83 (224.13)	1084.56 (325.19)	1064.97 (259.37)	1077.39 (296.76)	1122.94 (296.25)	1140.85 (367.69)	1062.15 (264.58)	1172.55 (397.56)	1008.35 (308.02)	1141.94 (468.09)	1142.17 (594.40)	1089.24 (368.56)
Low																
Discrepant positive affectivity	1067.29 (257.75)	1129.38 (278.84)	1063.22 (349.82)	1089.05 (292.60)	1078.61 (283.93)	1065.90 (199.88)	1051.12 (338.25)	1552.56 (2241.53)	1056.56 (258.59)	1052.69 (229.87)	1089.92 (226.04)	1081.48 (235.67)	1048.77 (211.85)	1078.88 (226.93)	1109.46 (312.27)	1221.82 (371.20)
Discrepant negative affectivity	961.82 (203.70)	950.08 (247.99)	1153.11 (937.70)	1040.91 (508.26)	913.31 (186.24)	976.33 (236.92)	963.77 (265.78)	954.66 (238.66)	1009.80 (480.46)	1036.81 (319.72)	987.79 (290.73)	936.08 (180.99)	1040.06 (298.78)	982.81 (213.48)	942.01 (183.81)	1078.09 (586.27)

TABLE 5
Attentional preference for negativity index under each experimental condition (*SDs* in parentheses)

Emotional vulnerability level and subtype	Anxious/relaxed		Sad/happy	
	Engagement bias index	Disengagement bias index	Engagement bias index	Disengagement bias index
500 ms exposure duration				
High				
Discrepant positive affectivity	−58.10 (347.85)	−25.91 (315.05)	84.47 (278.67)	−163.99 (324.47)
Discrepant negative affectivity	126.04 (503.33)	104.34 (459.13)	−153.85 (280.41)	−62.22 (381.37)
Low				
Discrepant positive affectivity	−103.51 (195.82)	−13.59 (401.74)	4.51 (306.71)	171.49 (357.88)
Discrepant negative affectivity	−129.87 (262.96)	−72.29 (248.72)	52.71 (350.13)	−101.22 (348.04)
1000 ms exposure duration				
High				
Discrepant positive affectivity	126.44 (230.24)	−62.28 (275.71)	−23.90 (213.59)	11.88 (474.04)
Discrepant negative affectivity	56.88 (380.14)	−74.30 (248.70)	−92.49 (265.03)	−186.56 (699.07)
Low				
Discrepant positive affectivity	33.48 (240.90)	3.80 (376.69)	17.23 (321.62)	74.26 (335.80)
Discrepant negative affectivity	100.46 (429.76)	−72.12 (252.28)	78.71 (487.53)	193.33 (508.76)

type (engagement bias index vs. disengagement bias index), stimulus domain (anxious/relaxed words vs. sad/happy words), and exposure duration (500 ms exposure vs. 1000 ms exposure). The hypothesis under test predicts a three-way interaction involving Emotional vulnerability level × Vulnerability type × Attentional bias type. If the pattern of effects predicted by the hypothesis is restricted to either the short or long exposure duration, or is evidenced more for one particular domain of emotional words, then such a three-way interaction would be modified by either or both of the other within-group factors.

The ANOVA revealed a significant two-way interaction between Emotional vulnerability level × Stimulus domain, $F(1, 75) = 7.98$, $p < .01$, $\eta^2 = .10$, and a significant three-way interaction between Attentional bias type × Stimulus domain × Exposure duration, $F(1, 75) = 4.31$, $p < .05$, $\eta^2 = .05$. Of more direct relevance to the particular issue under present scrutiny, these effects were subsumed within an overall five-way interaction involving Emotional vulnerability level × Vulnerability type × Attentional bias type × Stimulus domain × Exposure duration, $F(1, 75) = 5.19$, $p < .05$, $\eta^2 = .07$. Therefore, in order to understand the differing patterns of attentional engagement and disengagement exhibited by participants whose emotional vulnerability reflected either heightened negative affectivity or attenuated positive affectivity, we must decompose this complex higher order interaction to its component effect.

The contribution of exposure duration to the five-way interaction was straightforward. Neither the simple four-way interaction of the other factors, $F(1, 75) = 1.03$, *ns*, $\eta^2 = .01$, nor any other effects were evident under the 1000 ms exposure condition. However, this simple four-way interaction was significant under the 500 ms exposure condition, $F(1, 75) = 5.47$, $p < .05$, $\eta^2 = .07$. Thus, the differing patterns of attentional selectivity that distinguished the alternative types of emotional vulnerability were evident only when attention was assessed 500 ms after word onset.

We went on to explore the nature of the simple four-way interaction involving Emotional vulnerability level × Vulnerability type × Attentional bias type × Stimulus domain, observed using 500 ms word exposures. This involved breaking down the interaction to reveal the component effects shown by participants chosen on the basis of differing in alternative facets of emotional vulnerability. First, consider the pattern of attentional selectivity shown, at this 500 ms exposure duration, by those participants selected because of their discrepant levels of negative affectivity. Our hypothesis was that individuals whose heightened emotional vulnerability reflects elevated negative affectivity would show a similar attentional preference for negative information on both types of attentional bias measure. Hence we expected no impact of the attentional bias type factor for participants who differed in negative affectivity. Consistent with this expectation, the attentional bias type factor was not involved in any significant effects for this subgroup of participants. There was a significant effect of emotional vulnerability level for these participants, subsumed within an interaction that also involved stimulus domain, $F(1, 38) = 5.91$, $p < .05$, $\eta^2 = .14$. This two-way interaction, which was not further modified by attentional bias type, $F(1, 38) = 2.01$, ns, $\eta^2 = .05$, is shown in Figure 1.

As can be seen, the interaction reflected the fact that these high emotional vulnerability participants, characterised by heightened levels of negative affectivity, obtained higher attentional preference for negative information scores than did their low emotional vulnerability counterparts, but only when stimulus words fell within the anxious/relaxed domain ($M = 115.19$, $SD = 475.65$ vs. $M = 101.08$, $SD = 254.31$), $F(1, 38) = 5.26$, $p < .05$, $\eta^2 = .12$. There was no significant difference in the attentional preference for negative information scores shown by these high and low emotional vulnerability participants when stimulus words fell within the sad/happy domain, $F(1, 38) = 1.14$, ns, $\eta^2 = .03$. This pattern of results confirms that participants whose heightened emotional vulnerability reflected elevated negative affectivity showed greater attentional preference for negative information bias than did participants with lower levels of negative affectivity, and supports the prediction this attentional preference for negativity would be equally evident on measures of biased attentional engagement and disengagement. But it further demonstrates that the difference in attentional bias associated with discrepant levels of negative affectivity is especially evident on emotional information of particular relevance to anxiety.

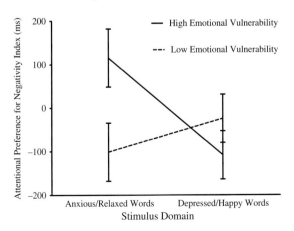

Figure 1. Interaction between Emotional vulnerability level × Stimulus domain at 500 ms exposure duration for participants discrepant in negative affectivity.

Next, consider the pattern of attentional selectivity shown, at this 500 ms exposure duration, by those participants selected because of their discrepant levels of positive affectivity. Our hypothesis predicts that individuals high in emotional vulnerability because of attenuated positive affectivity, will show greater attentional preference for negative information than their low emotional vulnerability counterparts only on the engagement bias measure. In contrast, on the disengagement bias measures they instead should demonstrate *reduced* attentional preference for negativity, relative to their low emotional vulnerability counterparts. This should give rise to a significant interaction between emotional vulnerability level and attentional bias type, for these participants. This two way interaction did indeed prove to be significant, $F(1, 37) = 4.81$, $p < .05$, $\eta^2 = .11$. This interaction effect was more evident for stimulus words falling in the sad/happy domain, rather than the anxious/relaxed domain, as evidenced by a three-way interaction also involving stimulus domain, $F(1, 37) = 4.20$, $p < .05$, $\eta^2 = .10$. This interaction is shown in Figure 2.

The simple two-way interaction of Emotional vulnerability level × Attentional bias type demonstrated on anxious/relaxed stimulus words, which is illustrated within Figure 2a, did not approach significance, $F < 1$. However, the simple interaction demonstrated on sad/happy stimulus words, which is illustrated within Figure 2b, was statistically reliable, $F(1, 37) = 8.72$, $p < .01$, $\eta^2 = .19$. The pattern of this simple two-way interaction, observed on emotional stimuli from the sad/happy domain, was generally consistent with predictions. On the engagement bias measure, the attentional preference for negativity score was nominally higher for the high emotional vulnerability participants than for the low emotional vulnerability participants ($M = 84.47$, $SD = 278.67$ vs. $M = 24.51$, $SD = 306.71$), though this effect fell short of statistical significance, $F < 1$. In direct contrast, on the disengagement bias measure these high emotional vulnerability participants instead demonstrated lower attentional preference for negativity scores than did the low emotional vulnerability group ($M = -163.99$, $SD = 324.47$ vs. $M = 171.49$, $SD = 357.88$), $F(1, 38) = 9.42$, $p = .01$, $\eta^2 = .20$.

These findings are consistent with the hypothesis that participants whose heightened emotional vulnerability reflects attenuated positive affectivity display greater attentional avoidance

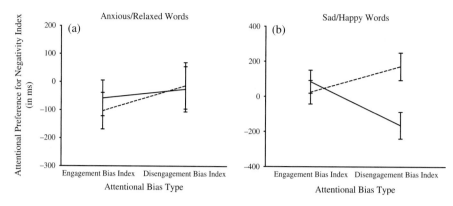

Figure 2. Interaction between Emotional vulnerability level × Attentional bias type × Stimulus domain at 500 ms exposure duration for participants discrepant in positive affectivity.

of negative information than do participants with higher levels of positive affectivity, but only as a result of facilitated attentional disengagement from such negative information. The results also indicate that the facilitated attentional disengagement from negative information, demonstrated by participants with attenuated levels of positive affectivity, is especially evident on emotional information that is of particular relevance to sadness.

DISCUSSION

The purpose of the present study was to test a novel hypothesis concerning the patterns of selective attentional engagement with, and disengagement from, negative emotional information, characteristic of emotional vulnerability that reflects either elevated negative affectivity or attenuated positive affectivity. In order to explain the previously observed robustness of the attentional preference for negative information in anxious participants, we proposed that heightened negative affectivity may be associated with a pervasive attentional preference for negativity, expressed both as relatively facilitated attentional engagement with, and impaired attentional disengagement from, negative information. In contrast, to explain the relative fragility of the attentional preference for negative information less commonly observed in depressed participants, we proposed that attenuated positive affectivity instead may be associated with reduced attention preference negativity that specifically reflects facilitated attentional disengagement from such information. In addition to potentially illuminating the similarities and differences between the attentional characteristics of anxiety

and depression, this hypothesis also may help to resolve the contradiction between conflicting theoretical accounts, which propose either that initial attention to negative information is followed by active avoidance of such information in emotionally vulnerable participants (Mogg & Bradley, 1998), or that negative information disproportionately holds attention in such individuals (Fox et al., 2001; Yiend, 2010). According to the present hypothesis, both accounts are valid, but each pattern of selective attentional disengagement is associated with a different underlying dimension of emotional vulnerability.

Using a new variant of the attentional probe task, designed to cleanly differentiate selective attentional engagement and disengagement, we found support for the hypothesis, though only when attention was assessed following 500 ms word exposures, as employed in the original version of the conventional dot probe task (MacLeod et al., 1986). Before discussing the pattern of attentional effects observed 500 ms after stimulus word onset, and their implications, it is appropriate to briefly reflect on the possible reasons why no group differences presently were evident when attention instead was assessed 1000 ms after stimulus word onset. As noted in the introduction, variants of the conventional probe task, using 1000 ms stimulus exposure durations, have sometimes found that emotionally vulnerable participants show evidence of attentional preference for negative information (e.g., Donaldson et al., 2007; Leyman, de Raedt, Schacht, & Koster, 2006). We can suggest two possible reasons why such previously observed effects may not have been evident in the present study. First, these previous studies have tested clinical participants diagnosed with emotional pathology. It is possible that the prolonged continuation of an attentional preference for threat stimuli, which remains evident 1000 ms after their onset, may be a characteristic of clinical pathology, not evidenced by nonclinical participants reporting elevated negative affectivity or attenuated positive affectivity. Second, these previous studies have employed pictorial stimuli, rather than words. The visual processing of word stimuli required to fully access their meanings can be completed very rapidly, but the visual processing of pictorial stimuli extends across a longer time span. Given that the visual processing required to fully extract meaning plausibly may extend beyond 1000 ms with pictorial images, but not with words, it may be that biased visual attention to emotionally charged pictorial images is more likely to remain evident at a 1000 ms SOA than will be the case for emotionally charged words. Future research could investigate the veracity of these alternative explanations, by systematically comparing the patterns of attentional selectivity observed 1000 ms after stimulus onset, when clinical and nonclinical participants are tested, and when verbal and pictorial stimuli are employed.

At the 500 ms exposure duration employed in the present study, there was clear evidence of group differences in selective attentional response to negative information, and the nature of the observed effects was consistent with our hypothesis. Elevated negative affectivity was associated with a pattern of response latencies suggesting attentional preference for negative words, on measures of both attentional engagement and disengagement. However, the pattern of response latencies associated with attenuated positive affectivity suggested attentional avoidance of negative words, restricted to the measure of disengagement bias, and reflecting enhanced attentional disengagement from negative words. It is also noteworthy that the attentional preference for negativity associated with elevated negative affectivity was evident primarily for emotional stimuli related to dimension of anxiety. In contrast, the attentional avoidance of negativity associated with attenuated positive affectivity, displayed on the measure of selective attentional disengagement, was evident primarily for emotional stimuli related to the dimension of depression. We believe these findings can shed new light on the nature of attentional selectivity likely to characterise heightened vulnerability to anxiety,

and to depression, respectively, and we will consider each emotion in turn.

Since heightened vulnerability to anxiety principally involves elevated negative affectivity, without attenuated positive affectivity, anxious individuals would be expected to reliably demonstrate the patterns of attentional selectivity we have found to characterise such negative affectivity. As we have noted, there is ample evidence that both high trait anxiety, and anxiety dysfunction, are associated with a robust attentional preference for negative words presented for durations of 500 ms (cf. Bar-Haim et al., 2007; Frewen et al., 2008). There is also evidence that anxious participants display this attentional selectivity primarily on emotional stimuli linked to their anxiety-related concerns (Becker, Rinck, Margraf, & Roth, 2001), consistent with the current observation that the attentional selectivity associated with heightened negative affectivity is most evident on anxiety-relevant stimuli. However, the question of whether anxiety-linked attentional selectivity reflects increased attentional engagement with negative stimuli, or impaired attentional disengagement from such stimuli, has not hitherto been resolved.

Some researchers previously have claimed that anxiety vulnerability is characterised only by enhanced attentional engagement with negative information (Massar, Mol, Kenemans, & Baas, 2011; Matsumoto, 2010); others instead have argued that it is characterised only by impaired attentional disengagement from negative information (Fox, Russo, & Dutton, 2002; Koster, Crombez, Verschuere, & de Houwer, 2004). The present methodology provides an especially powerful means of independently assessing both forms of attentional selectivity, by differentiating the attentional response to emotional stimuli that appear distally from initial attentional focus, and the attentional response to emotional stimuli that appear proximally to initial attentional focus. The findings invite the conclusion that elevated anxiety vulnerability, being marked principally by heightened negative affectivity, is likely to be simultaneously associated with both types of attentional selectivity. This accords with the theoretical position recently put forward by Ouimet, Gawronski, and Dozois (2009), who propose an integrative model of cognitive vulnerability to anxiety vulnerability, within which facilitated attentional engagement with, and impaired attentional disengagement from, negative information, both operate.

It may be the case that both forms of attentional preference for negative information are equally associated with the heightened negative affectivity characteristic of anxiety vulnerability, but this need not mean that biased attentional engagement and disengagement make an equivalent causal contribution to anxious symptomatology. In recent years, researchers have sought to determine the causal contributions of attentional bias by exposing participants to probe task variants designed to systematically modify selective attentional response to negative information, then examining the impact of such attentional change on anxiety symptoms (cf. Hakamata et al., 2010; Mathews & MacLeod, 2002). Although it usually has been unclear whether these bias modification procedures influence attentional engagement or disengagement, it repeatedly has been shown that reducing attentional preference for negative information serves to attenuate anxiety symptoms, suggesting that attentional selectivity causally contributes to anxiety (MacLeod, Rutherford, Campbell, Ebsworthy, & Holker, 2002; Schmidt, Richey, Buckner, & Timpano, 2009; See, MacLeod, & Bridle, 2009). In a recent variant of this approach, Hirsch et al. (2011) compared the impact of alternative bias modification variants, designed either to reduce attentional engagement with, or to increase attentional disengagement from, negative information, in a sample of self-selected worriers. Both procedures were equally effective in eliciting attentional change, but only the former procedure served to reduce the intensity of subsequently reported worry. Two possible accounts of these findings can be distinguished. One possibility is that only facilitated engagement with negative information causally contributes to anxiety, while impaired disengagement from negative information arises only as a consequence of this elevated anxiety. An alternative possibility is that facilitated attentional engagement with, and impaired disengagement from, negative information, may each make a causal contribution to differing dimensions of anxiety. For example, we have suggested elsewhere that the engagement bias may impact on the intensity of the anxiety response, whereas the disengagement bias may impact on its longevity (Rudaizky, MacLeod, & Page, 2011). Whatever their relative contribution to anxious symptomatology, it appears that heightened anxiety vulnerability is likely to be marked by attentional preference for negative information, on adequately sensitive measures of both selective attentional engagement and disengagement.

Let us turn now to consider how the present findings may shed light on the patterns of attentional selectivity that previous investigators have observed to characterise depressed participants. The results of the present study suggest that two dissimilar profiles of attentional selectivity will be combined in these participants; the profile associated with elevated negative affectivity, as just described, and the profile associated with attenuated positive affectivity. When an assessment task principally measures selective attentional engagement with negative information, then there will be no conflict between these two profiles of selectivity, and so depression should be characterised by facilitated attentional engagement with negative information. When an assessment task instead principally measures selective attentional disengagement, then the contradictory profiles of selectivity associated with elevated negative affectivity and attenuated positive affectivity will compete with each other, and their mutual negation may undermine the expression of depression-linked bias. Moreover, the present findings suggest that depressed participants' elevated negative affectivity should be associated with impaired disengagement from negative stimuli related to anxiety, while their attenuated positive affectivity should be associated with enhanced attentional disengagement from negative stimuli relatedness to sadness. This leads to the counterintuitive expectation that a depression-linked preference for negative information on attentional disengagement tasks will be most likely when this negative information is related to anxiety rather than to sadness.

We already have noted that, when attentional bias is assessed using tasks that do not distinguish selective engagement from disengagement, depression-linked effects are fragile and unreliable (Mathews & MacLeod, 2005; Gotlib & Joorman, 2010). However, in the past few years, a number of researchers have sought to specifically assess the patterns of selective attentional disengagement evidenced by depressed participants. Although their methodologies may always have not been optimal, there has indeed been evidence that depressed participants may display impaired attentional disengagement from negative information that is anxiety related. For example, when Leyman and colleagues (Leyman, de Raedt, & Koster, 2009; Leyman et al., 2006) employed hostile faces as negative stimuli, they concluded that their depressed participants showed impaired attentional disengagement from these images. Similar conclusions were drawn by Rinck and Becker (2005), who employed anxiety-related verbal stimuli, and by Caseras, Garner, Bradley, and Mogg (2007), whose negative stimuli included images of injured people, and individuals facing life threatening circumstances. In contrast, Karparova, Kersting, and Suslow (2005) employed negative stimuli related to sadness (sad faces), and concluded that the ability to disengage attention from such negative stimuli is not impaired in depression.

Although we have found evidence that attenuated positive affectivity is associated with enhanced attentional disengagement from sadness-related information, the causal basis of this relationship presently remains indeterminate. It is possible that this attentional effect may causally contribute to the maintenance of low positive affect, because it reduces the effective emotional processing of sadness-related information. Teasdale (1999) argues that when effective emotional processing of negative information is prevented, the consequence is sustained rumination, which serves to perpetuate depression. Alternatively, however, it also is possible that increased attentional disengagement from sadness-related information may be a consequence of low positive affect, perhaps adopted for the purpose of mood repair. Emotion regulation researchers contend that undesirable emotional states can trigger patterns of selective information processing that favour more desirable emotional states (cf. Gross, 2008). Speeded attentional disengagement from sadness-related information may thus represent an emotion regulation response, elicited by attenuated levels of positive affect, and serving to facilitate the elevation of positive affect. The validity of these alternative accounts could be empirically discriminated by future research delivering appropriate variants of the attentional bias modification procedure previously employed by Hirsch et al. (2011), to selectively manipulate this pattern of selective attentional disengagement. If it causally contributes to low positive affectivity then reducing the bias should lead to increased levels of positive affectivity. In contrast, if the bias is a consequence of low positive affectivity, then reducing it will not elevate positive affectivity. Indeed, if this attentional bias serves a mood repair function, then reducing it would instead lead to further attenuation of positive affect.

Another important avenue for future research will be to delineate the precise attentional mechanisms that underpin the presently observed individual differences in attentional engagement with, and disengagement from, negative information. Our paradigm permits us to conclude that participants with elevated negative affectivity demonstrate enhanced attentional engagement with negative information, in the sense that they exhibit an attentional preference for such information when it appears outside initial attentional focus. However, it is not yet possible to determine whether this reflects their elevated probability of moving attention to the locus of such distal negative information before the probe appears (thereby inflating their likelihood of attending here at the point of probe onset), or instead reflects their capacity to move attention with greater speed to the locus of the negative information, when the position of the probe indicates this to be required. Similarly, our paradigm permits conclusions concerning impaired (and enhanced) attentional disengagement from negative information, in the sense that such information is more (or less) likely to continue receiving attention 500 ms after having initially been the focus of attention. Once again, such differential disengagement could result from a variety of mechanisms. It may reflect the probability of participants moving attention away from negative information prior to probe onset, or might instead reflect the speed with which attention could be moved from the locus of the negative information when a distal probe appeared. It also is possible that individual differences in inhibition of return (IOR; cf. Klein, 2000) might contribute to the observed individual differences in attentional disengagement from negative information. For example, perhaps participants high in negative affectivity show continuing attention to negative information, 500 ms after they initially have attended to it, because they exhibit reduced inhibition of return effects for initially attended negative information (Perez-Duenas, Acosta, & Lupianez, 2009). By compromising their capacity to effectively sustain attentional disengagement from such negative information, such attenuated IOR would inflate the prospect of their subsequently displaying continued attention to it. Research employing eye-movement measures, to provide a more continuous record of attentional distribution during performance of this task, could shed valuable light on the contributions made by these various candidate mechanisms to the observed pattern of attentional effects (Buckner, Maner, & Schmidt, 2010).

Future research could also overcome a limitation of the current work, which prevents us from determining whether the presently observed attentional effects result from the selective processing of positive information, negative information, or both. Many previous attentional studies have contrasted only emotionally negative and neutral information, which has attracted the criticism that stimulus negativity has been confounded with stimulus emotionality (Rutherford, MacLeod, & Campbell, 2004). As noted by these critics, specific conclusions concerning selective attentional response to stimulus negativity requires contrasting equally emotional stimuli that differ only in terms of negativity. Our own design adopted this approach, thereby enabling us to draw conclusions concerning biased patterns of attention to negative information, relative to equally emotional positive information. However, such biases could, in principle, reflect selective attentional responding to positive material, rather than to negative material. Thus, for example, the relatively enhanced attentional engagement with negative words related to anxiety, which we observed in participants with elevated negative affectivity, could equally well be construed as relatively impaired attentional engagement with positive words related to relaxation. Similarly, the relatively enhanced attentional disengagement from negative words drawn from the sad/happy domain, which we observed in participants with attenuated positive affectivity, could also be described as relatively impaired attentional disengagement from positive words drawn from this domain. Studies that directly contrast attentional responses to negative, positive, and neutral stimuli could address this issue. Such designs also would permit researchers to examine how stimulus emotionality, as well as stimulus negativity, impacts on the patterns of attentional selectivity associated with individual differences in these two dimensions of affectivity.

Future investigations of this type seem certain to further advance understanding of the variations in attentional selectivity associated with individual differences in both negative and positive affectivity. For the moment, however, we can conclude that heightened emotional vulnerability involving elevated negative affectivity has a quite different attentional signature from heightened emotional vulnerability involving attenuated positive affectivity. Elevated negative affectivity is marked by an increase in attentional preference for negative relative to positive information, especially when it is anxiety related, and this bias reflects both facilitated attentional engagement with, and impaired attentional disengagement from, such information. Attenuated positive affectivity instead is marked by reduced attentional preference for negative information relative to positive information, especially when it is depression related, and this bias reflects only enhanced attentional disengagement from such information. Given the differing contributions made by negative and positive affectivity to anxiety and depression, anxious participants would be expected to consistently display the former pattern of attentional selectivity, whereas depressed participants would be expected to display a combination of both patterns of selectivity. The specific nature of this combination will depend upon the degree to which a given task assesses selective attentional engagement or disengagement, and the degree to which emotional stimuli are related to anxiety or to depression. We suggest that this may help explain why the patterns of attentional selectivity associated with elevated depression have proven to be less consistent than has the pattern associated with elevated anxiety.

REFERENCES

Amir, N., Elias, J., Klumpp, H., & Przeworski, A. (2003). Attentional bias to threat in social phobia: Facilitated processing of threat or difficulty disengaging attention from threat. *Behaviour Research and Therapy, 41*, 1325–1335.

Bar-Haim, Y., Lamy, D., Pergamin, L., Bakermans-Kranenburg, M. J., & van IJzendoorn, M. H. (2007). Threat-related attentional bias in anxious and nonanxious individuals: A meta-analytic study. *Psychological Bulletin, 133*, 1–24.

Beck, A. T., & Clark, D. A. (1997). An information processing model of anxiety: Automatic and strategic processes. *Behavior Research and Therapy, 35*, 49–58.

Beck, A. T., Emery, G., & Greenberg, R. (1985). *Anxiety disorders and phobias: A cognitive perspective.* New York, NY: Basic Books.

Becker, E. S., Rinck, M., Margraf, J., & Roth, W. T. (2001). The emotional Stroop effect in anxiety disorders: General emotionality or disorder specificity? *Journal of Anxiety Disorders, 15*, 147–159.

Bower, G. H. (1981). Mood and memory. *The American Psychologist, 36*, 129–148.

Bradley, B. P., Mogg, K., & Lee, M. (1997). Attentional biases for negative information in induced and naturally occurring dysphoria. *Behaviour Research and Therapy, 35*, 911–927.

Bradley, B. P., Mogg, K., Millar, N., & White, J. (1995). Selective processing of negative information: Effects of clinical anxiety, concurrent depression, and awareness. *Journal of Abnormal Psychology, 104*, 532–536.

Buckner, J. D., Maner, J. K., & Schmidt, N. B. (2010). Difficulty disengaging attention from social threat in social anxiety. *Cognitive Therapy Research, 34*, 99–105.

Caseras, X., Garner, M., Bradley, B. P., & Mogg, K. (2007). Biases in visual orienting to negative and positive scenes in dysphoria: An eye movement study. *Journal of Abnormal Psychology, 116*, 491–497.

Carlson, J. M., & Reinke, K. S. (2008). Masked fearful faces modulate the orienting of covert spatial attention. *Emotion, 8*, 522–529.

Cisler, J., Bacon, A. K., & Williams, N. L. (2009). Phenomenological characteristics of attentional biases towards threat: A critical review. *Cognitive Therapy and Research, 33*, 221–234.

Cisler, J., & Koster, E. H. (2010). Mechanisms of attentional biases towards threat in anxiety disorders: An integrative review. *Clinical Psychology Review, 30*, 203–216.

Clarke, P., MacLeod, C., & Guastella, A. J. (2011). Assessing the role of attentional engagement and disengagement in anxiety-linked attentional bias: A critique of current paradigms and suggestions for future research directions. *Manuscript under review.*

Crawford, J. R., & Henry, J. D. (2004). The Positive and Negative Affect Schedule (PANAS): Construct validity, measurement properties and normative data in a large non-clinical sample. *British Journal of Clinical Psychology, 43*, 245–265.

Donaldson, C., Lam, D., & Mathews, A. (2007). Rumination and attention in major depression. *Behavior Research and Therapy, 45*, 2664–2678.

Eysenck, M. W. (1979). Anxiety, learning, and memory: A reconceptualization. *Journal of Research in Personality, 13*, 363–385.

Eysenck, M. W. (1985). Anxiety and task performance. *Personality and Individual Differences, 6*, 579–586.

Eysenck, M. W. (1997). *Anxiety and cognition: A unified theory.* Hove, UK: Psychology Press.

Eysenck, M. W. (2010). Attentional control theory of anxiety: Recent developments. In A. Gruszka, G. Matthews, & B. Szymura (Eds.), *Handbook of individual differences in cognition: Attention, memory, and executive control* (pp. 195–204). New York, NY: Springer Science and Business Media.

Eysenck, M. W., & Derakshan, N. (2011). New perspectives in attentional control theory. *Personality and Individual Differences, 50*, 955–960.

Eysenck, M. W., Derakshan, N., Santos, R., & Calvo, M. G. (2007). Anxiety and cognitive performance: Attentional control theory. *Emotion, 7*, 336–353.

Fox, E., Russo, R., Bowles, R., & Dutton, K. (2001). Do threatening stimuli draw or hold visual attention in subclinical anxiety? *Journal of Experimental Psychology: General, 130*(4), 681–700.

Fox, E., Russo, R., & Dutton, K. (2002). Attentional bias for threat: Evidence for delayed disengagement from emotional faces. *Cognition and Emotion, 16*, 355–379.

Frewen, P. A., Dozois, D. J., Joanisse, M. F., & Neufeld, R. W. (2008). Selective attention to threat versus reward: Meta-analysis and neural-network modeling of the dot-probe task. *Clinical Psychology Review, 28*, 307–337.

Gotlib, I. H., & Joormann, J. (2010). Cognition and depression: Current status and future directions. *Annual Review of Clinical Psychology, 6*, 285–312.

Gotlib, I. H., Krasnoperova, E., Yue, D. N., & Joormann, J. (2004). Attentional biases for negative interpersonal stimuli in clinical depression. *Journal of Abnormal Psychology, 113*, 127–135.

Gross, J. J. (2008). Emotion and emotional regulation: Personality processes and individual differences. In P. Oliver, R. W. Robins, & L. A. Pervin (Eds.), *Handbook of personality psychology: Theory and research* (3rd ed), pp. 701–724). New York, NY: Guilford Press.

Hakamata, Y., Lissek, S., Bar-Haim, Y., Britton, J. C., Fox, N. A., Leibenluft, E., et al. (2010). Attention bias modification treatment: A meta-analysis toward the establishment of a novel treatment for anxiety. *Biological Psychiatry, 68*, 982–990.

Hirsch, C. R., MacLeod, C., Mathews, A., Sandher, O., Siyani, A., & Hayes, S. (2011). The contribution of attentional bias to worry: Distinguishing the roles of selective engagement and disengagement. *Journal of Anxiety Disorders, 25*, 272–277.

Howell, D. C. (2002). *Statistical methods for psychology* (5th ed.). Duxbury, UK: Wadsworth Group.

Joormann, J., & Gotlib, I. H. (2007). Selective attention to emotional faces following recovery from depression. *Journal of Abnormal Psychology, 116*, 80–85.

Karparova, S. P., Kersting, A., & Suslow, T. (2005). Disengagement of attention from facial emotion in unipolar depression. *Psychiatry and Clinical Neurosciences, 59*, 723–729.

Kessler, R. C., Gruber, M., Hettema, J. M., Hwang, I., & Sampson, N. (2010). Major depression and generalised anxiety disorder in the National Comorbidity Survey: Follow up survey. In D. D. Goldberg, K. S. Kendler, P. J. Sirovatka, & D. A. Regier (Eds.), *Diagnostic issues in depression and generalised anxiety disorder: Refining the research agenda for DSM-V* (pp. 139–170). Washington, DC: American Psychiatric Association.

Klein, R. M. (2000). Inhibition of return. *Trends in Cognitive Sciences, 4*, 138–147.

Koster, E. H., Crombez, G., Verschuere, B., & de Houwer, J. (2004). Selective attention to threat in the dot probe paradigm: Differentiating vigilance and difficulty to disengage. *Behaviour Research and Therapy, 42*, 1183–1192.

Koster, E. H., Leyman, L., de Raedt, & Crombez, G. (2006). Cueing of visual attention by emotional facial expressions: The influence of individual differences in anxiety and depression. *Personality and Individual Differences, 41*, 329–339.

Kucera, H., & Francis, W. N. (1967). *Computational analysis of present-day American English*. Providence, RI: Brown University Press.

Lee, A. C., Watson, D., & Mineka, S. (1994). Temperament, personality, and the mood and anxiety disorders. *Journal of Abnormal Psychology, 103*, 103–116.

Leyman, L., de Raedt, R., & Koster, E. H. (2009). Attentional biases for facial stimuli in currently depressed patients with bipolar disorder. *International Journal of Clinical and Health Psychology, 9*, 393–410.

Leyman, L., de Raedt, R., Schacht, R., & Koster, E. H. (2006). Attentional biases for angry faces in unipolar depression. *Psychological Medicine, 37*, 393–402.

MacLeod, C., Mathews, A., & Tata, P. (1986). Attentional bias in emotional disorders. *Journal of Abnormal Psychology, 95*, 15–20.

MacLeod, C., & Rutherford, E. (2004). Information-processing approaches: Assessing the selective functioning of attention, interpretation and retrieval. In R. G. Heimberg, C. L. Turk, & D. S. Mennin (Eds.), *Generalised anxiety disorder: Advances in research and practice* (pp. 109–142). New York, NY: Guilford Press.

MacLeod, C., Rutherford, E., Campbell, L., Ebsworthy, G., & Holker, L. (2002). Selective attention and emotional vulnerability: Assessing the causal basis of their association through the experimental manipulation of attentional bias. *Journal of Abnormal Psychology, 111*, 107–123.

Massar, S. A., Mol, N. M., Kenemans, J. L., & Baas, J. M. (2011). Attention bias in high- and low-anxious individuals: vidence for threat-induced effects on engagement and disengagement. *Cognition and Emotion, 25*, 805–817.

Matsumoto, E. (2010). Bias in attending to emotional facial expressions: Anxiety and visual search efficiency. *Applied Cognitive Psychology, 24*, 414–424.

Matthews, A., & Mackintosh, B. (1998). A cognitive model of selective processing in anxiety. *Cognitive Therapy and Research, 22*, 539–560.

Mathews, A., & MacLeod, C. (1994). Cognitive approaches to emotional disorders. *Annual Review of Psychology, 45*, 25–50.

Mathews, A., & MacLeod, C. (2002). Induced processing biases have causal effects on anxiety. *Cognition and Emotion, 16*, 331–354.

Mathews, A., & MacLeod, C. (2005). Cognitive vulnerability to emotional disorders. *Annual Review of Clinical Psychology, 1*, 167–195.

Mathews, A., Ridgeway, V., & Williamson, D. (1996). Evidence for attention to threatening stimuli in depression. *Behaviour Research and Therapy, 34*, 695–705.

Mogg, K., & Bradley, B. P. (1998). A cognitive-motivational analysis of anxiety. *Behavior Research and Therapy, 36*, 809–848.

Mogg, K., & Bradley, B. P. (2005). Attentional bias in generalized anxiety disorder versus depressive disorder. *Cognitive Therapy and Research, 29*, 29–45.

Mogg, K., Bradley, B. P., & Williams, R. (1995). Attentional bias in anxiety and depression: The role of awareness. *British Journal of Clinical Psychology, 34*, 17–36.

Mogg, K., Bradley, B. P., Williams, R., & Mathews, A. (1993). Subliminal processing of emotional information in anxiety and depression. *Journal of Abnormal Psychology, 102*, 304–311.

Mogg, K., Holmes, A., Garner, M., & Bradley, B. P. (2008). Effects of threat cues on attentional shifting, disengagement and response slowing in anxious individuals. *Behaviour Research and Therapy, 46*, 656–667.

Neshat-Doost, H. T., Moradi, A. R., Taghavi, M., Yule, W., & Dagleish, T. (2000). Lack of attentional bias for emotional information in clinically depressed children and adolescents on the dot probe task. *Journal of Child Psychology and Psychiatry, 41*, 363–368.

Ouimet, A. J., Gawronski, B., & Dozois, D. J. (2009). Cognitive vulnerability to anxiety: A review and an integrative model. *Clinical Psychology Review, 29*, 459–470.

Perez-Duenas, C., Acosta, A., & Lupianez, J. (2009). Attentional capture and trait anxiety: Evidence from inhibition of return. *Journal of Anxiety Disorders, 23*, 782–790.

Rinck, M., & Becker, E. S. (2005). A comparison of attentional biases and memory biases in women with social phobia and major depression. *Journal of Abnormal Psychology, 114*, 62–74.

Rudaizky, D., MacLeod, C., & Page, A. (2011). Anxiety reactivity and anxiety perseveration: Underlying dimensions of trait anxiety. *Manuscript under review*

Rutherford, E., MacLeod, C., & Campbell, L. (2004). Negativity selectivity effects and emotional selectivity effects in anxiety: Differential attentional correlates of state and trait variables. *Cognition and Emotion, 18*, 711–720.

Salemink, E., van den Hout, M. A., & Kindt, M. (2007). Selective attention and threat: Quick orienting versus slow disengagement and two versions of the dot probe task. *Behaviour Research and Therapy, 45*, 607–615.

Schmidt, N. B., Richey, J. A., Buckner, J. D., & Timpano, K. R. (2009). Attention training for generalized social anxiety disorder. *Journal of Abnormal Psychology, 118*, 5–14.

See, J., MacLeod, C., & Bridle, R. (2009). The reduction of anxiety vulnerability through the modification of attentional bias: A real-world study using a home-based cognitive bias modification procedure. *Journal of Abnormal Psychology, 118*, 65–75.

Taghavi, M., Neshat-Doost, H. T., Moradi, A. R., Yule, W., & Dalgleish, T. (1999). Biases in visual attention in children and adolescents with clinical anxiety and mixed anxiety-depression. *Journal of Abnormal Child Psychology, 27,* 251–223.

Teasdale, J. D. (1999). Emotional processing, three modes of mind and the prevention of relapse in depression. *Behavior Research and Therapy, 37,* S53–S77.

Watson, D., Clark, L. A., & Tellegen, A. (1988). Development and validation of brief measures of positive and negative affect: The PANAS scales. *Journal of Personality and Social Psychology, 54,* 1063–1070.

Watson, D., & Naragon-Gainey, K. (2009). On the specificity of positive emotional dysfunction in psychopathology: Evidence from the mood and anxiety disorders and schizophrenia/schizotypy. *Clinical Psychology Review, 30,* 839–848.

Watson, D., O'Hara, M. W., Simms, L. J., Kotov, R., Chmielewski, M., McDade-Montez, E., et al. (2007). Development and validation of the Inventory of Depression and Anxiety Symptoms (IDAS). *Psychological Assessment, 19,* 253–268.

Watson, D., & Tellegen, A. (1985). Toward a consensual structure of mood. *Psychological Bulletin, 98,* 219–235.

Weinberg, S. L., & Ambramowitz, S. K. (2008). *Statistics using SPSS: An integrative approach* (2nd ed.). New York, NY: Cambridge University Press.

Williams, J., Watts, F. N., MacLeod, C., & Mathews, A. (1988). *Cognitive psychology and emotional disorders.* Chichester, UK: Wiley.

Williams, J., Watts, F. N. , MacLeod, C., & Mathews, A. (1997). *Cognitive psychology and emotional disorders* (2nd ed.). Chichester, UK: Wiley.

Wilson, E. J., MacLeod, C., & Campbell, L. (2006). The information processing approach to emotion research. In J. A. Coan & J. J. B. Allen (Eds.) *The handbook of emotion elicitation and assessment* (pp. 184–202). Oxford, UK: Oxford University Press.

Yiend, J. (2010). The effects of emotion on attention: A review of attentional processing of emotional information. *Cognition and Emotion, 24,* 3–47.

Yiend, J., & Mathews, A. (2001). Anxiety and attention to threatening pictures. *Quarterly Journal of Experimental Psychology, 54A,* 665–681.

JOURNAL OF COGNITIVE PSYCHOLOGY, 2012, 24 (1), 54–65

Anxiety and selective attention to angry faces: An antisaccade study

M. L. Reinholdt-Dunne[1,2], K. Mogg[1], V. Benson[1], B. P. Bradley[1], M. G. Hardin[3], S. P. Liversedge[1], D. S. Pine[4], and M. Ernst[4]

[1]School of Psychology, University of Southampton, Southampton, UK
[2]Department of Psychology, University of Copenhagen, Copenhagen, Denmark
[3]Department of Human Development, University of Maryland, College Park, MD, USA
[4]Section of Developmental and Affective Neuroscience, National Institute of Mental Health, Bethesda, MD, USA

Cognitive models of anxiety propose that anxiety is associated with an attentional bias for threat, which increases vulnerability to emotional distress and is difficult to control. The study aim was to investigate relationships between the effects of threatening information, anxiety, and attention control on eye movements. High and low trait anxious individuals performed antisaccade and prosaccade tasks with angry, fearful, happy, and neutral faces. Results indicated that high-anxious participants showed a greater antisaccade cost for angry than neutral faces (i.e., relatively slower to look away from angry faces), compared with low-anxious individuals. This bias was not found for fearful or happy faces. The bias for angry faces was not related to individual differences in attention control assessed on self-report and behavioural measures. Findings support the view that anxiety is associated with difficulty in using cognitive control resources to inhibit attentional orienting to angry faces, and that attention control is multifaceted.

Keywords: Angry faces; Antisaccade; Anxiety; Selective attention.

According to cognitive models of anxiety, anxious individuals have an attentional bias for threatening information, which may cause and/or maintain their anxiety (e.g., Beck & Emery, 1985; Mogg & Bradley, 1998; Williams, Watts, MacLeod, & Mathews, 1997). This view has been supported by empirical studies showing that anxious persons have a greater attentional bias for threatening stimuli in comparison with nonanxious individuals (for review, see Bar-Haim, Lamy, Pergamin, Bakermans-Kranenburg, & van IJzendoorn, 2007), and by research suggesting that manipulation of the attentional bias for threat (by attentional training) modifies a person's vulnerability to subsequent emotional distress (MacLeod, Rutherford, Campbell, Ebsworthy, & Holker, 2002).

Thus, it is of theoretical and potential clinical importance to clarify the extent to which anxious individuals can use effortful ("top-down") processes in order to control their attentional bias for threat-related information (Bishop, 2007; Ochsner & Gross, 2005). Models from the neuroscience and cognitive literature argue that individuals differ in their ability to use attentional resources (i.e., "attention control") to suppress cognitive and affective responses to emotional stimuli (e.g., see reviews by Bishop, 2007; Eysenck, Derakshan, Santos, & Calvo, 2007; Ochsner &

Correspondence should be addressed to Karin Mogg, School of Psychology, University of Southampton, Highfield, Southampton SO17 1BJ, UK. E-mail: kmogg@soton.ac.uk

Gross, 2005). For example, it has been proposed that anxious individuals not only have an automatic or reflexive tendency to direct their attention towards threat (largely a "bottom-up", or stimulus-driven, process), but that they also have impaired ability to control their attentional response ("top-down", or goal-directed, process) (Eysenck et al., 2007).

The antisaccade task (Hallet, 1978) has become increasingly popular when assessing the effects of emotion on attentional control functions (e.g., Ansari & Derakshan, 2010; Ansari, Derakshan, & Richards, 2008; Derakshan, Ansari, Hansard, Shoker, & Eysenck, 2009; Hardin, Schroth, Pine, & Ernst, 2007; Jazbec, McClure, Hardin, Pine, & Ernst, 2005; Wieser, Pauli, & Mühlberger, 2009). The task requires participants to suppress the reflexive tendency to orient attention towards a cue that suddenly appears peripherally. Instead, participants are required to direct their gaze as quickly as possible to the opposite side of the visual display to that of the cue. In contrast, the prosaccade task requires participants to direct their gaze towards the suddenly appearing cue. Derakshan et al. (2009) recently used antisaccade and prosaccade tasks to examine attentional bias in anxiety; they found that high trait anxious individuals were slower in looking away from computer-generated images of angry faces compared to low anxious persons. This effect was greater for angry than happy or neutral cues (consistent with an anxiety-related attentional bias being specific to threat, rather than emotional information in general), and it was found in saccade latencies, but not errors. These results were in accord with Eysenck et al.'s (2007) attention control theory, which proposed that response latency reflects performance efficiency, which is impaired by anxiety, whereas errors reflect performance effectiveness, which is less sensitive to anxiety-related effects. Thus, these findings supported the view that anxiety is associated with difficulty in inhibiting attentional processing of threat (Eysenck et al., 2007).

Research using other paradigms has also indicated that attention control influences the association between anxiety and attentional bias for threat. Derryberry and Reed (2002) proposed that anxious individuals with poor attention control show an enhanced bias for threatening material, whereas anxious people with good attention control are able to control attention and therefore may show little or no threat bias (i.e., similar to nonanxious persons). Supportive

evidence for this view has been found in research using a spatial cueing task (Derryberry & Reed, 2002) and an emotional Stroop paradigm (Reinholdt-Dunne, Mogg, & Bradley, 2009). Thus, both anxiety and attention control may play important roles in regulating attentional responses to emotional information. It would seem important to investigate this further using eye movement methodology that allows precise assessment of top-down mechanisms of the control of attention allocation. Specifically, latency to onset of an antisaccade following appearance of a target stimulus provides a measure of the ability to engage resource-intensive cognitive strategies, in the service of control over reflexive attentional shifts (Hardin et al., 2007; Jazbec et al., 2005).

The current study complements recent research that has used the antisaccade paradigm to assess the effect of anxiety on the ability to control attentional responses to threat cues, as well as other work published during the course of the present investigation (Derakshan et al., 2009). Moreover, while Derkashan et al. (2009) relied on computer generated-images, the present study uses real-life photographic face images, as well as a wider range of emotional expressions. We assessed saccade latency and errors made on antisaccade versus prosaccade trials as a function of the emotional facial expression of the target stimulus (angry, fearful, and happy vs. neutral faces), and the trait anxiety level of the participants. It is well-established that saccade latency is typically longer for antisaccade than prosaccade trials, with this difference in latency being referred to as the antisaccade cost (e.g., Godijn & Kramer, 2008; Kristjánsson, Chen, & Nakayama, 2001). Although the exact underlying mechanisms are not fully understood, it is thought that cognitive processes that support reflexive prosaccades are engaged in both prosaccade and antisaccade tasks, though this reflexive prepotent (prosaccade) response must be inhibited in the antisaccade task, and a volitional (antisaccade) response executed instead. As such, the antisaccade task reflects the top-down (attentional) mechanisms involved in resolving the competition between this reflexive cognitive process and other cognitive processes involved in more deliberative, resource-intensive, voluntary saccade programmes. In the antisaccade task, relative to the prosaccade task, this competition is thought to result in longer latencies (Godijn & Kramer, 2008; Hutton & Ettinger, 2006; Kristjánsson, 2007; Olk & Kingstone, 2003). Consequently, the main aim of the study was to examine effects of anxiety and stimulus threat content on the antisaccade cost index of competition between reflexive and voluntary visual orienting (i.e., difference between antisaccade and prosaccade latencies; Godijn & Kramer, 2008).

A secondary aim of the study was to examine the relationship between the predicted selective attention bias (i.e., difficulty in orienting of gaze away from threat, reflected by antisaccade cost on threat vs. neutral trials) and individual differences in attention control, which is a broader construct, encompassing the ability to inhibit prepotent responses to distracting stimuli (Eysenck et al., 2007), that is typically assessed in situations where the stimulus information is free of emotional content. Individual differences in attention control were assessed using two separate measures: a self-report measure (Attention Control Scale, ACS; Derryberry & Reed, 2002) and a behavioural measure of attention control from the Attention Network Task (ANT; Fan, McCandliss, Sommer, Raz, & Posner, 2002). Importantly, unlike for our saccade measures, the ANT assesses attention control in a context free of emotionally salient distractors, such as evocative facial displays. In addition to assessing trait anxiety, we also obtained other self-reported indices of negative emotionality (state anxiety, social anxiety, social avoidance, negative affectivity, behavioural inhibition) given that the attentional bias for threat has been linked not only with trait anxiety, but also more generally with vulnerability to experiencing negative emotionality (MacLeod et al., 2002).

Based on a large body of work using antisaccade and prosaccade tasks, we expected that participants would generally make more errors, and have longer saccade onset latencies, on antisaccade than prosaccade trials (e.g., review by Hutton & Ettinger, 2006). In line with recent research (Derakshan et al., 2009), we hypothesised that participants with high trait anxiety would show greater difficulty in voluntary orienting of gaze away from angry faces, relative to neutral faces, compared with low trait anxious participants; i.e., increased antisaccade cost (slower latencies on antisaccade than prosaccade trials) for angry, relative to neutral, faces in anxious individuals. We also predicted that a similar anxiety-related bias would be found for fearful faces, but not happy faces. In addition, we used correlational analyses to examine whether the bias was associated with poorer attention control as measured by the Attentional Control Scale (Derryberry & Reed, 2002) and Attention Network Task (Fan et al., 2002).

METHOD

Participants

These were 55 undergraduate students (41 female; mean age of 21 years) from the University of Southampton. All participants had English as their primary language and were right-handed with normal or corrected vision. They received course credits for participating in the study. Participants were selected from a pool of approximately 119 volunteers on the basis of their scores on screening measures of trait anxiety (State Trait Anxiety Inventory, STAI; Spielberger, Gorsuch, Lushene, Vagg, & Jacobs, 1973) and subjective attention control (ACS; Derryberry & Reed, 2002), which were administered several weeks prior to the test session. Recruitment favoured those with high or low scores on each measure in order to minimise the proportion of participants with mid-range scores within the final sample. However, recruitment was not restricted only to those with extreme scores. Volunteers with mid-range scores were also included in order to avoid generating a sample with bimodally distributed anxiety and ACS scores, a feature that could complicate correlational analyses. The Kolmogorov-Smirnov test confirmed that the distributions of anxiety and ACS scores obtained from participants in the test session were not significantly different from normal ($ps = .38$ and $.66$, respectively).

Stimulus materials

Saccade task. The stimuli consisted of 16 faces from the NimStim picture set (available at www.macbrain.org, numbers: 05, 06, 07, 08, 09, 10, 14, 16, 23, 27, 33, 36, 37, 38, 40, and 42). Each face was shown with an angry, fearful, happy, and neutral expression resulting in 64 different images in total. Half of the faces were female and half were male. The faces were $4.5° \times 6.25°$ (Width $\times$ Height) with the inner edge located approximately $2°$ from the centre of the screen. For each trial, a centrally presented cue, one of two yellow letters (X or O), indicated the trial type (antisaccade or prosaccade) and the stimulus used for feedback was a solid green square; these stimuli were $1° \times 1°$. The feedback square was positioned approximately $2.5°$ from the centre of the screen. The stimuli were presented using experiment builder software (SR Research Ltd., Ontario, Canada) on a 19-inch ViewSonic (P227f) monitor. Participants' eye movements were recorded using an EyeLink 1000 tower-mounted eyetracking system (SR Research Ltd., Ontario, Canada), which had a 1 kHz sampling rate and a $< 0.01°$ spatial resolution. A headrest was used to minimise head movements. Raw eye movement data were analysed with Data Viewer software (SR Research Ltd., Ontario, Canada).

Attention network task. The stimuli were the same as those described by Fan et al. (2002). There was a warning display, where the warning cue was an asterisk (one of three different warning displays was presented, depending on the cue condition: no cue, one cue, or two cues). The response display comprised a target arrow and four flankers (two each side of the target), which were either four arrows or four lines. The stimuli were presented in white on a grey background. Each line or arrow was $2°$ and the contours of adjacent arrows or lines were separated by $1°$. The row of stimuli (i.e., a target and four flankers) was $14°$ in length. The warning cue, target, and flankers were presented either $3°$ above or below the central fixation point. Presentation software 10.0 (Neurobehavioral Systems Inc.) was used to display the stimuli and record response latency and accuracy. Manual RTs were collected via a parallel-port response box.

Procedure

Participants first gave written consent and were then assessed individually in a dimly lit room where they were seated 57 cm from the screen. The saccade task had 12 practice trials with neutral faces and 256 experimental trials, which consisted of an equal number of trials with angry, happy, fearful, and neutral faces. The experimental trials were divided into four blocks (A, B, C, and D) with a small rest break between each block. The eye-tracker was calibrated by presenting dots in a 3×3 array. Participants were told to look directly at the dot, and only move their gaze when the next dot appeared. After successful calibration, the trial block started. Each trial began with a centrally located cross with a contingent change fixation (i.e., trial would not continue unless the participant

was looking at the centre of the screen for a minimum duration of 200 ms). If contingency was met, the fixation cross was replaced by a yellow cue (either an X or an O) for a variable duration (between 1000 and 1500 ms). For two blocks of trials (A and C), cue X indicated a prosaccade trial, and O an antisaccade trial. For the other two blocks of trials (B and D), cue X indicated an antisaccade trial, and cue O a prosaccade trial. Thus, each block comprised a mixture of prosaccade and antisaccade trials, similar to the mixed-task condition used by Ansari et al. (2008), with the additional feature of cue type (X or O) being counterbalanced across blocks. Following the cue, the target face appeared either to the left side or to the right side of the screen for 1000 ms, and the trial ended with the green feedback square being displayed for 500 ms in the location the participant should have directed their gaze to if they made a correct response.[1] After a 500 ms intertrial interval (black screen), a new trial started. If eye calibration quality deteriorated during the block the calibration procedure was repeated. The order of the four trial blocks (A, B, C, and D) was counterbalanced using a Latin square design. All trials within each block were presented in a new random order for each participant (i.e., within each block, prosaccade and anti-saccade trial type and emotional face type were fully randomised). See Figure 1 for schematic representation of trial events.

The ANT was similar to that used in previous research (Fan et al., 2002; Reinholdt-Dunne et al., 2009) and comprised 24 practice trials followed by two buffer trials and 288 experimental trials. The task required participants to indicate whether a central arrow pointed left or right. Feedback (a beep if participants made an error and no beep if no error was made) was given on practice, but not experimental, trials.[2] The trials reflected the combination of the following conditions: warning cue (4: no cue, centre cue, double cue, or spatial

---

[1] The provision of feedback on antisaccade tasks is standard practice (e.g., Derakshan et al., 2009; Hardin et al., 2007; Jazbec et al., 2005). Thus, feedback was provided to help comparison with previous research findings and also make the task easier for participants, and keep errors to a minimum.

[2] Feedback was only provided on practice trials since the ANT is much simpler than, for instance, the antisaccade task (e.g., error rates were 22% on the antisaccade trials and 2% on the ANT). Using feedback on practice trials and not on experimental trials is also standard procedure (e.g., Fan et al., 2002; Reinholdt-Dunne et al., 2009), which allowed for comparison with findings from previous studies using the ANT.

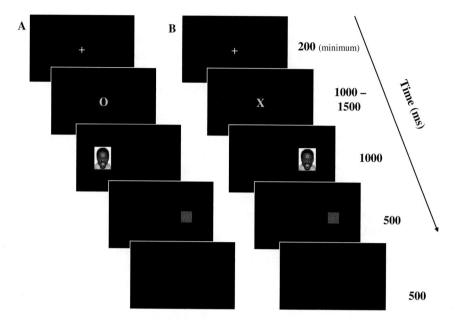

Figure 1. Illustration of (A) an antisaccade trial and (B) a prosaccade trial. See Method section for details.

cue), target-arrow location (2: top or bottom), target-arrow direction (2: left or right), flanker (3: neutral, congruent, or incongruent). There were six repetitions of each trial type. All trials were presented in a randomised order.

Each trial consisted of five events. First, there was a centrally located fixation cross, which appeared on the screen during the whole trial except when replaced by the centre cue. After a random interval (between 400 and 1600 ms), the warning condition was presented for 100 ms, which was either: (1) no warning cue, participants only saw the fixation cross for 100 ms; (2) single centre cue; (3) double cue, with one cue above and one below the fixation cross; or (4) single spatial cue, one cue either above or below the fixation cross. Next, the centrally located fixation cross was presented alone again for 400 ms, followed by the simultaneous appearance of five stimuli (target and four flankers) either above or below the central fixation cross. The target was a central arrow. The flankers (two each side of the target) were either arrows or lines, which determined the three flanker conditions: (1) neutral, where the flankers were lines (e.g., — — ← — —); (2) congruent, where the flankers were arrows pointing in the same direction as the central target arrow (e.g., ← ← ← ← ←); or (3) incongruent, where the flankers were arrows pointing in the opposite direction to the target arrow (e.g., → → ← → →). The target and flankers were presented

until the participant made a response, or a maximum duration of 1700 ms. Participants were asked to indicate the direction of the centre arrow (i.e., whether it was pointing left or right) and press the appropriate key as quickly and accurately as possible. After their response, the central fixation cross was displayed for a variable duration, such that the interval between target onset on one trial and warning cue onset on the next trial was 3500 ms).

Participants then completed several questionnaires including the state and trait versions of the State Trait Anxiety Inventory (STAI; Spielberger et al., 1983), Positive and Negative Affect Schedule (PANAS; Watson, Clark, & Tellegen, 1988), Behavioural Inhibition System/Behavioural Activation System Scales (BIS/BAS; Carver & White, 1994), Fear of Negative Evaluation (FNE; Leary, 1983), Social avoidance subscale of the Fear Questionnaire (FQ—social avoidance; Marks & Mathews, 1979), Social Desirability Scale (SDS; Crowne & Marlowe, 1964), and ACS (Derryberry & Reed, 2002).

Data preparation and analysis

Saccade task. Saccades were excluded if they were less than one degree in amplitude (i.e., response was too small to be stimulus driven).

They were also excluded if the start fixation point was more than 1° away from the centre of the screen (i.e., gaze was not centrally fixated), or if the saccade angle from the centre of the screen to either side was more than 45° above or below the target face (i.e., the fixation was not in the appropriate location of the screen). When determining correct and incorrect eye movements, only the first saccade following onset of the target stimulus was considered. *Saccade latency* was the time elapsed between the onset of the target face and the start of a saccade. To ensure that only task-relevant saccades were analysed, only those occurring between 80 ms and 850 ms after target onset were considered. Mean latencies were computed in each condition as a function of trial type (antisaccade, prosaccade) and face type (angry, fearful, happy, neutral) on trials with correct saccades. Data from five participants were excluded due to insufficient data for analyses (< 6 latencies per condition). In the final sample ($N = 50$), participants had latency data from > 190 190 trials (>75%).

Saccade latency bias scores were calculated by subtracting the mean difference in latency between antisaccade and prosaccade trials (antisaccade cost) when the face was neutral from the mean difference in latency between antisaccade and prosaccade trials when the face depicted an emotional expression (angry, fearful, or happy). Larger saccade latency bias scores reflect greater difficulty in shifting gaze away from emotional faces (angry, fearful, or happy) relative to neutral faces.

Attention network task. RTs from trials with errors (3%) and RT outliers (< 250 ms and > 3 *SD*s above each participant's mean; 1% of trials) were excluded. The task produced three attention network scores. *Attention control* (AC-ANT) scores were calculated by subtracting the mean RT of incongruent flanker trials (flanker arrows point in different direction to target arrow) from the mean RT of congruent flanker trials (flanker arrows point in same direction as target arrow). Thus, more positive values reflect better attention control, whereas greater negative values indicate poorer attention control (this score is the opposite of the attention conflict score calculated by Fan et al. (2002), but is more convenient here in order to allow comparison with the self-report attention control measures). *Alerting* scores were calculated by subtracting the mean RT of double-cue trials (i.e., trials with warning cue, but without

information about target location) from the mean RT of no-cue trials, such that positive values reflect better alerting skills. *Orienting* scores were calculated by subtracting the mean RT of spatial-cue trials (which signal the location of the target) from the mean RT of centre-cue (no information about target location), such that positive values reflect better orienting abilities. Each attention network score (i.e., attention control, alerting, and orienting) was entered into a 2 × 2 ANOVA with anxiety and attention control as between-subjects independent variables. Relationships between these scores and other variables were also examined using correlations.

RESULTS

The main hypotheses were evaluated in analyses of saccade latency bias scores, described earlier. However, before considering these, it is informative to examine briefly other data (i.e., group characteristics, saccade errors) that are relevant to the interpretation of results.

Group characteristics

Participants were divided into two groups based on trait anxiety, which was measured on the STAI in the experimental session (low anxious group had scores less than or equal to the median of 36; high anxious group had scores greater than 36). Mean questionnaire scores for each group are given in Table 1. The groups differed significantly on all questionnaire measures of self-reported attention control and negative emotionality, but not in BAS or social desirability scores (see Table 1 for results). The groups also did not differ significantly in gender ratio (20 women, eight men in low anxious group; 18 women, four men in high anxious group; Chi-squared = .72, $p = .39$).

Saccade errors

The percentage of trials with errors was calculated for each condition and participant. A 2 × 2 × 4 ANOVA of error data was carried out with trait anxiety group (high, low), trial type (prosaccade, antisaccade), and face type (angry, fearful, happy, neutral) as independent variables. This indicated a significant main effect of trial type: As expected, participants made more errors on antisaccade

TABLE 1
Mean questionnaire and attention network task (ANT) scores as a function of trait anxiety group

	Low trait anxiety		High trait anxiety		
	M	(SD)	M	(SD)	t(48)
Attentional control scale	53.8	(8.9)	47.5	(6.6)	2.75, p < .01
Trait anxiety	31.7	(4.2)	44.6	(5.2)	9.78, p < .01
State anxiety	33.5	(9.4)	36.7	(6.9)	2.12, p < .05
PANAS PA	28.5	(5.4)	24.1	(5.6)	2.82, p < .01
PANAS NA	5.4	(3.4)	11.3	(5.2)	4.81, p < .01
BIS	20.3	(3.8)	23.4	(3.0)	3.05, p < .01
BAS	41.2	(5.0)	39.6	(4.0)	1.20, p = .23
Fear of negative evaluation	11.8	(5.6)	20.4	(6.0)	5.17, p < .01
FQ—Social avoidance	9.9	(5.4)	14.6	(4.7)	3.25, p < .01
Social desirability scale	5.1	(1.6)	4.2	(2.4)	1.59, p = .12
Attention network task (ms)					
Attention control	−53.1	(17.7)	−60.3	(25.5)	1.17, p = .25
Alerting	42.4	(19.2)	32.1	(22.1)	1.75, p = .09
Orienting	25.8	(23.8)	29.6	(22.2)	0.58, p = .57

PANAS PA = Positive and Negative Affective Schedule—Positive Affect; PANAS NA = Positive and Negative Affective Schedule—Negative Affect; BIS = Behavioural Inhibition System; BAS = Behavioural Activation System; FQ = Fear Questionnaire.

($M = 22$) than prosaccade ($M = 2$) trials, $F(1, 48) = 140, p < .001$. There were no other significant results. Given the unequal variance across trial type (see Table 2), separate ANOVAs of errors from prosaccade and antisaccade trials were also conducted and these also showed no significant effects of face type or anxiety group.

Saccade latencies

A $2 \times 2 \times 4$ ANOVA of latency of first correct saccades was carried out with anxiety group (high, low), trial type (prosaccade, antisaccade), and face type (angry, fearful, happy, neutral) as independent variables. Results indicated a significant main effect of trial type, as participants showed significantly longer latencies on antisaccade ($M = 250$ ms) than prosaccade ($M = 161$ ms) trials, $F(1, 48) = 702, p < .001$. Additionally, there was a significant Anxiety group × Trial type interaction, $F(1, 48) = 11.36, p < .01$, and Anxiety group × Trial type × Face type interaction, $F(3, 144) = 4.29, p < .01$ (see Table 2).

To clarify the $2 \times 2 \times 4$ interaction for the saccade latency data, further analyses were conducted on the saccade latency bias scores. These scores had been calculated for each emotional face type and participant (see Data Preparation for calculation details, and Figure 2 for means). A 2×3 ANOVA of saccade latency bias scores with

anxiety group (high, low) and face type (angry, fearful, happy) as independent variables indicated a significant Anxiety group × Face type interaction, $F(2, 96) = 5.96, p < .001$. To clarify this interaction, we examined the effect of anxiety

TABLE 2
Mean percentage of trials with saccade errors and mean saccade latency (in ms) as a function of trial type and trait anxiety group

	Low trait anxiety		High trait anxiety	
	M	(SD)	M	(SD)
Errors (% of trials)				
ANTI fearful	23.7	(11.4)	17.4	(11.8)
ANTI angry	25.0	(17.3)	17.5	(13.6)
ANTI happy	24.0	(13.3)	21.2	(14.8)
ANTI neutral	24.0	(16.2)	18.5	(15.0)
PRO fearful	1.4	(2.6)	1.0	(2.8)
PRO angry	2.1	(4.4)	0.9	(2.1)
PRO happy	1.5	(2.5)	1.9	(3.2)
PRO neutral	1.9	(2.5)	2.0	(3.2)
Saccade latency (ms)				
ANTI fearful	262.8	(36.9)	239.8	(34.8)
ANTI angry	253.2	(30.5)	246.9	(47.9)
ANTI happy	254.9	(32.3)	239.5	(34.1)
ANTI neutral	255.8	(33.3)	239.2	(42.9)
PRO fearful	155.7	(25.3)	166.6	(33.7)
PRO angry	156.1	(24.0)	162.6	(26.4)
PRO happy	161.2	(29.4)	162.1	(26.6)
PRO neutral	158.1	(25.8)	167.8	(35.7)

ANTI = antisaccade trials; PRO = prosaccade trials.

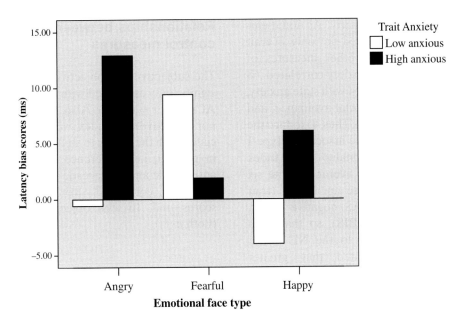

Figure 2. Mean saccade latency bias scores (in ms) for each emotional face type and trait anxiety group. Saccade latency bias scores are the mean antisaccade cost (i.e., mean difference in latency between correct antisaccade and prosaccade trials) for each emotional face type minus the mean antisaccade cost for neutral faces. Larger bias scores reflect greater difficulty in shifting gaze away from emotional faces (angry, fearful, or happy) relative to neutral faces.

on latency bias scores for each emotional face type separately.

Angry faces. The high anxious group showed significantly greater angry-face bias ($M = 13$ ms, $SD = 27$) than the low anxious group ($M = -1$ ms, $SD = 19$), $t(48) = 2.04$, $p < .05$, indicating that the anxious group had greater difficulty in shifting their gaze away from angry faces relative to neutral faces than the low anxious group. Angry-face bias was significant only in the high anxious (contrast vs. zero), $t(21) = 2.22$, $p < .05$, but not the low anxious group (contrast vs. zero), $t(27) = 0.16$, *ns.*

Fearful faces. There was no significant group difference in fearful-face bias, $t(48) = 1.19$, $p > .2$. Overall, participants showed a non significant trend to be slower to direct gaze away from fearful, relative to neutral, faces ($M = 6$ ms, $SD = 23$ ms; contrast versus zero), $t(49) = 1.94$, $p = .06$.

Happy faces. There was no significant group difference in happy-face bias, $t(48) = 1.50$, $p > .1$. Also, there was no overall bias for happy, relative to neutral, faces ($M = 0$ ms, $SD = 24$ ms).

Separate analyses of prosaccade and antisaccade latency data

ANOVAs were also conducted of prosaccade and antisaccade latency data separately, with anxiety group and face type as independent variables (see Table 2 for means). The 2 × 4 ANOVA of prosaccade latencies showed no significant results, e.g., Anxiety × Face type, $F(3, 144) = 2.18$, $p = .09$. However, the 2 × 4 ANOVA of antisaccade latencies showed a significant Anxiety × Face type interaction, $F(3, 144) = 2.92$, $p < .05$. The high anxious group was on average 8 ms slower to look away from angry than neutral faces, compared with the low anxious group who were 3 ms faster, Anxiety × Angry vs. neutral faces, $F(1, 48) = 3.70$, $p = .06$. There was no similar trend for an Anxiety × Face type interaction in antisaccade latencies for either fearful ($p = .29$) or happy faces ($p = .83$), relative to neutral faces.

Is the bias for angry faces influenced by individual differences in attention control?

Correlations were used to examine relationships between the measures of angry-face latency bias, emotionality, and attention control. As noted earlier, the anxiety groups differed not only in trait anxiety scores, but also on other measures of negative emotionality (trait anxiety correlated .68 with PANAS negative affect, .54 with state anxiety, .51 with FNE, .46 with FQ–social avoidance, and .37 with BIS scores, all $ps < .01$). Thus, to reduce the number of correlations and the associated Type-I error rate, a negative-emotionality (NE) index was calculated by taking the average of the six standardised scores for these measures (trait anxiety, state anxiety, PANAS negative affect, FNE, FQ–social avoidance, BIS), so that each measure contributed equally to the NE index. Correlational results indicated that greater difficulty in controlling orienting in response to threat cues (indexed by angry-face latency bias scores) was significantly associated with greater negative-emotionality, $r = .31$, $p < .05$. (In relation to the separate scores, the angry-face bias correlated .34 with PANAS negative affect, $p < .05$, and showed positive trends with other measures, e.g., .22 with trait anxiety, .21 with BIS, and .27 with FNE, $.15 > ps > .05$.)

The angry-face bias was not significantly associated with subjective attention control ($r = -.02$, ns, with ACS scores) or objective attention control ($r = -.15$, ns, with AC-ANT scores). The bias was also not associated with the interaction effect of attention control and negative-emotionality (i.e., angry-face bias correlated $-.01$, ns, with the product of standardised scores of NE and ACS; and $-.08$, ns, with the product of standardised scores of NE and AC-ANT scores).

The angry-face bias remained significantly associated with negative-emotionality independently of the effects of subjective or objective attention control (partial correlation controlling ACS: $r = .36$, $p < .05$; controlling AC-ANT: $r = .30$, $p < .05$). (Negative emotionality was associated with poor subjective attention control, $r = -.54$, $p < .05$, but not significantly with poor objective attention control, $r = -.14$, ns.)

The angry-face bias did not correlate significantly with saccade errors, i.e., with overall anti- or prosaccade error rates, or with the difference between them (the latter also did not correlate significantly with other measures of attention control or negative emotion).

Relationships between attention control measures

The subjective and objective AC scores were not significantly associated with each other (ACS with AC-ANT: $r = .08$, ns). Also, neither the subjective nor objective AC index were significantly associated with the ability to shift gaze away from faces in general, i.e., difference in latencies between antisaccade and prosaccade trials, averaged across face type, correlated $-.03$ with subjective ACS scores, and .16 with objective AC-ANT scores (both ns).

DISCUSSION

As expected, participants generally made more errors and had longer saccade latencies on antisaccade than prosaccade trials. This is consistent with previous research showing that performance on antisaccade trials requires inhibition of a reflexive tendency to look at the target stimulus (e.g., Hutton & Ettinger, 2006). Results also indicated that the difference in latencies between antisaccade and prosaccade trials (the "antisaccade cost") was influenced by an interactive effect of anxiety group and the emotional expression of faces. Further analyses, which clarified this interaction, showed that the high anxious group had a greater bias for angry faces (i.e., relatively greater difficulty in shifting gaze away from angry than neutral faces) than the low anxious group. There were no significant group differences in saccade bias for fearful or happy faces, relative to neutral faces. These findings support recent research indicating that high trait anxious individuals have greater difficulty directing their attention away from an angry face in comparison to a neutral face (e.g., Derakshan et al., 2009).

The present results extend the latter research in several ways. For example, they indicate that the difficulty in inhibiting eye movements to angry faces in anxious individuals is found when using photographs of real-life faces as stimuli. Thus, the present results confirm that findings for computer-generated images (Derakshan et al., 2009) generalise to naturalistic emotional facial expressions.

The present study also indicates that the anxiety-related bias is specific to angry faces, as the bias was not found for fearful faces. This contrasts with findings from other recent research examining biases in visual orienting to different facial expressions in high trait anxiety. A recent eye-tracking study found that high anxious individuals were more likely than low anxious individuals to direct gaze towards intense negative facial expressions (which were similar to the stimuli used here), irrespective of whether the faces were angry or fearful (Mogg, Garner, & Bradley, 2007). This suggests that both fearful and angry faces have a similar capacity to attract the attention of anxious individuals under free-viewing conditions, which do not require effortful inhibition of attentional biases. However, when anxious individuals attempt to recruit cognitive control processes to direct attention allocation (as in the antisaccade paradigm), they find it more difficult than low-anxious individuals to suppress an attentional bias for angry faces, but not for fearful faces. Anxious individuals' difficulty in suppressing the bias for angry faces may possibly be due to the threat potency of angry faces (i.e., angry faces represent a more direct source of threat than fearful faces). It may be helpful to evaluate this interpretation of findings from these different studies by examining attentional biases for angry and fearful faces in anxious individuals under both free-viewing and antisaccade conditions within the same study. Such research may help clarify the influences of stimulus-driven and cognitive control processes on attentional biases in anxious individuals.

Another aim of the present study was to investigate the associations between anxiety, ability to control attention towards threat, and objective and subjective measures of attention control. Correlational results suggested that poorer ability to control orienting towards angry faces was associated with greater levels of negative emotionality (as reflected by the summary index of trait, state, and social anxiety, negative affectivity, and behavioural inhibition). There was no evidence from the correlational analyses that the attentional bias for threat (assessed on the saccade task) was influenced by individual differences in attention control that were assessed by self-report or behaviourally on a nonemotional task (i.e., the angry-face bias was not associated with ACS or AC-ANT measures of attention control, or with interaction effects of negative emotionality and attention control). This is inconsistent with

previous findings (Derryberry & Reed, 2002; Reinholdt-Dunne et al., 2009) showing that the combination of high anxiety and poor attention control was a better predictor of threat bias than anxiety alone, and with findings showing an association between trait anxiety and AC-ANT scores (Pacheco-Unguetti, Acosta, Callejas, & Lupiáñez, 2010). It is important to note that, unlike the saccade-based tasks, the ANT assessed attention control in a context free of emotionally salient face-emotion displays. Considered from this perspective, the present results seem more consistent with the view that separate mechanisms underlie control of attentional responses to task-irrelevant *nonemotional* stimuli (e.g., as reflected by AC-ANT scores) versus attentional responses to task-irrelevant *threat* (as reflected by angry-face saccade latency bias scores). This highlights the distinction between general attention control versus specific attention control of threat processing.

A limitation of the present study concerns the use of a student sample, which may make it difficult to detect effects of individual differences in attention control on threat processing, given that university students are generally likely to have relatively high levels of attention control (e.g., compared to anxious patients). Thus, further investigation of the relationships between anxiety, attention control, and information-processing bias in a clinical sample would be useful.

Another interesting finding of this study was the lack of relationships between the various measures of attention control, which included subjective (ACS) and objective (AC-ANT) measures. In addition, neither measure was associated with slower saccade latencies on antisaccade versus prosaccade trials, which provide a further index of a person's ability to control attention. Previous research has also found nonsignificant or weak relationships between objective and subjective attention control measures (e.g., Austin & Hemsley, 1978; Muris, van der Pennen, Sigmond, & Mayer, 2008; Reinholdt-Dunne et al., 2009). Given the similar theoretical foundation between the attention control measures: ACS and AC-ANT (Derryberry & Reed, 2002; Fan et al., 2002), the lack of associations between them suggests that they reflect different constructs. Previous research suggests that attention control is a multifaceted construct, including distinct cognitive operations such as attentional shifting and inhibition of prepotent responses (e.g., Eysenck et al., 2007;

Miyake et al., 2000). Thus, it would be informative for future research to examine the processes underlying differing indices of attention control in more detail.

In conclusion, the results of this study support previous research indicating that high trait anxiety is associated with greater difficulty in using effortful control processes to shift gaze away from angry faces. Moreover, a novel finding of this study is that this difficulty in controlling attentional responses to threat-related cues in high trait anxiety is specific to angry, rather than fearful, faces. Additionally, poorer ability to control orienting in response to angry faces was associated with higher levels of negative-emotionality, but it was not influenced by individual differences in attention control (assessed on separate subjective and objective measures). The lack of association between the subjective and objective attention control measures highlights the need to take greater account of the multifaceted nature of attention control in future research into emotion-processing biases.

REFERENCES

Ansari, T. L., & Derakshan, N. (2010). Anxiety impairs inhibitory control but not volitional action control. *Cognition and Emotion, 24*, 241–254.

Ansari, T. L., Derakshan, N., & Richards, A. (2008). Effects of anxiety on task switching: Evidence from the mixed antisaccade task. *Cognitive, Affective, and Behavioral Neuroscience, 8*, 229–238.

Austin, S. V., & Hemsley., D. R. (1978). Objective and subjective measures of distractibility. *Bulletin of the Psychonomic Society, 12*, 182–184.

Bar-Haim, Y., Lamy, D., Pergamin, L., Bakermans-Kranenburg, M., & van IJzendoorn, M. (2007). Threat-related attentional bias in anxious and nonanxious individuals: A meta-analytic study. *Psychological Bulletin, 133*, 1–24.

Beck, A. T., & Emery, O. (1985). *Anxiety disorders and phobias: A cognitive perspective.* New York, NY: Basic Books.

Bishop, S. J. (2007). Neurocognitive mechanisms of anxiety: An integrative account. *Trends in Cognitive Science, 11*, 307–316.

Carver, C. S., & White, T. L. (1994). Behavioral inhibition, behavioural activation, and affective responses to impending reward and punishment: The BIS/BAS Scales. *Journal of personality and social psychology, 67*, 319–333.

Crowne, D. P., & Marlowe, D. (1964). *The approval motive: Studies in evaluative dependence.* New York, NY: Wiley.

Derakshan, N., Ansari, T., Hansard, M., Shoker, L., & Eysenck, M. W. (2009). Anxiety, inhibition, efficiency, and effectiveness: An investigation using the antisaccade task. *Experimental Psychology, 56*, 48–55.

Derryberry, D., & Reed, M. (2002). Anxiety-related attentional biases and their regulation by attentional control. *Journal of Abnormal Psychology, 111*, 225–236.

Eysenck, M. W., Derakshan, N., Santos, R., & Calvo, M. (2007). Anxiety and cognitive performance: Attentional control theory. *Emotion, 7*, 336–353.

Fan, J., McCandliss, B., Sommer, T., Raz, A., & Posner, M. (2002). Testing the efficiency and independence of attentional networks. *Journal of Cognitive Neuroscience, 14*, 340–347.

Godijn, R., & Kramer, A. F. (2008). The effect of attentional demands on the antisaccade cost. *Perception and Psychophysics, 70*, 795–806.

Hallet, P. E. (1978). Primary and secondary saccades to goals defined by instructions. *Vision Research, 18*, 1279–1296.

Hardin, M., Schroth, E., Pine, D., & Ernst, M. (2007). Incentive-related modulation of cognitive control in healthy, anxious, and depressed adolescents: Development and psychopathology related differences. *Journal of Child Psychology and Psychiatry, 48*, 446–454.

Hutton, S. B., & Ettinger, U. E. (2006). The antisaccade task as a research tool in psychopathology: A critical review. *Psychophysiology, 43*, 302–313.

Jazbec, S., McClure, E., Hardin, M., Pine, D. S., & Ernst, M. (2005). Cognitive control under contingencies in anxious and depressed adolescents: An antisaccade task. *Biological Psychiatry, 58*, 632–639.

Kristjánsson, A. (2007). Saccade landing point selection and the competition account of pro- and antisaccade generation: The involvement of visual attention—a review. *Scandinavian Journal of Psychology, 48*, 97–113.

Kristjánsson, Á., Chen, Y., & Nakayama, K. (2001). Less attention is more in the preparation of antisaccades, but not prosaccades. *Nature Neuroscience, 4*, 1037–1042.

Leary, M. R. (1983). A brief version of the ear of Negative Evaluation Scale. *Personality and Social Psychology Bulletin, 9*, 371–375.

MacLeod, C., Rutherford, E., Campbell, L., Ebsworthy, G., & Holker, L. (2002). Selective attention and emotional vulnerability: Assessing the causal basis of their association through the experimental manipulation of attentional bias. *Journal of Abnormal Psychology, 111*, 107–123.

Marks, I. M., & Mathews, A. M. (1979). Brief standard self-rating for phobic patients. *Behaviour Research and Therapy, 17*, 263–267.

Miyake, A., Friedman, N. P., Emerson, M. J., Witzki, A. H., Howerter, A., & Wager, T. D. (2000). The unity and diversity of executive functions and their contributions to complex "frontal lobe" tasks: A latent variable analysis. *Cognitive Psychology, 41*, 49–100.

Mogg, K., & Bradley, B. P. (1998). A cognitive-motivational analysis of anxiety. *Behavior Research and Therapy, 36*, 809–848.

Mogg, K., Garner, M., & Bradley, B. P. (2007). Anxiety and orienting of gaze to angry and fearful faces. *Biological Psychology, 76*, 163–169.

Muris, P., van der Pennen, E., Sigmond, R., & Mayer, B. (2008). Symptoms of anxiety, depression, and aggression in nonclinical children: Relationships with self-report and performance-based measures of attention and effortful control. *Child Psychiatry and Human Development, 39*, 455–467.

Ochsner, K. N., & Gross, J. J. (2005). The cognitive control of emotion. *Trends in Cognitive Sciences, 9*, 242–249.

Olk, B., & Kingstone, A. (2003). Why are antisaccades slower than prosaccades? A novel finding using a new paradigm. *NeuroReport, 14*, 151–155.

Pacheco-Unguetti, A. P., Acosta, A., Callejas, A., & Lupiáñez, J. (2010). Attention and anxiety: Different attentional functioning under state and trait anxiety. *Psychological Science, 21*, 298–304.

Reinholdt-Dunne, M. L., Mogg, K., & Bradley, B. P. (2009). Effects of anxiety and attention control on processing pictorial and linguistic emotional information. *Behaviour Research and Therapy, 47*, 410–417.

Spielberger, C. D. (1973). *Manual for the State-Trait Anxiety Inventory for Children.* Palo Alto, CA: Consulting Psychologists Press.

Watson, D., Clark, L. A., & Tellegen, A. (1988). Development and validation of brief measures of positive and negative affect: The PANAS scale. *Journal of Personality and Social Psychology, 54*, 1063–1070.

Wieser, M. J., Pauli, P., & Mühlberger, A. (2009). Probing the attentional control theory in social anxiety—An emotional saccade task. *Cognitive, Affective, and Behavioral Neuroscience, 9*, 314–322.

Williams, J. M. G., Watts, F. N., MacLeod, C., & Mathews, A. (Eds.). (1997). *Cognitive psychology and emotional disorders* (2nd ed.). Chichester, UK: Wiley.

JOURNAL OF COGNITIVE PSYCHOLOGY, 2012, 24 (1), 66–78

Psychology Press
Taylor & Francis Group

Anxiety and deficient inhibition of threat distractors: Spatial attention span and time course

Manuel G. Calvo, Aida Gutiérrez, and Andrés Fernández-Martín

University of La Laguna, Tenerife, Spain

We investigated whether anxiety facilitates detection of threat stimuli outside the focus of overt attention, and the time course of the interference produced by threat distractors. Threat or neutral word distractors were presented in attended (foveal) and unattended (parafoveal) locations followed by an unrelated probe word at 300 ms (Experiments 1 and 2) or 1000 ms (Experiment 2) stimulus–onset asynchrony (SOA) in a lexical decision task. Results showed: (1) no effects of trait anxiety on selective saccades to the parafoveal threat distractors; (2) interference with probe processing (i.e., slowed lexical decision times) following a foveal threat distractor at 300 ms SOA for all participants, regardless of anxiety, but only for high-anxiety participants at 1000 ms SOA; and (3) no interference effects of parafoveal threat distractors. These findings suggest that anxiety does not enhance *preattentive* semantic processing of threat words. Rather, anxiety leads to delays in the inhibitory control of *attended* task-irrelevant threat stimuli.

Keywords: Anxiety; Attention; Distractors; Eye movements; Parafoveal; Threat.

Theories of anxiety and attentional bias have proposed two major mechanisms by which anxiety affects cognitive processing (Derryberry & Reed, 2002; Eysenck, Derakshan, Santos, & Calvo, 2007; Mathews & Mackintosh, 1998; Mogg & Bradley, 1998; Williams, Watts, MacLeod, & Mathews, 1997). The first mechanism involves threat detection during early automatic processing stages, with the attentional system of anxious individuals (i.e., those high in the personality dimension of trait anxiety) being abnormally sensitive to threat. This leads anxious people to adopt a hypervigilant mode towards threat (Eysenck, 1992, 1997). A second mechanism involves maintenance of attention on the source of threat, which affects later processing stages. Anxious individuals dwell on threat cues, with delays and difficulties in attentional disengagement (Fox & Georgiou, 2005). A meta-analytic review by Bar-Haim, Lamy, Pergamin, Bakermans-Kranenburg, and van IJzendoorn (2007) has shown that both mechanisms are affected by anxiety: There is some evidence for a preattentive threat detection bias, although the effect size is larger for later selective allocation of attention to threat stimuli.

In the current study, we investigated two extensions of these attentional biases. First, regarding hypervigilance, we addressed the issue of whether anxiety facilitates the detection of threat stimuli outside the focus of overt attention, i.e., when they appear at extrafoveal locations in the visual field. There is considerable evidence for a lowered *temporal threshold* mechanism involved in hypervigilance, with high-anxiety individuals detecting threat words presented subliminally to a greater extent than nonanxious individuals (see Mayer & Merckelbach, 1999). This effect has been found even when threat words are displayed

Correspondence should be addressed to Manuel G. Calvo, Departamento de Psicología Cognitiva, Universidad de La Laguna, 38205, Tenerife, Spain. E-mail: mgcalvo@ull.es

This research was supported by Grant PSI2009-07245, from the Spanish Ministry of Science and Innovation.

too briefly, and/or backwardly masked, to be read or reported (MacLeod & Rutherford, 1992; Mogg, Bradley, & Williams, 1995). In contrast, the possibility of a hypervigilance mechanism involving the broadening of the *spatial* attentional span in high-anxious individuals has been scarcely investigated and therefore deserved further research in the current study. Presumably, if such a mechanism exists, it would permit processing of threat stimuli outside the focus of visual attention, i.e., stimuli that are more eccentric in the visual field.

Second, regarding the issue of attentional dwelling on threat stimuli, we investigated the time course of a deficient inhibitory control mechanism for threat distractors (both within and outside the focus of attention). In previous research, the role of anxiety on the inhibition of threat distractors has been investigated using mainly the emotional Stroop paradigm, where the relevant task involves naming the colour in which threat-related or neutral words are printed, while trying to ignore the word meaning (which thus becomes a task-irrelevant distractor). High-anxious individuals generally perform more slowly than low-anxious individuals when threat words are presented (see Bar-Haim et al., 2007; Williams, Mathews, & MacLeod, 1996). This suggests that anxiety impairs the ability to inhibit task-irrelevant threat processing. Nevertheless, in emotional Stroop tasks the relevant stimulus (word colour) and the distractor (word meaning) appear *simultaneously*, and so this paradigm serves to assess susceptibility to *concurrent* interference. In a complementary approach involving the presentation of a distractor *followed by* a task-relevant word, we aimed to determine whether interference *remains after* the threatening stimulus has disappeared, and for how long.

The processing of threat-related words outside the focus of overt attention has been investigated using a lexical decision task in a repetition priming paradigm (Calvo, Castillo, & Fuentes, 2006; Calvo & Eysenck, 2008). A threat-related, neutral, or positively valenced probe word was preceded by a parafoveal prime word (2.2° away from fixation; 150 ms display) which was identical or unrelated to the probe. In the Calvo et al. (2006) study, the effect of emotional *state* was examined. Results showed facilitation in lexical decision times for probe threat words if primed by an identical (relative to an unrelated) parafoveal word, when a negative emotional state (anxiety or sadness) was induced by means of unpleasant

visual scenes prior to the word task. Calvo and Eysenck (2008) investigated the effects of *trait* anxiety. Parafoveal prime threat words facilitated lexical decision responses to identical (vs. unrelated) threat words for individuals high in trait anxiety. Nevertheless, although these selective priming effects appeared for threat (in comparison with positive and neutral) words, the repetition priming paradigm does not allow us to disentangle semantic from orthographic effects. Repetition priming served to determine that parafoveal threat words were especially likely to be *detected*, but not *what* type information was obtained from them. An alternative paradigm is needed to demonstrate that *meaning* is extracted from parafoveal threat words.

Interference paradigms are useful for addressing the two major issues that we aim to investigate, i.e., the effects of anxiety on the semantic processing of threat-related words outside the focus of overt attention, and the deficient inhibition of threat distractors. In such paradigms, distractor cues are presented that are unrelated to the probe and, therefore, task-irrelevant. If threat distractors are processed semantically, they will grab attention. As a result, if there is deficient inhibition of attention to the distractor, there will be impaired processing of the probe stimulus presented simultaneously or subsequently. The attention-grabbing power and interference of emotionally negative words has been demonstrated when the words are presented at fixation, for samples of participants unselected as a function of anxiety (Calvo & Castillo, 2005; Harris & Pashler, 2004; Pratto & John, 1991; White, 1996). Such interference with the processing of neutral words presented concurrently or subsequently probably occurs because attention is drawn and/or held by the meaning of the distractor. Accordingly, if high-anxious individuals are more likely than low-anxious ones to process parafoveal threat words semantically, the former will exhibit larger interference effects than the latter when threat (relative to neutral) parafoveal word distractors are presented. In contrast, if only the orthographic codes are processed, then parafoveal threat words will not produce any interference.

Previous research using interference paradigms to investigate the effects of anxiety on parafoveal processing has not produced clear findings. Fox (1993, 1994) used an emotional Stroop task in which colour patches were presented at fixation concurrently with threat words spatially separated from the patch. Fox (1993) found that high-anxious participants exhibited interference with colour naming when threat words were presented, but Fox (1994) did not. Fox, Russo, Bowles, and Dutton (2001) used a cueing procedure. Typically, in this task, a cue (e.g., a threat word) appears at one of two sides of a central fixation point, followed by a target (e.g., a circle) in the precued location (valid trials) or the opposite location (invalid trials). Impaired performance (i.e., longer target localisation times) on invalid trials indicates difficulties in disengagement from the cue word. In the Fox et al. (2001, Exp. 1) study, participants took longer to localise the target when the cue was a threat word than when it was a positive or a neutral word. While this indicates parafoveal capture of attention by the threat words, the interference effect of these words was similar for the high- and the low-anxious participants. Broomfield and Turpin (2005) also used a cueing paradigm and found slowed disengagement (i.e., slower to detect invalidly cued targets) from threat words than from neutral words for both high- and low-anxiety groups, in Experiment 1. However, in Experiment 2, high-anxiety participants showed faster disengagement from threat cue words (i.e., faster to detect invalidly cued targets) relative to neutral words, and low-anxiety participants showed no facilitation or interference.

In summary, no consistent findings have appeared regarding the possibility that anxiety is especially associated with parafoveal threat processing and deficient inhibition of threat word distractors. Clarification of this issue probably requires consideration of the time course of the underlying processes. Fox et al. (2001) used a short 150 ms cue–target stimulus–onset asynchrony (SOA), whereas Broomfield and Turpin (2005) used a 500 ms SOA. It is possible that, at very early stages, the threat meaning is active for most individuals, but that it is inhibited later by those low in anxiety, whereas their high-anxiety counterparts continue to attend to threat. Whereas a 150 ms SOA represents early stages, a 500 ms SOA may represent a time between early and late stages, involving both automatic and strategic processes. If so, at 500 ms from the onset of the threat cue, a mixture of effects may occur. Presumably, clearer strategic effects on attentional dwelling on threat as a function of anxiety only appear later than 500 ms. These speculations indicate the importance of investigating the time course of a deficient inhibitory control mechanism in high anxiety.

With this in mind, we used an interference paradigm in the current study in which the onset asynchrony between a distractor word and a probe word was varied. A threat-related or a neutral distractor were presented foveally (at fixation) or parafoveally (displaced 2.2° of visual angle to the right or left), followed by a foveal neutral probe word for lexical decision at short (300 ms; Experiments 1 and 2) or long (1000 ms; Experiment 2) SOAs. The distractor was always task-irrelevant, as it was unrelated to the probe meaning and form. The critical comparison involves the probe lexical decision latencies when the distractor is a threat word relative to when it is a neutral word. If the meaning of the threat word distractor is processed, it should capture attention and so interfere with the processing of the probe word. This would be reflected in slowed responses to the probe when preceded by a threat distractor, relative to a neutral distractor. A deficient inhibitory control mechanism for threat would manifest itself in slowed responses not only at the short but also at the long SOA for high-anxiety participants, while the interference effect would not occur at the longer SOA for those low in anxiety.

EXPERIMENT 1

Eye movements were monitored while threat-related and neutral words were presented as distractors foveally or parafoveally for 150 ms, followed by neutral probe words at 300 ms SOA. Some studies have demonstrated that individuals high in trait anxiety show a bias in overt orienting (i.e., eye movements) towards threat words outside of foveal vision (Broomfield & Turpin, 2005). Accordingly, to determine that there is truly parafoveal processing of threat words, it is important to prevent eye fixations on the parafoveal distractors (while allowing such fixations in the foveal condition). To achieve this, we used a gaze-contingent-display change technique (see Calvo & Nummenmaa, 2009). With this technique, when the eyes of the participant move away from the fixation point beyond a prespecified boundary, the parafoveal word is replaced by a row of Xs. This ensures that the distractor word cannot be fixated foveally, yet it remains available parafoveally. Hypervigilance will occur if there are more saccades towards the parafoveal threat distractors

ANXIETY AND THREAT PROCESSING   69

than to neutral distractors, and/or slower lexical decisions to the probe words following the parafoveal threat distractors than following neutral distractors.

Method

Participants. Sixteen psychology undergraduates high in trait anxiety (12 female) and 16 low in trait anxiety (12 female) participated for course credit. They were selected from a group of 91 students as a function of their high ($M = 54.6$, $SD = 4.4$) or low ($M = 34.4$, $SD = 3.1$), $t(30) = 15.95$, $p < .0001$, scores in the trait scale (ranging from 20 to 80) of the STAI (State-Trait Anxiety Inventory; Spielberger, Gorsuch, & Lushene, 1982). This inventory was administered under nonstressful, nonthreatening conditions (in a large group, anonymously, in a classroom, during a demonstration of the use of questionnaire measures). To encourage honest responses (and minimise the potential influence social desirability) in this self-report measure, each questionnaire was identified by an anonymous code, rather than by the participant's name. Furthermore, the students were told in advance that each would score his/her own responses, and then they would be provided with instructions about how to interpret them. We assumed all this would contribute to reliable trait anxiety assessment.

Stimuli. As target distractors, 48 threat-related words and 48 neutral words were presented (see Appendix). As probes, 96 neutral words were used, all of which were semantically and orthographically unrelated to the distractors. In addition, 48 nonword stimuli (i.e., pseudowords in which one letter of a valid word was changed) were presented as probes, preceded by 48 additional word distractors. The target words have been validated and used in previous studies (e.g., Calvo & Castillo, 2005; Calvo et al., 2006).The threat and the neutral word distractors were matched in length and were practically identical in lexical frequency (threat: $M = 36.96$ occurrences per million; neutral: $M = 36.31$).

Apparatus. The verbal stimuli were presented on a 21-inch monitor with a 120 Hz refresh rate, connected to a Pentium IV computer. Participants' eye movements were recorded with an EyeLink II tracker (SR Research Ltd., Mississauga, Ontario,

Canada). The sampling rate of the eyetracker was 500 Hz and the spatial accuracy was better than $0.5°$, with a $0.01°$ resolution in pupil tracking mode. A chin and forehead rest was used at a 60 cm viewing distance from the monitor.

The distractor words (in lowercase) subtended a visual angle between $1.3°$ and $1.8°$, depending on the number of letters (five to seven). The probe string (in capital letters) subtended a visual angle between $1.4°$ and $2.0°$. In the foveal condition, the distractor appeared at fixation at the same time as a string of xx + xx ($1.4°$) appeared parafoveally. In the parafoveal condition, the string of xx + xx appeared at fixation at the same time as the distractor appeared parafoveally. The distance between the respective centres of the two stimuli (i.e., distractor word and string of xx + xx) was $2.2°$. In the parafoveal condition, a gaze-contingent-display change was implemented such that the initial and the last x of the central fixation of xx + xx constituted a boundary. When the centre of the foveal fixation of the viewer crossed these boundaries, the parafoveal word turned to a string of five Xs in a row.

Design and procedure. The design involved a combination of trait anxiety (low vs. high), distractor valence (threat vs. neutral), and distractor location (foveal vs. parafoveal); visual field (left vs. right) of distractor was also included in the parafoveal condition. Anxiety was a between-subjects factor; the others were within-subjects factors. Each participant was presented once with half of the threat distractors and half of the neutral distractors in the foveal condition, and the other half in the parafoveal condition. Assignment of distractors to the foveal and the parafoveal condition was counterbalanced across participants. Each participant was presented with 96 probe word trials, and 48 nonword trials, plus 30 practice trials. The experimental trials were randomly assigned to two blocks and randomly presented within each block for each participant.

Figure 1 depicts the sequence of events on each trial. A central white circle ($0.8°$) served for drift correction. When the participant fixated this circle, the distractor display appeared for 150 ms, with one foveal word at the centre of fixation or a parafoveal word to the left or right of fixation. Following a 150 ms blank interval, a probe word (or nonword) appeared in the centre, for a lexical decision response. Accordingly, there was a 300 ms distractor–probe SOA. The probe

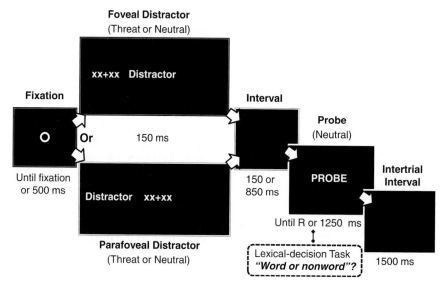

Figure 1. Sequence of events on each trial in Experiments 1 and 2.

remained visible for 1250 ms or until the participant responded whether it was a word or a nonword. Participants responded to the probe as rapidly as possible by pressing one of two keys of a response box. After the response, there was a 1500 ms intertrial interval. Participants were instructed to look at the centre, as the relevant stimulus for lexical decision would appear on that location.

Measures. The following measures assessed eye movements: the probability of initiating a saccade towards the parafoveal distractor, the saccade latencies (i.e., the time to initiate an eye movement from the central fixation point towards the distractor), and the end time (i.e., the time taken to land on the location of the distractor). In the foveal condition, no eye-movement measure was of particular interest, given the short display at fixation. For the probe words, accuracy and reaction times in the lexical decision task served to assess interference effects.

Results

Saccades towards the parafoveal distractors. Saccades were analysed in 2 (anxiety) $\times 2$ (valence of distractor) $\times 2$ (visual field of distractor) ANOVAs. The duration of fixations on the distractor area was also examined when there was any fixation. There was no significant effect on the probability of saccades towards the distractor: all $Fs < 1$, for anxiety (low $M = 0.131$, high

$M = 0.123$), valence (threat $M = 0.128$, neutral $M = 0.126$), and visual field (left $M = 0.124$, right $M = 0.130$). In addition, neither saccade latencies nor the end times of the saccades landing on the distractor location were significantly affected by any factor (all $Fs < 1$). The mean *start* time of these saccades was 138 ms ($SD = 7.80$), and the mean *end* time was 160 ms ($SD = 10.8$). Given that the parafoveal word was displayed for 150 ms, these results imply, first, that the prime words were parafoveally available (i.e., not yet covered by the gaze-contingent five-X mask) during most of the 150 ms display time, even on the 12.7% of trials with eye movements; and, second, on most of the trials with eye movements, the parafoveal word had actually disappeared (or else it was masked) by the time the fixation landed on the word location, and so the word itself was not fixated. Thus, the conditions allowed for parafoveal processing without foveal processing of the words.

Lexical decision performance on the probe. Response accuracy and latencies of correct responses in the lexical decision task were analysed in two 2 (anxiety) $\times 2$ (valence of distractor) $\times 2$ (distractor location) ANOVAs. Visual field was not included initially, as it was involved in the parafoveal but not in the foveal condition.

Response accuracy was not significantly affected by any factor (M probability of correct responses $= 0.974$; all $Fs < 1$). A main effect of valence on lexical decision times emerged, $F(1, 30) = 11.76$, $p < .01$, $\eta_p^2 = .282$, which was qualified by a valence by location interaction, $F(1, 30) = 10.97$, $p < .01$, $\eta_p^2 = .268$. Post hoc contrasts were conducted to decompose the interaction. In the foveal condition, responses to probe words were 25 ms slower following threat distractors ($M = 686$ ms) than following neutral distractors ($M = 661$), $t(15) = 5.37$, $p < .0001$, whereas in the parafoveal condition response times were equivalent (-3 ms) following threat ($M = 661$) and neutral ($M = 664$) distractors. The effect of anxiety was not significant ($F < 1$), nor were any of the interactions in which anxiety was involved (all Fs < 1). The mean correct lexical decision times on probe words are shown in Table 1.

We decided to examine further the possibility that visual field made a contribution or modulated the effects of threat words, in view of the evidence of a right visual field advantage in word recognition (Calvo & Nummenmaa, 2009; Kanne, 2002) and in threat word processing (Calvo & Eysenck, 2008). Accordingly, we included visual field (in addition to valence and anxiety) as a factor in a further ANOVA on response times in the parafoveal distractor condition. No significant effects appeared, including interactions with visual field (all Fs < 1). The interference scores (i.e., threat–neutral distractor) on response times to the probe words were close to zero (i.e., no interference) and equivalent when the threat word was presented in the right ($M = -4$ ms) and the left ($M = -2$ ms) visual fields. The interference scores also did not differ as a function of anxiety ($M = -3$ ms for both high- and low-anxiety groups).

Discussion

Threat word distractors in foveal vision interfered with the processing of subsequent neutral words,

and this occurred similarly for low- and high-anxiety participants. This can be inferred from the longer lexical decision times on a neutral probe following a threat distractor relative to a neutral distractor. Such a main interference effect of threat words has been frequently reported in prior research using different paradigms, with participants unselected as a function of anxiety (e.g., Pratto & John, 1991; Stormark, Nordby, & Hugdahl, 1995; White, 1996). This suggests that threat words presented at fixation can generally grab attention and interrupt other ongoing processes for most viewers, regardless of anxiety. Nevertheless, this is apparently not consistent with the hypothesis that anxiety is especially characterised by deficient inhibition of threat distractors (Eysenck et al., 2007), or difficulties in disengaging from threat stimuli (Fox & Georgiou, 2005). It is, however, possible that the effects of anxiety depend on the time course of the inhibitory mechanism. In fact, with participants unselected as a function of anxiety, Calvo and Castillo (2005) found that the interference effect of threat distractors occurred at 300 ms SOA (as in the current experiment) but disappeared at 1000 ms SOA. Accordingly, it is important to investigate whether the defective inhibition of threat distractors extends over time for high- but not for low-anxiety individuals. This issue was addressed in Experiment 2, by manipulating the distractor–probe SOA.

In contrast, parafoveal threat words did not cause any interference, even in conditions (i.e., right visual field) that facilitate lexical access (Calvo & Nummenmaa, 2009). This lack of effects cannot be attributed to insufficient capture of cognitive resources by the threat words, as interference did occur when they were presented foveally. It is possible that words were not semantically processed in parafoveal vision and that threat words are not especially likely to be perceived by high-anxiety individuals outside the focus of overt attention. However, this conclusion would be at odds with the hypervigilance hypothesis, according to which anxiety should broaden spatial attention—or the span of effective vision—for threatening stimuli (Eysenck et al., 2007), and also with prior data showing facilitation effects of parafoveal prime threat words on probe threat words, for high anxiety subjects (Calvo & Eysenck, 2008). Given the need to account for such inconsistencies, we conducted Experiment 2.

TABLE 1

Mean lexical decision times (in ms) for probe words as a function of location and valence of distractor word, for low and high trait anxiety groups, in Experiment 1

	Foveal location				Parafoveal location			
	Low anxiety		High anxiety		Low anxiety		High anxiety	
Distractor valence	M	SD	M	SD	M	SD	M	SD
Threat	680	106	692	103	659	130	662	102
Neutral	662	111	660	100	662	118	665	103

EXPERIMENT 2

Experiment 2 was concerned with the time course of the interference that the processing of foveal or parafoveal threat distractors may produce. We varied the SOA between the distractor and the probe (either 300 or 1000 ms), with the distractor display kept constant at 150 ms. This allows us to examine whether interference involves only initial capture of attention or whether it also affects later attentional engagement. The use of two SOAs permits the exploration of a defective inhibition mechanism for threat-related information, according to which high-anxious individuals show delayed disengagement from threat stimuli. Slowed lexical decision times on the probe words following a threat (relative to a neutral) distractor were assumed to indicate deficient inhibitory control. The prediction is that the interference effects of threat words in high-anxious participants will occur at 1000 ms as well as 300 ms SOA, whereas interference will occur for low-anxious participants only at 300 ms SOA.

Method

Participants. Twenty-four psychology undergraduates high in trait anxiety (18 female) and 24 low in trait anxiety (18 female) participated for course credit. They were selected from a group of 142 students as a function of their high ($M = 54.5$, $SD = 4.0$) or low ($M = 33.4$, $SD = 3.3$), $t(46) = 16.87$, $p < .0001$, scores in the trait scale of the STAI (Spielberger et al., 1982), with the same criteria as in Experiment 1.

Other methodological characteristics. The apparatus, stimuli, design, and procedure resembled those used in Experiment 1, with the following differences. First, no eyetracker was used now, given the negligible number of saccades that landed on the parafoveal word location during the 150 ms display in Experiment 1. Second, a new distractor–probe 1000 ms SOA was added. The distractor word and the string of xx + xx were always presented concurrently for 150 ms, followed by either an 850 ms blank interval (1000 ms SOA) or a 150 ms blank interval (300 ms SOA) before the onset of the probe. The design involved a combination of trait anxiety (low vs. high), SOA (300 vs. 1000 ms), distractor valence (threat vs. neutral), and distractor location (foveal vs. parafoveal). For each participant, half of the threat distractors and half of the neutral distractors were randomly assigned to each SOA condition, with each SOA condition assigned to either the first or the second block in a counterbalanced order. Anxiety was a between-subjects factor, whereas the others were within-subjects factors.

Results

Response accuracy was not significantly affected by any factor (M probability of correct responses = 0.977; all $Fs < 1$). Mean correct lexical decision times for probe words (see Table 2) were initially analysed in an Anxiety $\times$ SOA $\times$ Valence $\times$ Location ANOVA. The main effects of valence, $F(1, 46) = 16.54$, $p < .0001$, $\eta_p^2 = .265$, and SOA, $F(1, 46) = 43.58$, $p < .0001$, $\eta_p^2 = .486$, with no effects of anxiety ($F < 1$) or location ($p = .22$), were qualified by the following interactions: Anxiety $\times$ Valence, $F(1, 46) = 9.63$, $p < .01$, $\eta_p^2 = .173$, Location $\times$ Valence, $F(1, 46) = 48.46$, $p < .0001$, $\eta_p^2 = .513$, Anxiety $\times$ Valence $\times$ Location, $F(1, 46) = 9.44$, $p < .01$, $\eta_p^2 = .170$, Valence $\times$ SOA, $F(1, 46) = 12.45$, $\eta_p^2 = .213$, and Anxiety $\times$ Valence $\times$ SOA, $F(1, 46) = 6.43$, $p < .025$, $\eta_p^2 = .123$.

To examine the meaning of these interactions (see Figure 2), we analysed the effects of valence for each location, SOA, and anxiety group. When threat distractors appeared *foveally* at the shorter (300 ms) SOA, responses to the probe words were slower than when neutral distractors were presented, for both the low-anxious, $t(23) = 4.45$,

TABLE 2
Mean lexical decision times (in ms) for probe words as a function of location and valence of distractor word in the 300 ms and the 1000 ms SOA conditions, for low and high trait anxiety groups, in Experiment 2

	Stimulus–onset asynchrony							
	Foveal location				Parafoveal location			
	300 ms		1000 ms		300 ms		1000 ms	
Distractor valence	M	SD	M	SD	M	SD	M	SD
Low anxiety								
Threat	669	103	630	97	648	109	641	97
Neutral	644	93	639	99	652	99	647	99
High anxiety								
Threat	686	93	671	93	652	97	643	96
Neutral	653	91	645	90	657	96	647	97

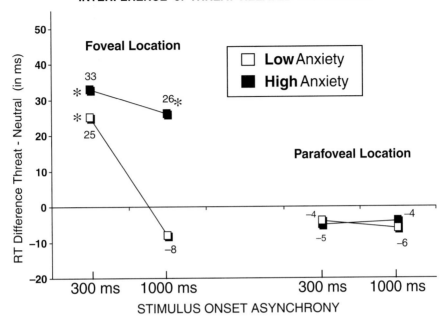

Figure 2.   Interference scores (i.e., lexical decision times for the probe following a threat distractor word minus RTs following a neutral distractor). Positive scores indicate interference. Asterisks show significant differences between the threat and the neutral condition.

$p < .0001$, and the high-anxious, $t(23) = 7.10$, $p < .0001$, group. However, at the longer (1000 ms) SOA, this effect remained significant only for the high-anxious group, $t(23) = 4.35$, $p < .0001$.

In contrast, when the distractors were presented *parafoveally*, there was no significant effect of valence at either SOA and for either anxiety group. We further included visual field as a factor in the ANOVA. The interference scores were close to zero (i.e., no interference) when the threat word distractor was presented in the right visual field (M low anxiety $= -3$ ms vs. high anxiety $= -2$ ms), and were not different from those in the left visual field (M low anxiety $= -7$ ms vs. high anxiety $= -6$ ms). No interaction was significant ($Fs < 1$).

Discussion

Foveal threat word distractors generally slowed down lexical decision responses to neutral probes at the shorter (300 ms) SOA. This reveals initial attentional *capture* by threat stimuli, which occurs generally for most individuals regardless of anxiety. In addition, foveal threat distractors continued to produce interference at the longer (1000 ms) SOA for high-anxiety participants, but the effect disappeared for low-anxiety participants. This

reveals attentional *engagement*, or longer dwelling, on the threat source only for high anxiety individuals. The fact that foveal interference remained for the high-anxious group at 1000 ms SOA confirmed the prediction that this group would be slower to disengage from threat words, which could be either an attentional effect or a response effect. It was as if high-anxiety participants were "cognitively frozen" by the threat distractors, whereas low-anxiety participants could "get rid of" such distractors earlier and reallocate attention to the probe. This is consistent with the hypothesis that high-anxiety individuals are characterised by difficulties in disengaging from threat-related stimuli (Fox & Georgiou, 2005), and that they have deficient inhibitory control of attention to such stimuli (Eysenck et al., 2007). In contrast, parafoveal threat distractors did not produce any interference at either SOA or for either anxiety group, which suggests that threat word meaning was not processed outside the focus of overt attention (see the next section for an explanation of discrepancies).

GENERAL DISCUSSION

The current study has yielded three major findings. First, high trait anxiety was not associated with enhanced saccades towards parafoveal threat word distractors, relative to neutral distractors and to low anxiety. Second, threat distractors appearing at fixation produced immediate interference with the processing of neutral probe words for both high- and low-anxiety groups, but threat distractors produced delayed interference only for those high in anxiety. And, third, threat distractors did not cause any interference when they were presented parafoveally. These findings are relevant to three important issues, respectively: biased overt orienting to threat-related stimuli, deficient delayed inhibitory control of threat distractors, and semantic processing of threat cues outside the focus of overt attention.[1]

Initial orienting and deficient inhibitory control of attention to threat distractors

In their meta-analytic review of attentional bias, Bar-Haim et al. (2007) concluded that two prominent cognitive characteristics of anxiety involve initial preattentive threat detection and later allocation of attention to threat. These characteristics can be linked to the hypervigilance and the deficient inhibition hypotheses, which are central in models of anxiety and cognitive functioning (Eysenck et al., 2007; Fox & Georgiou, 2005; Mathews & Mackintosh, 1998; Mogg & Bradley, 1998; Williams et al., 1997). Anxiety would facilitate threat detection through hypervigilance to threat cues, which, once detected, would be difficult to suppress or ignore—even if they are task-irrelevant—due to deficient inhibitory control.

Early threat detection can be accomplished by means of a hypervigilance mechanism through eye movements to threat stimuli appearing outside the focus of attention. Some studies have investigated eye movements to lateralised emotional faces (Bradley, Mogg, & Millar, 2000) or scenes (Calvo & Avero, 2005) as a function of trait anxiety. In the only study with words as stimuli of which we have knowledge, high-anxious participants were more likely to make eye movements to lateralised threat words, relative to nonthreat words (Broomfield & Turpin, 2005). In contrast, in the current study (see also Calvo & Eysenck, 2008), high-anxious participants had no more eye movements to threat than to nonthreat words, and did not make more such movements than low-anxious participants. These empirical discrepancies cannot be attributed to our use of gaze-contingent masking, which might have discouraged participants from looking at the parafoveal words. The reason is that the percentage of trials with (uninstructed) saccades towards the words in our study was higher (13%) than in the Broomfield and Turpin experiments (6%, on average). Accordingly, it is possible that hypervigilance can be accomplished by alternative—though compatible—means: Anxiety could broaden the attentional spatial span through covert attention (and hence no overt saccades would be necessary to process parafoveal words; Calvo & Eysenck, 2008), or anxiety could induce eye-movement scanning through overt attention (Broomfield & Turpin, 2005).[2]

A mechanism of defective inhibition of attention to threat has been investigated by means of task-irrelevant distractors (see Eysenck et al., 2007). In our study, the fact that interference persisted following threat word distractors longer for high- than for low-anxiety participants reveals difficulties in inhibiting attention to threat. This is consistent with research using the emotional Stroop task (see Williams et al., 1996), where

---

[1]Theory and research on anxiety and cognitive bias has focused on attention to *threat*-related stimuli as a specific characteristic of anxiety. In the current study, we aimed to extend the views on the mechanisms involved, i.e., hypervigilance and deficient inhibition of threat stimuli, and therefore we used threat-related words (and neutral words, for comparison). We might, nevertheless, consider whether the processing of other types of emotional stimuli, mainly positively valenced, is also affected by hypervigilance and attentional control in anxious individuals. Thus far, there is minimal evidence of the involvement of these mechanisms in the processing of positive stimuli, as a function of anxiety (see Bar-Haim et al., 2007). Furthermore, in a related study, Calvo and Eysenck (2008) found no significant differences in positive-word processing between high- and low-anxiety participants.

[2]We have assumed that anxiety-driven hypervigilance can involve broadening of perceptual span to facilitate detection of threatening stimuli appearing eccentrically in the visual field. Although this assumption has received some support (Keogh & French, 1999; Shapiro & Lim, 1989), there is also controversy about it. Positive emotions have been proposed to broaden the scope of attention, whereas negative emotions, including anxiety, could produce narrowing (Derryberry & Tucker, 1994; Fredrickson & Branigan, 2005; see Clore & Huntsinger, 2007, for a review). It must, nevertheless, be noted that, in these studies, broadening and narrowing were conceptualised in a general sense encompassing a wide range cognitive processes; furthermore, attentional span was not strictly defined in terms of the functional field of view, with no manipulation of stimulus eccentricity.

anxious individuals find it difficult to ignore the content of threat words. Our findings add to these studies by showing that threatening information not only can draw attention, but that threat holds attention even when the stimulus is *no longer* present. Whereas in Stroop studies the task-relevant word colour and the task-irrelevant word meaning are presented simultaneously, in the current paradigm, the task-irrelevant distractor was presented *before* the task-relevant probe. Beyond concurrent interference (Stroop studies), we have thus shown *poststimulus* interference. Other paradigms in which threat cue words and probe words are presented in a sequential manner have also provided evidence of defective inhibition in anxiety (Fox et al., 2001; Wood, Mathews, & Dalgleish, 2001; with cue angry faces or unpleasant scenes, see Derakshan, Ansari, Hansard, Shoker, & Eysenck, 2009; Fox, Russo, & Dutton, 2002; and Yiend & Mathews, 2001). The current study makes a contribution by showing the time course of this mechanism, i.e., how threat interferes automatically for all individuals at an initial stage, whereas interference either persists or is controlled at later strategic stages as a function of anxiety.

In summary, of the two major characteristics regarding the processing of threat-related information by high-anxiety individuals, i.e., hypervigilance and early orienting to threat, and later allocation and deficient inhibitory control of attention to threat, we have found clear evidence supporting the latter, but not the former (at least, no selective orienting in *overt* visual attention to threat words).[3] It must, nevertheless, be noted that our study was designed to investigate the role of *trait* rather than state anxiety. Bishop (2009), and Pacheco-Unguetti, Acosta, Callejas, and Lupiáñez (2010) have shown that the effects of trait and state anxiety on attentional mechanisms are not the same. Bishop (2009); see also Bishop, 2007) found high trait anxiety to be linked to impoverished recruitment of prefrontal attentional control mechanisms (especially the dorsolateral prefrontal

cortex and the ventrolateral prefrontal cortex) to inhibit distractor processing; furthermore, this effect remained after controlling for state anxiety. In contrast, elevated state anxiety is associated with increased amygdala responsiveness, and therefore hypervigilance to threat (see Bishop, 2007). Also, Pacheco-Unguetti et al. have demonstrated that, whereas state anxiety is associated with an overfunctioning of alertness and orienting in attentional networks, trait anxiety is mainly related to deficiencies in the executive control of attention. This is consistent with our own findings, in that trait anxiety is more related to deficient inhibitory control than to hypervigilance (which might be more affected by state anxiety; see Calvo et al., 2005).

Semantic versus nonsemantic parafoveal processing of threat words

In spite of the clear interference caused by foveal threat distractors immediately (300 ms SOA; all participants) and with delay (1000 ms SOA; only high-anxiety participants), the same threat words in parafoveal vision produced no interference. If we take the threat vs. neutral interference difference as indicative that threat meaning was processed (see introduction and later), the lack of effects suggests that parafoveal threat words were not semantically analysed by low- or high-anxiety participants. This is in apparent conflict with the findings obtained by Calvo and Eysenck (2008). These authors used a repetition priming paradigm to investigate facilitation effects of parafoveal prime words on the processing of identical versus unrelated probe words. They found faster lexical decision responses for probe threat words following parafoveal threat words for high- than for low-anxiety participants, relative to neutral and positive words. These facilitation effects would demonstrate that threat words are especially likely to be perceived in parafoveal vision by high-anxiety individuals.

It must, however, be noted that repetition priming indicates that the prime words are processed, but does not reveal what kind of information is extracted, that is responsible for the facilitation effects. Although repetition priming is sensitive to word meaning (i.e., the prime–probe semantic relatedness; e.g., Gollan, Forster, & Frost, 1997), it can be influenced by the prime-probe orthographic similarity. In fact, prior

---

[3]The null effect on anxiety on visual orienting in the current study cannot be attributed simply to the use of words. In a recent study, Derakshan and Koster (2010) recorded eye movements in a visual search task using face stimuli with angry, happy, and neutral expressions. Trait anxiety was not associated with number of fixations or time spent on crowd faces *before* fixating the angry (i.e., threat) targets, thus showing no facilitated orienting to threat. This adds to the debate about the extent to which anxiety affects early threat detection (Bar-Haim et al., 2007).

research has shown that word form codes are more likely than semantic codes to be obtained parafoveally (see Rayner, 1998). Accordingly, the priming effects found by Calvo and Eysenck (2008) could have been determined more by orthographic similarity rather than by meaning. These authors explicitly acknowledged this possibility as an alternative explanation of the priming advantage for parafoveal threat words in high-anxiety individuals. Furthermore, this orthographic advantage hypothesis is compatible with an additional finding. Namely, in the Calvo and Eysenck study, anxiety was associated with greater familiarity with threat words, and the parafoveal priming effects were significantly reduced when differences in word familiarity were removed. At a more general level, this is also consistent with the suggestion that the preattentional bias to threat words may have more to do with their disproportionate usage in anxious people than with the processing of the actual emotional word valence (see Fox & Georgiou, 2005, p. 11).

Accordingly, it is possible to interpret and integrate the empirical discrepancies between the lack of interference (current study) and the facilitation (Calvo & Eysenck, 2008) effects of parafoveal threat words. High-anxious individuals would be more likely than low-anxious ones to process threat words orthographically due to greater familiarity with them. This would explain why high-anxious participants showed a parafoveal threat priming effect (Calvo & Eysenck, 2008). Due to greater familiarity with threat words, their orthographic form would become more accessible in parafoveal vision and produce repetition priming, i.e., *facilitation* in the processing of an orthographically overlapping probe word. However, the mere orthographic representation of threat words (*not* involving threatening *meaning*—hence, not grabbing attention) would not *interfere* with the semantic processing of an unrelated neutral probe word. Thus, orthographic processing of parafoveal threat distractors would be insufficient on its own to interfere with lexical decisions on unrelated neutral probes (the current experiments), but would be enough to produce repetition priming (Calvo & Eysenck, 2008).

CONCLUSIONS

We investigated two extensions of attentional bias in anxiety: (1) preattentive processing of threat-related stimuli in parafoveal vision, and (2) the time course of defective inhibition of attention to threat distractors. First, the lack of selective orienting to, and interference from, parafoveal threat word distractors suggests that anxiety does not facilitate the semantic processing of threat-related information outside the focus of overt attention, i.e., preattentively or prior to fixation on the words. In contrast, second, anxiety strongly affects attentional engagement on threat content *after* a threat-related stimulus has been fixated. When threat word distractors were presented at fixation, they slowed down lexical decisions on neutral probe words immediately (300 ms SOA) for all participants, but such an interference effect remained at a later stage (1000 ms SOA) only for high-anxiety participants. This suggests anxious people have difficulties in inhibiting attention to threat distractors, even after these are no longer present as stimuli.

REFERENCES

Bar-Haim, Y., Lamy, D., Pergamin, L., Bakermans-Kranenburg, M. J., & van IJzendoorn, M. H. (2007). Threat-related attentional bias in anxious and non-anxious individuals: A meta-analytic study. *Psychological Bulletin, 133*, 1–24.

Bishop, S. J. (2007). Neurocognitive mechanisms of anxiety: An integrative account. *Trends in Cognitive Sciences, 7*, 307–316.

Bishop, S. J. (2009). Trait anxiety and impoverished prefrontal control of attention. *Nature Neuroscience, 12*, 92–92.

Bradley, B., Mogg, K., & Millar, N. H. (2000). Covert and overt orienting of attention to emotional faces in anxiety. *Cognition and Emotion, 14*, 789–808.

Broomfield, N. M., & Turpin, G. (2005). Covert and overt attention in trait anxiety: A cognitive psychophysiological analysis. *Biological Psychology, 68*, 179–200.

Calvo, M. G., & Avero, P. (2005). Gaze direction and duration in the time course of attention to emotional pictures in anxiety. *Cognition and Emotion, 19*, 433–451.

Calvo, M. G., & Castillo, M. D. (2005). Foveal vs. parafoveal attention-grabbing power of threat-related information. *Experimental Psychology, 52*, 150–162.

Calvo, M. G., Castillo, M. D., & Fuentes, L. J. (2006). Processing of "unattended"threat-related information: Role of emotional content and context. *Cognition and Emotion, 20*, 1049–1075.

Calvo, M. G., & Eysenck, M. W. (2008). Affective significance enhances covert attention: Roles of anxiety and word familiarity. *Quarterly Journal of Experimental Psychology, 61*, 1669–1686.

Calvo, M. G., & Nummenmaa, L. (2009). Word identification by covert attention in the right visual field: Gaze-contingent foveal masking. *Laterality: Asymmetries of Body, Brain and Cognition, 14*, 178–195.

Clore, G. L., & Huntsinger, J. R. (2007). How emotions inform judgment and regulate thought. *Trends in Cognitive Sciences, 11*, 393–399.

Derakshan, N., Ansari, T. L., Hansard, M., Shoker, L., & Eysenck, M. W. (2009). Anxiety, inhibition, efficiency, and effectiveness. *Experimental Psychology, 56*, 48–55.

Derakshan, N., & Koster, E. (2010). Processing efficiency in anxiety: Evidence from eye-movements during visual search. *Behaviour Research and Therapy, 48*, 1180–1185.

Derryberry, D., & Reed, M. (2002). Anxiety-related attentional biases and their regulation by attentional control. *Journal of Abnormal Psychology, 111*, 225–236.

Derryberry, D., & Tucker, D. M. (1994). Motivating the focus of attention. In P. M. Niedenthal & S. Kitayama (Eds.), *The heart's eye: Emotional influences in perception and attention* (pp. 167–196). San Diego, CA: Academic Press.

Eysenck, M. W. (1992). *Anxiety: The cognitive perspective*. London, UK: Lawrence Erlbaum Associates Ltd.

Eysenck, M. W. (1997). *Anxiety and cognition: A unified theory*. Hove, UK: Psychology Press.

Eysenck, M. W., Derakshan, N., Santos, R., & Calvo, M. G. (2007). Anxiety and cognitive performance: Attentional control theory. *Emotion, 7*, 336–353.

Fox, E. (1993). Attentional bias in anxiety: Selective or not? *Behaviour Research and Therapy, 31*, 487–493.

Fox, E. (1994). Attentional bias in anxiety: A defective inhibition hypothesis. *Cognition and Emotion, 8*, 165–195.

Fox, E., & Georgiou, G. A. (2005). The nature of attentional bias in human anxiety. In R. W. Engle, G. Sedek, U. von Hecker, & D. N. McIntosh (Eds.), *Cognitive limitations in aging and psychopathology* (pp. 249–274). Cambridge, UK: Cambridge University Press.

Fox, E., Russo, R., Bowles, R., & Dutton, K. (2001). Do threatening stimuli draw or hold visual attention in subclinical anxiety? *Journal of Experimental Psychology: General, 130*, 681–700.

Fox, E., Russo, R., & Dutton, K. (2002). Attentional bias for threat: Evidence for delayed disengagement from emotional faces. *Cognition and Emotion, 16*, 355–379.

Fredrickson, B., & Branigan, C. (2005). Positive emotions broaden the scope of attention and thought-action repertories. *Cognition and Emotion, 19*, 313–332.

Gollan, T., Forster, K. I., & Frost, R. (1997). Translation priming with different scripts: Masked priming with cognates and noncognates in Hebrew-English bilinguals. *Journal of Experimental Psychology: Learning, Memory, and Cognition, 23*, 1122–1139.

Harris, C. R., & Pashler, H. E. (2004). Attention and the processing of emotional words and names: Not so special after all. *Psychological Science, 15*, 171–178.

Kanne, S. (2002). The role of semantic, orthographic, and phonological prime information in unilateral visual neglect. *Cognitive Neuropsychology, 19*, 245–261.

Keogh, E., & French, C. C. (1999). The effect of trait anxiety and mood manipulation on the breadth of attention. *European Journal of Personality, 13*, 209–223.

MacLeod, C., & Rutherford, E. M. (1992). Anxiety and the selective processing of emotional information: Mediating roles of awareness, trait and state variables, and personal relevance of stimulus materials. *Behaviour Research and Therapy, 30*, 479–491.

Mathews, A., & Mackintosh, B. (1998). A cognitive model of selective processing in anxiety. *Cognitive Therapy and Research, 22*, 539–560.

Mayer, B., & Merkelbach, H. (1999). Unconscious processes, subliminal stimulation, and anxiety. *Clinical Psychology Review, 19*, 571–590.

Mogg, K., & Bradley, B. (1998). A cognitive-motivational analysis of anxiety. *Behaviour Research and Therapy, 36*, 809–848.

Mogg, K., Bradley, B., & Williams, R. (1995). Attentional bias in anxiety and depression: The role of awareness. *British Journal of Clinical Psychology, 34*, 17–36.

Pacheco-Unguetti, A. P., Acosta, A., Callejas, A., & Lupiáñez, J. (2010). Attention and anxiety: Different attentional functioning under state and trait anxiety. *Psychological Science, 21*, 298–304.

Pratto, F., & John, O. P. (1991). Automatic vigilance: The attention-grabbing power of negative social information. *Journal of Personality and Social Psychology, 61*, 380–391.

Rayner, K. (1998). Eye movements in reading and information processing: 20 years of research. *Psychological Bulletin, 124*, 372–422.

Shapiro, K. L., & Lim, A. (1989). The impact of anxiety on visual attention to central and peripheral events. *Behaviour Research and Therapy, 27*, 345–351.

Spielberger, C. D., Gorsuch, R. L., & Lushene, R. E. (1982). *Cuestionario de Ansiedad Estado-Rasgo [State Trait Anxiety Inventory]*. Madrid, Spain: TEA Ediciones.

Stormark, K. M., Nordby, H., & Hugdahl, K. (1995). Attentional shifts to emotionally charged cues: Behavioural and ERP data. *Cognition and Emotion, 9*, 507–523.

White, M. (1996). Automatic affective appraisal of words. *Cognition and Emotion, 10*, 199–211.

Williams, J. M. G., Mathews, A., & MacLeod, C. (1996). The emotional Stroop task and psychopathology. *Psychological Bulletin, 120*, 3–24.

Williams, J. M. G., Watts, F. N., MacLeod, C., & Mathews, A. (1997). *Cognitive psychology and emotional disorders* (2nd ed). Chichester, UK: Wiley.

Wood, J., Mathews, A., & Dalgleish, T. (2001). Anxiety and cognitive inhibition. *Emotion, 2*, 166–181.

Yiend, J., & Mathews, A. (2001). Anxiety and attention to threatening pictures. *Quarterly Journal of Experimental Psychology, 54A*, 665–681.

APPENDIX

Threat words and neutral words

Threat words

Coffin (ataúd)	Poison (veneno)	Rape (violar)
Hate (odiar)	Thief (ladrón)	Suffocation (asfixia)
Fight (pelea)	Alarm (alarma)	Drowned (ahogado)
Tumour (tumor)	Panic (pánico)	Help! (Socorro)
Cruel (cruel)	Cry (llanto)	Malignant (maligno)
Tomb (tumba)	Wound (herida)	Shot (disparo)
Bomb (bomba)	Crime (crimen)	Torture (tortura)
Kill (matar)	Horror (horror)	Stroke (infarto)
Virus (virus)	Suffer (sufrir)	Murder (asesino)
Die (morir)	Terror (terror)	Punishment (castigo)
Pain (dolor)	Jail (cárcel)	Corpse (cadáver)
Fear (miedo)	Cancer (cáncer)	Enemy (enemigo)
Lash (azotar)	Fire! (¡fuego!)	Ill (enfermo)
Viper (víbora)	Blood (sangre)	Danger (peligro)
Mugging (atraco)	War (Guerra)	
Beating (paliza)	Victim (víctima)	
Agony (agonía)	Shoot (fusilar)	

Neutral words

Hat (gorro)	Bag (bolso)	Beard (barba)
Add (sumar)	Cable (cable)	Ear (oreja)
Poem (poema)	Bird (pájaro)	Bricklayer (albañil)
Walk (andar)	Trial (ensayo)	Broom (cepillo)
Nose (nariz)	Moustache (bigote)	Keyboard (teclado)
Look (mirar)	Shoulder (hombro)	Form (impreso)
Letter (carta)	Tent (tienda)	Concrete (cemento)
Floor (suelo)	Close (cerrar)	Cotton (algodón)
Smooth (alisar)	Bridge (puente)	Track (sendero)
Paintbrush (brocha)	Harbour (puerto)	Pavement (asfalto)
Cheque (cheque)	Theatre (teatro)	February (febrero)
Horseman (jinete)	Model (modelo)	Paint (pintura)
Bronze (bronce)	Path (camino)	Similar (similar)
Cardboard (cartón)	Morning (mañana)	Message (mensaje)
Shoe (zapato)	Mountain (montaña)	Next (próximo)
Light (ligero)	Approach (acercar)	Liquid (líquido)

Note: Original Spanish Words in parenthesis.

JOURNAL OF COGNITIVE PSYCHOLOGY, 2012, 24 (1), 79–91

The effect of cognitive load in emotional attention and trait anxiety: An eye movement study

Nick Berggren[1], Ernst H. W. Koster[2], and Nazanin Derakshan[1]

[1]Department of Psychological Science, Birkbeck University of London, London, UK
[2]Department of Psychology, Ghent University, Ghent, Belgium

There is extensive debate on the automaticity of attentional processing of emotional information. One core feature of automaticity is the independence of processing emotion from factors that can affect attention such as cognitive load. In the present study we investigated whether processing of emotional facial expressions was dependent on cognitive load using a visual search paradigm. Manual responses as well as eye movements were recorded. Although both measures showed that emotional information captured attention more strongly than neutral information, manual responses indicated that load slowed reaction times only for "pop-out" emotion conditions; no increase was seen for all-emotional displays. This suggests that the saliency of emotion was reduced, but eye movement data showed that effects were caused by improvements for all-emotional displays in target processing efficiency. Additionally, trait anxiety did not influence threat processing, but costs were observed under load that were not present for nonanxious subjects. Our results suggest that while load can interfere with task performance, it may not affect emotion processing. Our findings highlight the importance of eye movement measures in accounting for differences in manual response data and provide novel support to theories of anxiety.

Keywords: Anxiety; Attention; Emotion; Eye movement; Visual search.

It has been argued that the cognitive processing of emotional, and especially threat-related, information has a special status in animals and humans (Oatley & Johnson-Laird, 1987); an important characteristic being its reflexive orienting of attention to threat and the prioritisation of threat over other stimuli and task demands. Evolutionary accounts of threat processing dictate that such prioritisation can be considered adaptive, hard-wired, and present in all individuals (Lang, Bradley, & Cuthbert, 1997; Mathews & Mackintosh, 1998; Mogg & Bradley, 1998; see Öhman et al., in press). There is also emerging evidence from electrophysiological recordings to indicate that early visual components are influenced by the emotional significance of stimuli (e.g., Stolarova, Keil, & Moratti, 2006). Indeed threat-related stimuli have been shown to activate amygdala response even when presented subliminally (Morris, Öhman, & Dolan, 1996).

If emotional material is processed preattentively, and can have potent effects on the orienting of attention, attention itself will not influence initial emotion processing. However, recent challenges (see, e.g., Pessoa, 2005) have led to considerable debate about how threat is processed and whether it depends on attentional resources. For example, Stein, Peelen, Funk, and Seidl (2010) saw that the advantage for conscious detection of threat images in the attentional blink

Correspondence should be addressed to Dr Nazanin Derakshan, Affective and Cognitive Control Lab, Department of Psychological Science, Birkbeck University of London, Malet Street, London WC1E 7HX, UK. E-mail: n.derakhshan@bbk.ac.uk

This work was partially supported by a Royal Society Joint International Grant awarded to Nazanin Derakshan and Ernst Koster. Nick Berggren is supported by a 1 + 3 ESRC PhD studentship. We are grateful to Leor Shoker for assistance with programming and data extraction.

paradigm, compared to positive images, was abolished when attention was consumed by another visual task. Pessoa, Kastner, and Ungerleider (2002) also found that amygdala response to emotion was hampered when attentional resources were taxed, and similar findings were reported by Bishop, Jenkins, and Lawrence (2007). But there is also evidence that emotion can activate the amygdala irrespective of the focus of attention (see Vuilleimer, Armony, Driver, & Dolan, 2001), and indeed this position is seen as the more traditional belief on the basis of influential theories of automaticity such as by LeDoux (1995).

An important distinction must be made between how emotion may be impacted upon by early attention, and how it may interact with later cognitive facets and working memory. Models of selective attention such as Load Theory (e.g., Lavie, 2005) propose that visual demands on attention reduce early resources available to process additional information, extended to include emotional content by others (Bishop et al., 2007; Pessoa et al., 2002). Whether or not demands on early attention (i.e., perceptual load) can modulate emotion processing, far less emphasis has been paid on what happens when perceptual demands on attention are low. Under this circumstance, it is presumed that emotion will be processed automatically, regardless of one's view about the importance of early attention. Thus, information processing depends upon later cognitive influences such as central executive control.

Working memory is believed to be a major process in keeping one's goals in mind, and for coordinating between tasks (Shallice & Burgess, 1996). For example, in visual search, working memory is believed to be used to maintain target information (Duncan & Humphreys, 1989). Therefore, loading working memory should disrupt one's ability to maintain task goals and lead to increased likelihood of distraction by irrelevant information. Consistent with this, cognitive load has been shown to disrupt performance in the antisaccade task (Roberts, Hager, & Heron, 1994), increase the likelihood of attentional capture (Lavie & de Fockert, 2005), and result in greater interference by response-competing distractors (de Fockert, Rees, Frith, & Lavie, 2001). Individuals lower in working memory capacity have also shown evidence of generally greater distraction outside of load manipulations (see Kane & Engle, 2002).

With this in mind, working memory may also interact with emotion. Previous work has focused on how cognitive load can affect response to negative emotion in a more thought-driven manner. For instance, whilst conducting working memory tasks like digit rehearsal or math problems, feelings towards concurrently presented negative images are reduced in intensity (van Dillen, Heslenfeld, & Koole, 2007), and amygdala activity to negative emotion can be reduced either by reappraisal and down-regulating negative feelings, or equally by distracting oneself with another task (McRae et al., 2010). However, such previous work examines how loading working memory can affect emotional responses in the sense of thinking about negative emotion; when verbal processes are engaged, it is known that additional thought generation or mind wandering is reduced (Teasdale et al., 1995). Thus, evidence that negative emotions are attenuated through occupying working memory are interesting, but clearly cannot be applied to the idea that the ability of threatening information to capture and orient attention is affected by working memory.

That said, recent studies have proposed that simple threat processing in attention tasks can be hampered under cognitive load, though studies investigating this topic are few in number. Van Dillen and Koole (2009) induced a cognitive load, either through concurrent mathematics or digit rehearsal of one or eight digits, while participants responded to the gender identity of angry or happy faces. The authors found that angry faces took longer to respond to than happy ones, presumably through the angry faces capturing and holding attention, reducing processing efficiency in responding. Under high load, however, the difference between angry and happy trial reaction times was abolished. The authors argued that cognitive load may promote the processing of task-relevant information and reduce the disruptive effect of threat. We note, however, that this interpretation is somewhat at odds with previous work suggesting that a cognitive load should increase distraction, and also that in their experiments reaction times increased under load more for happy than angry trials. Therefore, it is difficult to interpret the finding that load increased reaction times to negative emotion to a lesser extent than it did for reaction times to positive emotion as evidence that load hampered threat processing. Another study by Pecchinenda and Heil (2007) found little impact of cognitive load on emotion. In their task (Experiment 3) participants responded to the valence of a target word, either positive or negative, superimposed over angry, happy, or neutral faces. The authors primarily looked for increases in response-competition under load, having replicated the effects on wholly neutral stimuli seen by de Fockert et al. (2001). However, the authors failed to replicate the load effect in this experiment, finding a compatibility effect under both load conditions yet no increase, suggesting that emotional distraction may be processed independently from working memory manipulations. Whether or not load affected reaction times differently for each particular expression was not assessed, as the authors' focus was on compatibility effects when collapsing across distractor expression. Moreover, whether cognitive load could increase distraction within the same experiment for nonemotional material could not be gleaned.

In appreciating these findings, the possible role of working memory in emotion processing has thus far found little empirical support. As with nonemotional items, a cognitive load may enhance threat processing by reducing one's ability to regulate and override threat's effect in pulling our attention. Equally, attending to emotion may be disrupted if cognitive resources are taxed and attentional reactions to threat require working memory to initiate. Finally, threat may grab attention in an automatic manner, overriding task goals and orienting attention outside of cognitive control. In the present study, we sought to investigate the value of these accounts in a visual search task modulating levels of cognitive load.

Two points set our study apart from previous investigations. First, we aimed to assess levels of trait anxiety and how load may affect individuals high or low in such a trait differently. Trait anxiety has been associated with a preferential bias in attention towards threatening information (see Bar-Haim, Lamy, Pergamin, Bakermans-Kranenburg, & van IJzendoorn, 2007, for a review). Interestingly, Bar-Haim et al. (2007) found that, when anxiety is measured, there seems to be a consistent lack of a threat bias for individuals with low levels of anxiety. This point is intriguing considering that threat processing is often seen as hard-wired and automatic. It may be that low anxious individuals process threat but simply control their attention through working memory and prevent orienting of attention towards such items to occur, or that responses are simply attenuated when arousal caused by the threat is diminished. A load on early attention has been shown to attenuate threat processing in the amygdala even for high anxious subjects (Bishop et al., 2007), but how cognitive load may affect threat processing is an unanswered question when taking into account anxiety. Second, in addition to behavioural responses, we also measured eye movements. Comparing manual response times are a good measure of distractibility, but some authors have argued that the presence of threat can speed up behavioural response (Flykt, 2006), and others have suggested that threat might disrupt responding (Mogg, Holmes, Garner, & Bradley, 2008). Additionally, Derakshan and Koster (2010) demonstrated that eye tracking can reveal saccades to distractor items before the target is fixated, and after target fixation prior to the manual response being given. Thus, recording eye movements can give additional insights into attentional biases that may be masked by simply behavioural reaction time data.

THE CURRENT INVESTIGATION

The present study was designed to examine attentive processing of threat under cognitive load, taking previous limitations into account. To reduce ambiguity over the dependent measure of attentive processing of threat, we used manual reaction times as well as eye movements as dependent variables in a visual search paradigm. In this task, participants can be provided with different type of instructions. In the present study we used the "odd-one-out" instructions where individuals were instructed to see whether a display of eight faces contained a face (target) with a different emotional expression. By manipulating the emotional expression of the target and the crowd, one can investigate speeded threat detection as well as impaired disengagement from threat through the examination of response latencies in high versus low anxious individuals. For example, an angry face (target) can be presented in a display of neutral faces (crowd) to investigate speeded threat detection. Conversely, a neutral face (target) can be presented among an angry crowd to examine attentional disengagement. In previous research, the visual search task has shown to be a sensitive paradigm to capture effects of emotional attention and modulation of anxiety-related individual differences (e.g., Byrne

& Eysenck, 1995; Öhman, Lundqvist, & Esteves, 2001; Rinck, Reinecke, Ellwart, Heuer, & Becker, 2005).

The following hypotheses were tested in this study. First, if attentive processing is an automatic process mainly related to bottom-up characteristics, emotional attention will be observed under conditions of cognitive load in similar magnitude. Contrarily, if working memory is involved in facilitated detection of threat, emotional attention will be reduced by cognitive load as suggested by previous work on thought regulation and response competition. We examined facilitated detection of threat (on trials with threatening targets) and disengagement from threat (on trials with threatening distractors) under load. Considering cognitive load has been shown to increase interference from distracting information, and working memory is involved in modulating attention, this could theoretically also result in reduced ability to disengage from threat while facilitation itself is unhindered. Finally, we tested whether individual differences in trait anxiety influence the attentive processing of threat under cognitive load.

METHOD

Participants

A sample of 63 participants[1] (39 female) was recruited via advertisements posted around the University of London colleges. Participants had a mean age of 28.71 ($SD = 5.89$). All had normal to corrected-to-normal vision and were asked to wear their glasses or contact lenses if necessary. Participants were paid £5 for participating in the experiment.

Stimuli

Eight angry, eight happy, and eight neutral facial expressions of emotion (half male and half female) were selected from three sources of databases of facial expressions, including the Ekman and Friesen database (Ekman & Friesen, 1978), the NimStim database (Tottenham et al., 2008) and the Karolinska Directed Emotional faces set (Lundqvist & Öhman, 1998). The faces

---

[1] The data for two participants were discarded due to poor calibration.

were presented in greyscale and positioned against a black background. The visual angle subtended by each face, when fixated, was $2°$ $29' \times 4° 29'$. Basic image statistics were computed and found to be similar for all three expressions. The standard deviation of the individual mean luminances, as a fraction of the overall mean, was computed. This "coefficient of variation" was approximately 1%.

Visual search task

Eight faces, arranged in a circle, were simultaneously shown on each trial. All faces were in the same frontal (and upright) orientation. The faces were shown in the eight "compass points". The eccentricity of each face, when fixating the central cross (i.e., the radius of the circle) was $8° 15'$.

For each of the three possible target expressions, there were two alternative nontarget (crowd) expressions. This produced six distinct target/crowd pairings, which were: angry target/happy crowd, angry target/neutral crowd, happy target/angry crowd, happy target/neutral crowd, neutral target/angry crowd, and neutral target/happy crowd. Each target expression appeared on any of the eight faces in the circle, equally often. Hence, there were 48 distinct target/crowd screens. The design also incorporated catch trials, on which eight identical faces (i.e., angry, happy, or neutral) were presented. The presentation of all trials was randomised for every participant. Participants completed six blocks (three under cognitive load and three under no load) of 60 trials (48 target/crowd trials and 12 catch trials). A trial began with a fixation cross (width and height of 33 pixels) that appeared in the centre of the screen for 1250 ms. This was followed by the stimulus screen until a response was made or, in case of no response, for 5000 ms.

Eye-tracking device and controlling software

The LC Technologies "Eyegaze" system was used to track eye movements (LC Technologies, 2003). This system uses the Pupil-Centre Corneal Reflection method (PCCR; Mason, 1969; Merchant & Morrisette, 1973). The eyes are lit by an infrared source and the resulting image of (one of) the eyes is monitored. The gaze point (intersection of the optic axis with the screen) is estimated from the image of the pupil, in conjunction with the corneal reflection of the light source.

The screen position of the gaze point is estimated at 60 Hz, with a typical root mean square error of less than $0.6°$ (38′). The Eyegaze system estimates participants' fixations by spatial averaging over groups of gaze points. A minimum duration of an individual fixation is defined as 100 ms and the maximum fixation radius is defined as $0.6°$ (38′).

The stimuli were presented in 24-bit colour on a 1024×768 LCD (ViewSonic 700b, cell response time 35 ms). The presentation of the stimuli was controlled by the DMDX program (Forster & Forster, 2003), which ensures millisecond timing accuracy. Responses were recorded from a button box (PIO-12 interface), monitored at 1000 Hz by DMDX. The eyetracking system was automatically synchronised to DMDX at the beginning of each trial. The eye-gaze system is tolerant of small head movements (up to 32 mm in any direction) and able to resume tracking after larger movements.

Procedure

The experiment took place in a dimly lit room that housed the eyetracker in the Laboratory of Affective and Cognitive Neuroscience at Birkbeck University of London. Upon arrival at the laboratory participants completed a measure of trait anxiety (Spielberger, Gorsuch, Lushene, Vagg, & Jacobs, 1983). They were seated at a distance of 60 cm from the eyetracking device. Participants were instructed to press the corresponding button as quickly as possible whenever a face in the circle depicted a different expression. They were asked not to respond if all the faces showed the same expression. Cognitive load was manipulated in a within-subject design: On half of the blocks, a two digit number appeared at the beginning of the trial. Participants were asked to count backwards in threes, out loud, from that number, until the end of that trial.[2] The remaining three blocks did not involve any manipulation of load. Orders of blocks were counterbalanced across participants. Speed and accuracy of response, as well as the need to attend to the

---

[2]Participants' performance while counting was monitored by the experimenter who sat outside the testing cubicle, and prompted the participant if counting incorrectly. All participants performed the counting task at ceiling level.

fixation cross whenever it appeared on the screen throughout the experiment, were emphasised.

Instructions were followed by practice trials for both load and no load conditions with the visual search task depicting different faces to those that appeared in the main experimental task. The eyetracking calibration procedure was then run, requiring the participant to fixate a series of 12 points on the screen. The main experimental task began as soon as the calibration procedure was completed. Participants were thanked and debriefed at the end of the session.

RESULTS

Participants had a mean trait anxiety score of 39.7 ($SD = 11.10$; min = 20, max = 77). To test the effects of anxiety participants were divided into low ($N = 29$) and high-trait anxious ($N = 32$) groups based on a median split on the trait anxiety score: Those scoring 37 and below were classified as low anxious, and those scoring above 37 were classified as high anxious. Mean trait anxiety for the low anxious group was 30.86 ($SD = 4.23$) and for the high anxious group it was 47.72 ($SD = 9.09$). The two groups differed significantly on trait anxiety levels, $t(59) = 9.42$, $p < .001$.

Manual responses (reaction times)

Reaction times were recorded from the onset of the face array. Less than 3% of the data was lost due to outliers (reaction times less, or greater, than 3 SD of each participant mean). Figure 1 shows mean reaction times for target detection in each of the six conditions as a function of cognitive load.

A $6 \times 2 \times 2$ Mixed ANOVA with condition and load as within-subjects factor and anxiety group as between-subject factor revealed main effects of condition, $F(5, 295) = 130.35$, $p < .001$, $\eta^2 = .69$, with participants being slowest to detect an angry target in a happy crowd and a happy target in an angry crowd that seemed to be unaffected by load. There was a main effect of load, $F(1, 59) = 6.55$, $p < .02$, $\eta^2 = .10$, with longer reaction times under load ($M = 1803$, $SD = 386$) than no load ($M = 1721$, $SD = 327$). There was also a Condition $\times$ Load interaction, $F(5, 295) = 3.12$, $p < .02$, $\eta^2 = .05$.

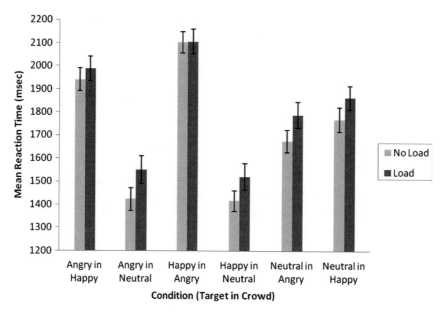

Figure 1. Mean reaction times to target as a function of target and crowd emotional expression in low and high anxious groups (bars indicate standard errors).

Corroborating this interaction, we tested if (1) facilitated detection of threat is influenced by cognitive load, and (2) if cognitive load interferes with disengagement from threat processing. Analysis showed that load interfered with facilitated detection of angry, $t(60) = 2.75, p < .01$, as well as happy targets, $t(60) = 3.05, p < .004$, when in neutral crowd. Accordingly, participants were slower to detect emotional targets under load (angry: $M = 1552, SD = 468$; happy: $M = 1522, SD = 440$) compared with no load (angry: $M = 1423, SD = 384$; happy: $M = 1417, SD = 352$). Analysis also showed that load interfered with both the disengagement from threat on trials with a neutral target and an angry crowd (no load: $M = 1675, SD = 372$; load: $M = 1788, SD = 439$), $t(60) = 2.85, p < .007$, but equally to find a neutral target amongst a happy crowd (no load: $M = 1769, SD = 410$; load: $M = 1864, SD = 388$), $t(60) = 2.39, p = .02$. Finally, load had no significant effect on finding an angry target in a happy crowd, $t(60) = 1.22, p > .2$, or vice versa, $t < 1$.

Analysis showed a main effect of anxiety, $F(1, 59) = 5.17, p < .03, \eta^2 = .08$, as well as a significant Load × Anxiety interaction, $F(1, 59) = 5.87, p < .02, \eta^2 = .09$. Although low and high anxious individuals did not differ in their reaction times under the no load condition, $t(59) = 1.38, p > .1$, high anxious individuals showed significantly longer reaction times under load, $t(59) = 2.81, p < .01$. Moreover, low anxious individuals showed no actual increase in reaction times generally under load (no load: $M = 1661, SD = 297$; load: $M = 1665, SD = 316$), $t(28) = 0.138, p = .89$, whereas high anxious individuals showed increased costs (no load: $M = 1776, SD = 347$; load: $M = 1929, SD = 405$), $t(31) = 2.97, p < .007$. The three-way interaction of Load × Condition × Anxiety was not significant, $F(5, 295) = 1.69, p = .16$.

Eye movement data

Table 1 shows the descriptive statistics for the following indices as a function of condition and load. For the eye movement data we presented several indices related to initial target detection, attentional disengagement target processing efficiency and fixations made after the target was located. Although other indices can also be examined (e.g., Derakshan & Koster, 2010), for reasons of parsimony, we selected the indices that most directly related to our hypotheses.

Time taken to fixate target

This was defined as the time participants spent on crowd faces prior to fixating the target, i.e., the elapsed time between onset of visual display and fixating target. A 6 (condition) × 2 (load) × 2 (anxiety group) mixed ANOVA revealed a main effect of condition, $F(5, 295) = 120.56, p < .001$,

$\eta^2 = .67$, which was qualified by a quadratic trend to indicate that participants took longer to fixate target when target and crowd were both emotional, followed by conditions where crowd was emotional and target neutral, and emotional targets in neutral crowds, $F(1, 59) = 37.42$, $p < .001$. There was a main effect of load, $F(1, 59) = 28.05$, $p < .001$, $\eta^2 = .32$, with participants taking longer to fixate a target under load ($M = 1173$, $SD = 225$) than under no load ($M = 1050$, $SD = 150$). Load did not interact with condition, $F < 1$. A two-way interaction of Anxiety $\times$ Load was observed, $F(1, 59) = 12.44$, $p = .001$, $\eta^2 = .17$. This showed that load affected the time taken to fixate target for the high anxious group (no load: $M = 1043$, $SD = 150$; load: $M = 1241$, $SD = 247$), $t(31) = 5.09$, $p < .001$, more than it did in the low anxious group (no load: $M = 1059$, $SD = 153$; load: $M = 1098$, $SD = 174$), $t(28) = 2.05$, $p = .05$. No other main effects or interactions were significant.

Mean crowd dwell time

This was defined as the mean time participants spent on each individual face in the crowd before fixating target. This index defined the attention grabbing power of each crowd face, i.e., attentional dwell time. A 6 (condition) $\times$ 2 (load) $\times$ 2 (anxiety group) mixed ANOVA on this data revealed a main effect of condition, $F(5, 295) = 33.43$, $p < .001$, $\eta^2 = .36$, qualified with a significant cubic trend, $F(1, 59) = 5.09$, $p < .03$, to indicate that angry crowd faces grabbed more attention than

happy crowd faces followed by neutral crowd faces ($M = 208$ vs. $M = 201$ vs. $M = 187$, respectively). There was a Load $\times$ Anxiety interaction, $F(1, 59) = 6.10$, $p < .02$, $\eta^2 = .09$. High anxious individuals showed a tendency to spend longer fixating each face under load ($M = 205$, $SD = 38$), compared with no load ($M = 198$, $SD = 24$) but this difference was not significant, $t(31) = 1.68$, $p = .10$. On the other hand, low anxious individuals spent less time fixating each face under load ($M = 195$, $SD = 25$) compared with no load ($M = 200$, $SD = 23$), $t(28) = 2.08$, $p < .05$. No other effects reached significance.

Target processing efficiency

This was defined as the elapsed time between landing fixation on target and behavioural reaction time as assessed by button press, and was used to assess the time taken to process the target. A 6 (condition) $\times$ 2 (load) $\times$ 2 (anxiety group) mixed ANOVA revealed a significant main effect of condition, $F(5, 295) = 33.67$, $p < .001$, $\eta^2 = .36$, with slowest target processing times for when both target and crowd were emotional and fastest target processing times for when an emotional target was embedded in a neutral crowd. There was no main effect of load, $F(1, 59) = 2.49$, $p = .12$, but a Load $\times$ Condition interaction, $F(5, 295) = 2.83$, $p < .03$, $\eta^2 = .05$. This interaction showed that load enhanced processing efficiency of an angry target in a happy crowd (no load: $M = 780$, $SD = 283$; load: $M = 708$, $SD = 261$), $t(60) = 2.44$, $p < .02$, as well as enhanced processing of a happy

TABLE 1

Patterns of eye movements prior to, and after, fixating target as a function of valence of target and crowd, and load

Eye movement index		Condition (target in crowd)					
		Angry in happy M (SD)	Angry in neutral M (SD)	Happy in angry M (SD)	Happy in neutral M (SD)	Neutral in angry M (SD)	Neutral in happy M (SD)
Time taken to fixate target (in ms)	NL	1194 (196)	836 (194)	1292 (203)	843 (186)	1058 (194)	1081 (216)
	L	1304 (248)	948 (296)	1384 (306)	977 (267)	1201 (269)	1226 (250)
Crowd attentional dwell time (in ms)	NL	203 (27)	185 (24)	212 (26)	188 (28)	208 (30)	198 (29)
	L	205 (35)	188 (43)	210 (34)	191 (37)	205 (36)	205 (38)
Number of crowd fixations made after landing target	NL	1.58 (0.83)	0.95 (0.61)	1.68 (0.83)	1.00 (0.63)	1.04 (0.59)	1.23 (0.72)
	L	1.16 (0.70)	1.03 (0.61)	1.36 (0.89)	0.93 (0.58)	0.88 (0.51)	1.04 (0.72)

NL = no load, L = Load.

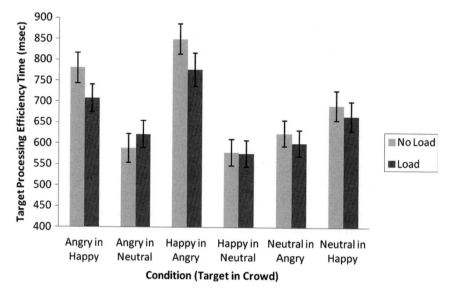

Figure 2. Target processing efficiency as a function of load (bars indicate standard errors).

target in an angry crowd (no load: $M = 850$, $SD = 283$; load: $M = 777$, $SD = 314$), $t(60) = 2.29$, $p < .03$. This pattern of findings is depicted in Figure 2. There was also a main effect of anxiety, $F(1, 59) = 6.89$, $p = .011$, $\eta^2 = .11$, with high anxious individuals generally slower in target processing ($M = 1142$, $SD = 172$) when compared to low anxious individuals ($M = 1079$, $SD = 155$). Anxiety did not interact with load or condition.

Number of crowd fixations after fixating target

This was defined as the number of fixations participants made on crowd faces after fixating target, complimenting target processing time by showing how much of time spent between target detection and pressing a manual response was taken up by processing/fixating distractor crowd faces (see Table 1). A 6 (condition) × 2 (load) × 2 (anxiety group) mixed ANOVA revealed a main effect of load, $F(1, 59) = 11.27$, $p = .001$, $\eta^2 = .16$, with fewer fixations made on distractor crowd faces following fixation on target under load (no load: $M = 1.25$, $SD = 0.58$; load: $M = 1.07$, $SD = 0.56$). There was also a main effect of condition, $F(5, 295) = 29.35$, $p < .001$, $\eta^2 = .33$, with a cubic trend showing more posttarget fixations made on displays with angry targets and happy crowds and vice versa compared to all other conditions, $F(1, 59) = 11.49$, $p = .001$, $\eta^2 = .16$. A Load × Condition interaction was also seen, $F(5, 295) = 6.41$, $p < .001$, $\eta^2 = .10$,

qualified by a significant cubic trend, $F(1, 59) = 4.14$, $p < .05$, indicating fewer posttarget fixations on crowd items in all-emotional displays under load, followed by neutral target in emotional displays, and finally emotional target in neutral displays.

Last, there was a main effect of anxiety, $F(1, 59) = 5.91$, $p = .02$, $\eta^2 = .09$, whereby high anxious participants made more crowd fixations following landing on target compared to low anxious participants (low anxious: $M = 0.99$, $SD = 0.36$; high anxious: $M = 1.31$, $SD = 0.61$). Once more, anxiety did not interact with load or condition.

DISCUSSION

The current study examined whether threat processing is affected by cognitive load. In theoretical models of threat processing there is extensive discussion on the degree to which threat processing is influenced by bottom-up characteristics, such as stimulus saliency, versus top-down mechanisms such as goal-directed behaviour and working memory processes in identifying task-relevant and task-irrelevant information (Cisler & Koster, 2010; Eysenck, Derakshan, Santos, & Calvo, 2007; Mathews, Mackintosh, & Fulcher, 1997). Examining whether threat processing is affected by cognitive load provides a partial answer to the question of whether threat processing occurs in an automatic fashion, independent from the availability of cognitive resources or alternatively is influenced by shared resources with other aspects of working memory (Pessoa et al., 2002), or can be suppressed by cognitive control. In order to obtain a fine-grained picture of the influence of cognitive load on various components of attentive processing of threat we combined a visual search paradigm with eye-registration methodology. The results of this study indicate that emotional information captures and holds attention more strongly than neutral information, that cognitive load appeared to hamper emotion processing, and that anxiety was associated with greater costs to performance under load. These findings are discussed next.

Emotion captures and holds attention

In the current study manual response time as well as eye movement data indicate that emotional information captured attention. That is, emotional targets in neutral crowds were responded to faster than neutral targets in emotional crowds. Moreover, initial target fixation to emotional targets was faster than to neutral targets, and attentional dwell time was longer for emotional crowds compared with neutral crowds. Interestingly, in our data there was little evidence for a threat superiority effect, which has been observed in several previous studies (e.g., Fox et al., 2000). In this regard, it is worth mentioning that several studies now indicate that valence per se is not the most important determining factor for attentional capture but that the arousal value of stimuli is associated with attentional capture (Schimmack, 2005; Vogt, de Houwer, Crombez, Koster, & van Damme, 2008), which also argues against the notion of threat superiority.

Emotion processing under load

With regard to our specific predictions of threat processing under load, we found that threat processing was hampered under cognitive load at the level of manual responses and, through eyetracking data, that this effect was driven by an increased time to fixate the target, but crucially not due to more fixations made on distractors. Thus, our findings suggest that diverting cognitive resources between the visual search and counting tasks caused a general slow-down in responses.

Interestingly, examining manual responses, load appeared to slow reaction times in all conditions except when a happy face was presented in an angry crowd or vice versa. Superficially, this would suggest that load may have disrupted the emotional saliency of information; an angry/happy face in a neutral crowd would take longer to find if the saliency of the emotional target was reduced, and equally a neutral target in an emotional crowd would stand out less if target to nontarget similarity is increased (Duncan & Humphreys, 1989). For trials already requiring serial search, however, such as all-emotional displays, if load hampered emotional saliency then reaction times would be less affected as the target cannot "pop-out" as easily to begin with.

However, with the aid of eye-movement measurement, we were able to pinpoint this discrepancy precisely; load appeared to improve target processing efficiency time for all-emotional displays, explaining why reaction times suffered in all other conditions but not these, and why there was no interaction of load and condition in time taken to fixate target. Thus, although the cost of load seemed to affect conditions differently, as indicated by increased response times, our eye movement data shows that we cannot solely rely on manual response times to determine emotion-specific attentive processing. Rather, under increased cognitive demands, all displays were simply more difficult to efficiently complete regardless of emotional valence (in the sense of time to fixate target), demonstrating that target items involving emotion are not immune to cognitive interference caused by cognitive load and yet are not differentially affected.

Why target processing efficiency for all-emotional displays was enhanced under load is unclear, but when measuring fixations made to other crowd items following landing fixation on target, we saw that load not only reduced this interference to processing efficiency but reduced it most for all-emotional displays. Thus, once participants had fixated a discrepant emotional target in an emotional crowd, they were faster to respond and made fewer follow-up eye movements under load than in other conditions.

Interactions of emotion and cognition

Although the differences in condition response times under load were pinpointed by differences in target processing efficiency, performing a concurrent task did not increase or decrease the saliency of emotional relative to neutral targets. However, a general cost in time to fixate target was observed under load regardless of valence. In this sense, our data suggests that cognitive load does have an effect on emotion processing, but only in affecting the cognitive factors involved in visual search and orienting attention such as the role of working memory in keeping the target template in mind during such tasks (Duncan & Humphreys, 1989).

With regard to whether cognitive resources are required in processing emotion, our manual response data supported this assumption by suggesting that emotion lost its salient qualities under load, though this finding was negated by the vital inclusion of eye movement recording. Thus, we cannot conclude that emotion processing does require cognitive resources and, as outlined in our introduction, there is inconclusive evidence to suggest that it does. It remains possible that our load manipulation, counting back in multiples of three, was not a strong enough demand and that a more potent load may have caused differences seen in emotion processing. What is clear, however, is that load can have differential effects on conditions in target processing efficiency in visual search tasks. As a consequence, future work may benefit from utilising eyetracking as a measure, as our data provides a cautionary note in interpreting purely behavioural responses that showed an interaction of load and condition that was not seen in eye movement latencies to fixate targets.

Anxiety under cognitive load

Finally, our findings with regard to the influence of trait anxiety require some consideration. In previous work, individual differences in anxiety levels were often neglected, which is problematic as the automaticity of threat processing may vary between high and low anxious individuals (see Bar-Haim et al., 2007; Fox, Russo, & Georgiou, 2005). If threat processing is more automatic in high anxious individuals, this would be less affected by cognitive load in high compared with low anxious individuals. In the current study we tested a relatively large sample and used a median-split procedure to explore influences of anxiety on threat processing. Overall, we failed to find that high anxious individuals' threat processing was less affected by cognitive load compared with low anxious individuals, and indeed no marked difference even under the no-load condition.

However, we found that anxious subjects were generally slower in reaction times in the visual search task. Eye movement data showed that high anxious subjects also demonstrated reduced target processing efficiency between fixating target and responding, which was likely driven by further fixations on distractors once the target had been fixated. This may suggest that anxious subjects were more likely to doubt their choice on finding the target, and so increased the likelihood of checking nearby distractor faces prior to manual response. Crucially, we also noted a number of interesting interactions with anxiety under load for both manual responses and eye movements. When a load was imposed, high anxious subjects experienced slower response times, whereas low anxious individuals showed no evidence of a cost. Eye movement data demonstrated that this effect was caused by longer latencies before landing fixation on target, possibly explained by increased fixations on crowd items under load that just missed significance, whereas the low anxious made significantly fewer crowd fixations under load.

Taken together, our findings support theories of trait anxiety such as Attentional Control Theory (ACT; Eysenck et al., 2007), which posits that anxiety is associated with reduced cognitive efficiency. Moreover, our findings of increased detriments to performance under load also support ACT's prediction that anxious individuals can attempt to compensate for reduced cognitive efficiency by utilising cognitive effort to placate this. With the imposition of cognitive load, compensatory strategies may have been disrupted as resources were diluted across two concurrent tasks, explaining why anxious participants showed costs under load, whereas nonanxious participants did not. Thus, manipulations of cognitive load may be a useful tool in elucidating attentional control deficits in anxiety that may sometimes be camouflaged under less demanding conditions by compensatory cognitive strategies (see Ansari & Derakshan, 2011).

CONCLUSIONS

The findings of the current investigation contribute to the literature in several important ways. First, in a visual search paradigm that is suitable to find attentional capture and holding effects of threat, we observed that emotional information in general demands attention. There was no evidence for threat specificity at any of the attentional indices, although processing of angry and happy faces did differ strongly at the level of target processing. These findings argue against a threat superiority effect which is in line with several recent studies that have observed little evidence for strong automatic threat processing (Calvo, Gutiérrez, & Fernández-Martín, in press; Huijding, Mayer, Koster, & Muris, 2011). Moreover, the results of the present study are of importance to the debate on the automaticity of threat processing; that is, strong claims have been put forward about the automaticity of threat processing. Our data provide important evidence that threat processing can be affected by cognitive load at the level of attentive processing in terms of a slowdown, but that emotion advantages in prioritising attention are generally maintained across conditions. Furthermore, our data indicate that threat processing is also perhaps not more automatic in anxious individuals. Last, our data point to a cost in task performance and reaction time in anxiety that is further revealed by cognitive load.

Clearly several limitations require consideration here. First, although stimulus material was carefully selected, one could argue that visual search was mainly performed through analysis of visual features of discrepant faces rather than the emotional expression of the faces, with a feature-based search not being divergent in high versus low anxious individuals. Yet, this account cannot explain the specific divergent pattern of eye movements with and without cognitive load and the findings at the level of the target processing index. The latter findings suggest some degree of emotion processing during visual search instead of a purely feature-based search. Second, we presented the analyses based on median split to ensure appropriate statistical power. It is important that we recognise some of the problems noted with regard to median-split analysis; however, similar effects were obtained when using more extreme scores on anxiety (tertiary split).

In sum, the current study shows that cognitive load can hamper effective visual search, including when that search involves emotion, arguing against strong claims of automaticity in emotional items capturing attention immediately and unaffected by current cognitive demands. However, emotion processing itself was relatively unaffected under load, with manual response differences explained through the use of eye movement data, and suggesting that process of emotion capturing attention may not be dependent upon cognitive resources, but simply slowed down. With the benefits of eye movement data, we were able to localise the effects of load on both differences in emotion conditions and in trait anxiety performance, finding specific effects on target search time under load, and more general effects on target processing efficiency. Utilising similar methodologies, future work may produce a more fine-grained analysis of how attentional processes are influenced by variables such as emotion, cognitive load, and anxiety.

REFERENCES

Anderson, A. K. (2005). Affective influences on the attentional dynamics supporting awareness. *Journal of Experimental Psychology: General, 134*, 258–281.

Ansari, T. L., & Derakshan, N. (2011). The neural correlates of cognitive effort in anxiety: Effects on processing efficiency. *Biological Psychology, 86*, 337–348.

Bannerman, R. L., Milders, M., & Sahraie, A. (2009). Processing emotional stimuli: Comparison of saccadic and manual choice-reaction times. *Cognition and Emotion, 23*, 930–954.

Bar-Haim, Y., Lamy, D., Pergamin, L., Bakermans-Kranenburg, M. J., & van IJzendoorn, M. H. (2007). Threat-related attentional bias in anxious and non-anxious individuals: A meta-analytic study. *Psychological Bulletin, 133*, 1–24.

Byrne, A., & Eysenck, M. W. (1995). Trait anxiety, anxious mood, and threat detection. *Cognition and Emotion, 9*, 549–562.

Calvo, M. G., Gutiérrez, A., & Fernández-Martín, A. (in press). Anxiety and deficient inhibition of threat distractors: Spatial attention span and time course. *Journal of Cognitive Psychology*.

Cisler, J. M., & Koster, E. H. W. (2010). Mechanisms underlying attentional biases towards threat: An integrative review. *Clinical Psychology Review, 30*, 203–216.

Corbetta, M., & Shulman, G. L. (2002). Control of goal-directed and stimulus-driven attention in the brain. *Nature Reviews Neuroscience, 3*, 215–229.

Derakshan, N., & Eysenck, M. W. (2009). Anxiety, processing efficiency and cognitive performance: New developments from attentional control theory. *The European Psychologist, 14*, 168–176.

Derakshan, N., & Koster, E. H. W. (2010). Processing efficiency in anxiety: Evidence from eye-movements during visual search. *Behaviour Research and Therapy, 48*, 1180–1185.

De Ruiter, C., & Brosschot, J. F. (1994). The emotional Stroop interference effect in anxiety: Attentional bias or cognitive avoidance? *Behaviour Research and Therapy, 32*, 315–319.

Desimone, R., & Duncan, J. (1995). Neural mechanisms of selective attention. *Annual Review of Neuroscience, 18*, 193–222.

Ekman, P., & Friesen, W. V. (1978). *The facial action coding system.* Palo Alto, CA: Consulting Psychologists Press.

Eysenck, M. W., & Calvo, M. G. (1992). Anxiety and performance: The processing efficiency theory. *Cognition and Emotion, 6*, 409–434.

Eysenck, M. W., Derakshan, N., Santos, R., & Calvo, M. G. (2007). Anxiety and cognitive performance: The processing efficiency theory. *Emotion, 7*, 336–353.

Flykt, A. (2006). Preparedness for action: Responding to the snake in the grass. *American Journal of Psychology, 119*, 29–43.

Forster, K. I., & Forster, J. C. (2003). DMDX: A Window display program with millisecond accuracy. *Behavior Research Methods, Instruments and Computers, 35*, 116–124.

Fox, E. (2004). Maintenance or capture of attention in anxiety-related biases. In J. Yiend (Ed.), *Emotion, cognition, and psychopathology.* Cambridge, UK: Cambridge University Press.

Fox, E., Lester, V., Russo, R., Bowles, R. J., Pichler, A., & Dutton, K. (2000). Facial expressions of emotion: Are angry faces detected more efficiently? *Cognition and Emotion, 14*, 61–92.

Fox, E., Russo, R., Bowles, R., & Dutton, K. (2001). Do threatening stimuli draw or hold visual attention in subclinical anxiety? *Journal of Experimental Psychology: General, 130*, 681–700.

Fox, E., Russo, R., & Georgiou, G. (2005). Anxiety modulates the degree of attentive resources required to process emotional faces. *Cognitive, Affective and Behavioral Neuroscience, 5*, 396–404.

Gerdes, A., Pauli, P., & Alpers, G. W. (2009). Toward and away from spiders: Eye-movements in spider-fearful participants. *Journal of Neural Transmission, 116*, 725–733.

Hermans, D., Vansteenwegen, D., & Eelen, P. (1999). Eye movement registration as a continuous index of attention deployment: Data from a group of spider anxious students. *Cognition and Emotion, 4*, 419–434.

Huijding, J., Mayer, B., Koster, E. H. W., & Muris, P. (2011). To look or not to look: An eye-movement study of hypervigilance during change detection in high and low spider fearful students. *Emotion, 11*, 666–674.

Koster, E. H. W., Crombez, G., Verschuere, B., van Damme, S., & Wiersema, J.-R. (2006). Components of attentional bias to threat in high trait anxiety: Facilitated engagement, impaired disengagement, and attentional avoidance. *Behaviour Research and Therapy, 44*, 1757–1771.

Lavie, N. (2005). Distracted and confused? Selective attention under load. *Trends in Cognitive Sciences, 9*, 75–82.

MacLeod, C., Koster, E. H. W., & Fox, E. (2009). Whither cognitive bias modification research: A commentary on the special section. *Journal of Abnormal Psychology, 118*, 89–99.

Mason, K. A. (1969) *Control apparatus sensitive to eye-movement.* US Patent #3, 462, 604

Mathews, A., Mackintosh, B., & Fulcher, E. (1997). Cognitive biases in anxiety and attention to threat. *Trends in Cognitive Science, 1*, 340–345.

McRae, K., Hughes, B., Chopra, S., Gabrieli, J. D. E., Gross, J. J., & Ochsner, K. N. (2010). The neural bases of distraction and reappraisal. *Journal of Cognitive Neuroscience, 22*, 248–262.

Merchant, J., & Morrisette, R. (1973). *A remote oculometer permitting head movement* (Report No. AMRL-TR-73-69). Wright-Patterson Air Force Base, Aerospace Medical Research Laboratory, OH.

Miltner, W. H. R., Krieschel, S., Hecht, H., Trippe, R., & Weiss, T. (2004). Eye movements and behavioral responses to threatening and nonthreatening stimuli during visual search in phobic and non-phobic subjects. *Emotion, 4*, 323–339.

Mogg, K., & Bradley, B. P. (1998). A cognitive-motivational analysis of anxiety. *Behaviour Research and Therapy, 36*, 809–848.

Mogg, K., Holmes, A., Garner, M., & Bradley, B. P. (2008). Effects of threat cues on attentional shifting, disengagement and response slowing in anxious individuals. *Behaviour Research and Therapy, 46*, 656–667.

Öhman, A., Lundqvist, D., & Esteves, F. (2001). The face in the crowd revisited: A threat advantage with schematic stimuli. *Journal of Personality and Social Psychology, 80*, 381–396.

Öhman, A., Soares, S., Juth, P., Lindstrom, B., & Esteves, F. (in press). Evolutionary derived modulations of attention to two common feared stimuli: Serpents and hostile humans. *Journal of Cognitive Psychology.*

Parke, F. I., & Waters, K. (1996). *Computer facial animation.* A. K. Peters Ltd.

Pashler, H., Johnston, J., & Ruthruff, E. (2001). Attention and performance. *Annual Review of Psychology, 52*, 629–651.

Pecchinenda, A., & Heil, M. (2007). Role of working memory load on selective attention to affectively valent information. *European Journal of Cognitive Psychology, 19*, 898–909.

Pessoa, L., Kastner, S., & Ungerleider, L. G. (2002). Attentional control of the processing of neutral and emotional stimuli. *Cognitive Brain Research, 15*, 31–45.

Posner, M. I. (1980). Orienting of attention. *Quarterly Journal of Experimental Psychology, 32A*, 3–25.

Raes, A. K., Koster, E. H. W., van Damme, S., Fias, W., & de Raedt, R. (2010). Aversive conditioning under conditions of restricted awareness: Effects on spatial cueing. *Quarterly Journal of Experimental Psychology, 63*, 2336–2358.

Rinck, M., & Becker, E. S. (2006). Spider fearful individuals attend to threat, then quickly avoid it: Evidence from eye movements. *Journal of Abnormal Psychology, 115*, 231–238.

Rinck, M., Reinecke, A., Ellwart, T., Heuer, K., & Becker, E. S. (2005). Speeded detection and increased distraction in fear of spiders: Evidence from eye movements. *Journal of Abnormal Psychology, 114*, 235–248.

Shapiro, K. L., Caldwell, J., & Sorensen, R. E. (1997). Personal names and the attentional blink: A visual "cocktail party" effect. *Journal of Experimental Psychology: Human Perception and Performance, 23*, 504–514.

Spielberger, C. C., Gorsuch, R. L., Lushene, R., Vagg, P. R., & Jacobs, G. A. (1983). *Manual for the State–Trait Anxiety Inventory.* Palo Alto, CA: Consulting Psychologists Press.

Teasdale, J. D., Dritschell, B. H., Taylor, M. J., Proctor, L., Lloyd, C. A., Nimmo-Smith, I., & Baddeley, A. D. (1995). Stimulus independent thought depends upon central executive resources. *Memory and Cognition, 28*, 551–559.

Tipples, J., Young, A., & Atkinson, A. P. (2002). The raised eyebrow: A salient social signal. *Emotion, 2*, 288–296.

Van Dillen, L. F., Heslenfeld, D. J., & Koole, S. L. (2009). Tuning down the emotional brain: An fMRI study of the effects of cognitive load on the processing of affective images. *NeuroImage, 45*, 1212–1219.

Van Dillen, L. F., & Koole, S. L. (2009). How automatic is "automatic vigilance"? The role of working memory in interference of negative information. *Cognition and Emotion, 23*, 1106–1117.

Vogt, J., de Houwer, J., Crombez, G., Koster, E. H. W., & van Damme, S. (2008). Examining the attentional bias to emotional stimuli: A crucial role for arousal level. *Emotion, 8*, 880–885.

Waters, K. (1987). A muscle model for animating three-dimensional facial expression. *Computer Graphics (Proc. SIGGRAPH '87), 21*, 17–24.

Weierich, M. R., Treat, T. A., & Hollingworth, A. (2008). Theories and measurement of visual attentional processing in anxiety. *Cognition and Emotion, 22*, 985–1018.

Williams, J. M. G., Watts, F. N., MacLeod, C., & Mathews, A. (1988). *Cognitive psychology and emotional disorders.* Chichester, UK: Wiley.

JOURNAL OF COGNITIVE PSYCHOLOGY, 2012, 24 (1), 92–105

Effects of modifying the interpretation of emotional ambiguity

Andrew Mathews[1,2]

[1]Department of Phycology, University of California, Davis, CA, USA
[2]Kings College, London, UK

People vary in how they perceive emotionally ambiguous events: For example, anxious individuals are particularly likely to interpret emotional ambiguity in a threatening way. Experimental studies have shown that such processing styles are malleable, and when modified can lead to corresponding changes in emotional reactivity. The methods used to modify processing and to assess subsequent changes in emotional reactivity are described and theoretical accounts of the mechanism underlying such changes are discussed. Recent application of related methods to modifying clinical problems demonstrates their utility, but beyond such practical applications, the approach provides new ways of probing the nature of the relationship between cognition and emotion.

Keywords: Emotion; Interpretation; Modification.

Suppose you venture an opinion on current events to a group of acquaintances and notice that some of them are smiling. Most of us would take that as a sign of approval, or at least a degree of positive interest. In contrast, people who are prone to feeling anxious in social situations are quite likely to interpret the smiles of others as indicating derision, and feel embarrassed rather than pleased. As this example is intended to illustrate, the interpretation of emotional information sometimes seems to influence how we feel, although it is probably also true that how we feel can influence how we interpret events. In the present paper, after a brief and necessarily selective review of the evidence for such an association, experiments are described that support the hypothesis of a causal relationship between how ambiguous information is interpreted and emotional reactivity, and that suggest mechanisms that may underlie this relationship.

The methods used to investigate this relationship open up new ways of studying cognition–emotion interactions, as well as new approaches for treating or preventing emotional problems.

INDIVIDUAL DIFFERENCES IN THE INTERPRETATION OF EMOTIONAL AMBIGUITY

A collaborative research programme with Michael Eysenck and others, beginning around two decades ago, has established the existence of systematic variations in how people varying in emotionality process ambiguity for affective information and events. Whereas most people tend towards a slight bias favouring benign interpretations of emotionally ambiguous events, those who are prone to anxiety or depression do not—at least when the ambiguity concerns personally

Correspondence should be addressed to Andrew Mathews, Department of Psychology, University of California, One, Shields Avenue, Davis, CA 95616, USA. E-mail: andrew.mathews@sbcglobal.net

I am grateful to the many collaborators who have provided ideas and much of the work reported here, but of course especial thanks are due to Michael Eysenck, who began the whole thing.

http://dx.doi.org/10.1080/20445911.2011.584527

relevant emotional meanings. In a seminal early investigation of interpretation of emotional ambiguity, Eysenck, Mogg, May, Richards, and Mathews (1991) showed that, relative to a nonanxious control groups, individuals with Generalised Anxiety Disorder were more likely to remember ambiguous sentences in terms of their more threatening meanings,. In two experiments, participants listened to recorded sentences, some of which were neutral fillers, while others were ambiguous and could be interpreted in either a negative or a benign manner. Subsequently, they were asked to endorse (Experiment 1) or rate (Experiment 2) recognition items having related threatening or nonthreatening meanings as being similar to those heard earlier (for examples, see Table 1). The key finding was that nonanxious controls were more likely to endorse nonthreatening than threatening interpretations of ambiguous items presented earlier, whereas currently anxious individuals were equally likely to endorse threatening as nonthreatening meanings. A signal detection analysis (in Experiment 2) showed that these results reflected variations in recognition accuracy—implying real interpretation differences—rather than just a response bias reflecting a tendency to endorse all items of a particular affective valence, irrespective of whether or not they corresponded to a possible interpretation.

Subsequent evidence provided further support for the idea that nonanxious individuals tend to favour positive inferences about ambiguity, but that this bias is conspicuously absent in anxious groups. For example, in experiments reported by Hirsch and Mathews (1997, 2000), socially anxious and nonanxious participants read descriptions of job interviews and, at ambiguous points in the text (when the outcome still remained unclear) were required to make speeded lexical decisions about words related to possible inferences concerning negative or positive outcomes. Nonanxious individuals were consistently faster to endorse words related to positive outcomes, whereas socially anxious individuals were equally fast to endorse words matching either positive or negative outcomes. Thus, consistent with the individual differences found by Eysenck et al. (1991) in how ambiguous sentences are recalled, similar differences can be detected "online", that is, around (or very shortly after) the time that ambiguous information is first encountered (see also Calvo, Eysenck, & Castillo, 1997; MacLeod & Cohen, 1993; Richards & French, 1992). It is important to note that the critical finding in all these experiments was of an interaction revealing interpretation *differences* between anxious and nonanxious groups, rather than showing that either group was necessarily biased in the sense of departing from objective outcome probabilities (that remain unknown). It is clear, however, that increased anxiety levels are associated with a *relatively* greater tendency to perceive the more threatening meaning of emotionally ambiguous information.

There is somewhat less consistent evidence for an association between depression and the interpretation of emotional ambiguity. Using a similar method to that of Hirsch and Mathews (1997, 2000), Lawson and MacLeod (1999) failed to find differences in naming time for target words matching negative or benign inferences between depressed and control groups (see also Bisson & Sears, 2006). However, clear differences did emerge in a later experiment using startle modulation as a measure of how ambiguous word cues had been interpreted (Lawson, MacLeod, & Hammond, 2002). Mixed results were reported by Mogg, Bradbury, and Bradley (2006), again with a failure to show depression related differences in reading latencies, but differences being revealed in a task involving the interpretation of homophones. Overall, these results provide support for the suggestion made by Lawson and MacLeod (1999) that emotion-related differences of interpretation between depressed and nondepressed groups may often be obscured in reaction time tasks (due to general slowing in depression), but do emerge when interpretation is assessed in other ways.

TABLE 1

Sample ambiguous and recognition items from Eysenck et al. (1991, Exp. 2)

Original ambiguous sentence	"Your boss calls you to their office to discuss the quality of your recent work."
Threatening interpretation probe item	"Your boss calls you to their office to say that your work is not up to standard."
Nonthreatening interpretation probe item	"Your boss calls you to their office to congratulate you on your work."
Threatening distractor item	"Your boss calls you to their office to ask you why you are not getting on with your colleagues."
Nonthreatening distractor item	"Your boss calls you to their office to offer you a pay rise."

These and other related findings invite the hypothesis that interpretative processing style is a *cause* of emotional vulnerability, although until recently there was little or no experimental evidence directly supporting this possibility. The present paper summarises findings on the emotional consequences of experimentally modifying interpretations that provide the strongest evidence to date that cognitive processing style is a *cause* of emotional vulnerability. Similar methods of modifying interpretational style can be used to ameliorate clinical conditions such social phobia, and more generally, have important implications for understanding cognition–emotion interactions. Before returning to these general issues, however, in the next section the most commonly used methods for modifying emotional interpretative style will be described.

METHODS FOR MODIFYING INTERPRETATION OF EMOTIONAL AMBIGUITY

Interpretational style can be modified using tasks based on measures already described but with the variation that ambiguity is consistently resolved in either a negative or benign direction according to group allocation, rather than varying unpredictably. In an initial study, we (Grey & Mathews, 2000) presented unselected volunteers with a series of homographs having both threatening and nonthreatening meanings, followed by a to-be-completed word fragment associated with either meaning (e.g., "batter" followed by "ass_ult" or "p_ncake"; see left-hand side of Table 2 for more

examples). Participants were instructed to use the first word (the homograph) as a clue to help identify the associated fragment and to press a key as soon as they had done so. Groups allocated to either consistently threatening or nonthreatening associates were thus encouraged to generate either the negative or benign interpretations of the homographs to help them resolve the word fragment. Subsequent to this first phase, training effects were investigated by allocating half of each group to a test block of new associate-fragments having the same or different emotional valence to those seen earlier. Results showed that, as expected, reactions were faster when the valence of these test fragments was consistent with prior experience.

Subsequent experiments showed that (with sufficient training) this result generalised to test homographs not seen previously and to novel tasks, such as making lexical decisions for associates primed by new homographs. In a final experiment, designed to clarify whether these changes required active generation of interpretations, or could follow from repeated priming of an emotional category, already completed associates were presented *prior* to the homographs and participants were required to identify whether the two words were related or unrelated in meaning. This task does not require participants to generate interpretations of the homographs for themselves, because the required meaning has already been supplied by the preceding associate—but, nonetheless, groups differed on a subsequent test of interpretation to at least the same extent as in the previous experiments. It thus appeared that the results could be explained in terms of a persistent priming effect enhancing

TABLE 2
Sample material used to train interpretative style

(a) Ambiguous words		(b) Ambiguous event descriptions
Batter:	pancake/assault	You have decided to go caving even though
Committed:	dedicated/breakdown	you feel nervous about being in an enclosed
Stalk:	flower/pursue	space. You get to the caves before anyone
Tense:	verb/nervous	else arrives. Going deep inside the cave you
Cross:	church/angry	realise you have completely lost your (way/fear).
Odd:	number/weird	Are you feeling afraid in the cave?
Threat/nonthreat homographs with associates corresponding to their benign or threatening meanings, presented as to-be-completed fragments, or as words to be judged for their relatedness to the homograph. Groups are assigned to either negative or benign associates.		Ambiguous text with the final word presented as to-be-completed fragment (e.g., w_y/ fe_r), that resolves the text meaning in either a benign or negative way depending on group assignment. Answering the (yes/no) question that follows requires participants to further endorse the resolved meaning.

access to meanings consistent with the previously presented associates, rather than necessarily requiring the active generation of interpretations. However, as will be discussed later, such a conclusion now seems premature, or only partially correct.

In parallel experiments using ambiguous text descriptions rather than single words (Mathews & Macintosh, 2000), repeated exposure to negative or benign event outcomes similarly modified the later interpretation of novel descriptions that remained ambiguous. In this method, nonanxious volunteers read and imagined themselves in emotionally ambiguous situations that were resolved in a negative or benign way only by the final word, presented as a to-be-completed fragment (see right-hand side of Table 2 for an example). The effects of training were tested by presenting novel descriptions that remained ambiguous, and then requiring participants to rate sentences that embodied possible interpretations for their similarity to the original. Results showed that nonanxious volunteers trained using negative (as opposed to benign) resolutions can be induced to make interpretations resembling those of the clinically anxious group studied by Eysenck et al. (1991). Furthermore, the negatively trained volunteers tended to become more anxious during training, whereas the benign-trained volunteers did not. Subsequent experiments suggested that such effects on mood depended on having participants actively generate negative meanings (e.g., by completing the resolving fragment and endorsing a related question; see Table 1), because when the same valenced outcome was written into the text to be read, the differential mood effect disappeared, although effects on the interpretation of novel test items persisted. Thus, it seemed that, rather than induced mood producing the observed effect on interpretations (and further evidence against this possibility is discussed later), mood effects may be the result of participants selecting threatening meanings of ambiguous descriptions. However, before discussing the evidence for this hypothesis more fully, it is first necessary to consider experiments establishing that modification of interpretation can enhance subsequent later emotional reactivity, even when there are no obvious mood changes during training itself.

EFFECTS OF MODIFYING INTERPRETATION STYLE ON EMOTIONAL VULNERABILITY

In a pioneering exploration of effects of training visual attention to threatening or benign words, MacLeod, Rutherford, Campbell, Ebsworth, and Holker (2002) showed that subsequent exposure to a mildly stressful experience (such as failing to solve apparently easy anagrams) revealed congruent differences in emotional reactivity. That is, those who had previously been trained to attend to threatening rather than benign words subsequently reported greater increases in anxiety. This important finding allowed the conclusion that the manipulation of selective attention towards or away from threatening meanings can influence later emotional response to a stressful event. The implication is that induced styles of cognitive processing (e.g., selective attention to threat in this case) can influence subsequent emotional vulnerability, presumably via the recapitulation of the induced processing style when a related emotional event is encountered. That is, practice in selectively attending to threatening meanings during training may have led to attention being similarly deployed to threatening meanings in the stress test.

Application of related methods to interpretation training has led to similar conclusions. For example, in a study of training in which presentation of homograph cues was followed by to-be-completed fragments corresponding to either their threatening or nonthreatening meanings, greater emotional reactivity to a video of serious accidents was observed in the group that had practised accessing threatening rather than benign meanings (Wilson, MacLeod, Mathews, & Rutherford, 2006). Those who had made threatening interpretations in training responded to the subsequent video with greater increases in rated anxiety than did those who had made benign interpretations. Again, it seems likely that the differential emotional vulnerability was due to participants tending to interpret the accident video in a manner consistent with their prior training experience. That is, those who had practiced making negative interpretations may have similarly focused on the more threatening meanings of the accident video (e.g., their potentially traumatic consequences), whereas those who had practiced benign interpretations may have focused more on positive aspects (e.g., that victims survived thanks to the coura-geous efforts of their rescuers).

ALTERNATIVE EXPLANATIONS FOR THE EFFECTS OF INTERPRETATION TRAINING

Although the findings discussed here are consis-tent with the view that subsequent emotional reactivity differences depend on the recapitula-tion of the induced interpretative style, they do not provide any direct evidence for it. One alternative explanation that has been offered is that emotional effects might simply reflect per-sisting (even if undetected) mood-related changes due to greater exposure to emotionally evocative material. Indeed, there is evidence that mood state manipulations alone can sometimes influ-ence the interpretation of ambiguity (e.g., Halber-stadt, Niedenthal, & Kushner, 1995; although see later discussion of negative findings). However, even when no mood change was observed during training (as is typical with methods involving single ambiguous words), differential emotional reactivity has been revealed via responses to a subsequent stress task (e.g., Hoppitt, Mathews, Yiend, & Mackintosh, 2010b; Wilson et al., 2006). Other recent studies have directly manipulated mood to investigate whether changes comparable to those observed during interpretation training can be induced by mood state induction alone. In an initial experiment, Standage, Ashwin, and Fox (2010) confirmed that modifying interpretation using the method used by Mathews and Mack-intosh (2000) produced training-congruent differ-ences on a test requiring the resolution of ambiguous word strings as either a positive or negative sentence (the scrambled sentence test; see Rude, Vladez, Odom, & Ebrahimi, 2003, for evidence that this test can predict later depres-sion). Then, in a second experiment, Standage et al. showed that inducing contrasting emotional states using a musical mood manipulation failed to produce any differential change on the same task. Similarly, Salemink, van den Hout, and Kindt (2010b) independently varied the valence of interpretation training and a subsequent musi-cal mood induction and found that the direction of mood manipulation did not alter the effects of

training on the interpretation test used by Math-ews and Mackintosh.

Furthermore, delays between training and test, sufficient for dissipation of any transient mood effects, do not appear to abolish changes in later emotional reactivity. In one experiment, practice with descriptions resolved in a benign or negative way (as used by Mathews & Mackintosh, 2000) induced congruent changes in the interpretation of new ambiguous descriptions, despite context changes between training and test (i.e., in location and auditory or visual presentation). More criti-cally, viewing an accident video 24 hours later elicited greater emotional responses in negative than benign training groups, in the absence of any mood differences prior to viewing the video (Mack-intosh, Mathews, Yiend, Ridgeway, & Cook, 2006).

Although possible demand effects have not been as systematically studied as have mood effects, they have been routinely assessed using postexperiment interviews in most of the studies of interpretation modification discussed here, and in every case have been rejected on the grounds that the vast majority of participants were unable to correctly report the purpose of the experiment and denied seeing any link between the training phase and their later responses to test items. It seems implausible to suppose that demand effects can provide an adequate account of findings when the participants themselves seem to be unaware of either the purpose of the experiment or of its expected effects. Furthermore, demand effects cannot easily account for the faster latencies to identify words having an emotional valence con-gruent with training (e.g., Grey & Mathews, 2000; Wilson et al., 2006) or improvements in working memory capacity following positive training in anxious participants (see later discussion; Hirsch, Hayes, & Mathews, 2009). Nonetheless, it is clearly desirable to investigate the effects of interpretation training on other objective indices, such as avoidance behaviour, although the few studies of this sort have not yet proved definitive (Lange et al., 2010; Teachman & Addison, 2008).

If neither the persistence of mood or demand effects is insufficient to explain the observed effects of interpretation training, what alternative mechanisms could account for them? We have considered two alternative (but not mutually exclusive) explanations: semantic priming of a category of affective meanings, and transfer of a learned form of processing from training to test. Priming seems able to account for the short-term facilitation of responses typically found with novel test items matching the affective valence of meanings previously accessed during training. For example, participants trained to make negative interpretations are faster to identify negative words in a lexical decision task, and vice versa for positive trained participants, although this effect apparently requires the presentation of a related prime prior to the to-be-identified word (Grey & Mathews, 2009; Hoppitt et al., 2010b; Wilson et al., 2006). Thus, rather than showing that words of a particular emotional valence are always more accessible, these results suggest that they come to be more readily primed by related cues. Furthermore, priming explanations encounter difficulty when trying to explain why emotional vulnerability effects can endure across longer periods than are usually associated with semantic priming (e.g., 24 hours in the study reported by Mackintosh et al., 2006). The finding that associated emotional effects can be reactivated by a novel threatening event in a completely different context and after a long delay seems difficult to accommodate within an explanation based only on semantic priming as usually understood.

Consequently, rather than priming alone, we have suggested that an additional critical factor is required to elicit emotional effects; specifically, learning to actively seek and select affective meanings. That is, when training requires participants to actively seek for and select either positive or negative meanings, then a subsequent ambiguous event may be more likely to elicit the same active mode of processing, even when the task itself does not demand it. Training that involves accessing semantic meanings within a specific affective category, but does not require an active search and selection process may still facilitate access to related meanings in response to an associated prime when performing a cognitive task that requires semantic access (e.g., the lexical decision task). However, when encountering a realistic and potentially more emotional event, such as failing on a seemingly easy task or viewing serious accidents, training of this type is less likely to elicit emotional reactivity differences that depend on going beyond semantic understanding of the event itself. In contrast, a learned tendency to actively search for and select one type of emotional meaning is likely to be deployed even when no longer demanded by the task, leading to more personally relevant emotional meanings being accessed and having consequences for emotional reactivity.

In a test of the active search and selection hypothesis, Hoppitt, Mathews, Yiend, and Mackintosh (2010a) required participants to read and imagine themselves in initially ambiguous situations that were resolved by positive or negative endings that were provided for them, or by having to actively resolve the valence of the same outcomes for themselves. The latter was achieved by presenting a final resolving word fragment to be completed (with only one solution being possible) followed by a question that required participants to endorse that resolution, whereas the former (passive) group simply read the completing word and the question rephrased as a statement and incorporated into the text. In a later test of emotional reactivity, participants imagined novel ambiguous test items: Training-congruent emotional reactivity differences were observed in the active, but not in the passive training groups.

In a second experiment, active groups saw homograph cues followed by fragments to be completed as words associated with either their negative or benign meanings, whereas control groups saw unambiguous synonyms corresponding to the assigned homograph meaning, again followed by the same to-be-completed fragment. Thus, all groups were exposed to the same emotional meanings, but only the active groups were required to actively select those meanings themselves. A subsequent lexical decision task revealed equivalent priming effects for new words that shared the emotional valence promoted in training, irrespective of active and passive training conditions. In contrast, training-congruent emotional reactivity differences to a video of accidents were confined to the active training groups (Hoppitt et al., 2010b).

In sum, although "passive" training leads to facilitation of semantic priming effects, it seems to be insufficient to modify later emotional reactions. Rather, the critical process influencing emotional vulnerability appears to be the unintentional reenactment of an acquired processing style—actively seeking and selecting specific types of emotional meaning—when encountering real potentially emotional events. In some ways this can be seen as related to the "transfer-appropriate processing" framework (Blaxton, 1989) in memory research, in which recall is influenced by the type of encoding used when first encountering a to-be-remembered item.

Appropriate recall cues lead to the transfer of processing operations used when encoding an item to how recall cues are processed, influencing the extent and type of information recalled. Similarly, a later event related to that experienced in training may lead to transfer of previously practiced processing to the new event. According to the present hypothesis, active selection of emotional meanings in training is more likely to lead to active search and selection of similar (but more emotive) meanings when later encountering a potentially emotional event, even when no such selection is required. It is striking to find that a simple task like the interpretation of homographs can sometimes influence the emotional reaction to a very different event such as watching videos, and presumably to other naturalistic events, although (as will be discussed later) such transfer does not always occur. Being able to predict when transfer will or will not occur is important for both practical applied reasons and to help us understand the mechanisms involved.

AUTOMATIC AND CONTROLLED INFLUENCES ON INTERPRETATION BIAS AND TRAINING

In an earlier model of attentional and interpretation biases, we (Mathews & Mackintosh, 1998) argued that both types of bias depended on the interaction of automatic (bottom-up) and strategic (top-down) influences acting on preconscious representations of competing threatening and nonthreatening meanings. According to this account, threatening representations are strengthened by anxiety and related habitual processing styles, sometimes overwhelming the opposing influence of strategic control and leading to the dominance of threatening meanings of ambiguity. More recent accounts have similarly suggested that interpretative biases result from an interaction of automatic and strategic processes (Ouimet, Gawronski, & Dozois, 2009).

However, the terms automatic and strategic can be taken to imply several distinct properties that are often disassociated. For example, labelling a process as automatic carries the implication that it is fast, uncontrollable, unintended, nonconscious, invariable, and resource-independent, although these properties may vary independently (Moors & de Houwer, 2006). The evidence that both threat and nonthreat meanings of

ambiguous words are initially activated, but that it takes longer (about 750 ms or more) for one meaning to become dominant and enter awareness, has been taken to imply that interpretation bias results from mainly strategic processes (Richards, 2004). Furthermore, the finding that interpretation biases are relatively malleable (in training experiments) suggests that they are not strongly automatic, at least in the sense that they can be readily altered. However, although interpretation bias is thus clearly not an invariable process, subjective reports in such experiments indicate that participants are typically unaware of being influenced by training and deny intentionally controlling the interpretations they make of ambiguous test items (e.g., Hirsch et al., 2009). Furthermore, those with clinical conditions such as Generalised Anxiety Disorder typically seek treatment because they see their anxiety and worry as uncontrollable, apparently unaware of the contribution made by threatening interpretations of ambiguous future outcomes to their own distress, and (before treatment or training) find it difficult to perceive alternative positive interpretations (Hayes, Hirsch, Krebs, & Mathews, 2010). It appears that awareness of the processes underlying emotional interpretations is very limited, as is the perception that such interpretations can be controlled, although with the appropriate guidance and practice, they can indeed be modified.

Emotional interpretations are thus not strategic in the sense of being intentional, nor are the processes involved readily available to consciousness, so that the individuals concerned typically perceive them as being inevitable rather than deliberate. At the same time, emotional interpretations are not wholly automatic, in the sense that they are not invariable (contrary to how they are often perceived by anxious individuals) but can be brought under control by deliberate practice in rehearsing more desirable meanings of ambiguity. Thus, in common with many other complex cognitive operations, interpretation bias is probably best understood as the outcome of processes having both automated and strategic attributes.

WHEN DOES INTERPRETATION TRAINING GENERALISE TO OTHER TASKS OR DOMAINS?

Training with items within a particular domain of emotional concern does not always generalise to tests of interpretation having content drawn from another emotional domain. For example, training with descriptions of ambiguously threatening social situations sometimes generalises to a limited extent to the interpretation of test items involving physically threatening situation (involving possible crime or disease) but sometimes not (Mathews & Mackintosh, 2000; Salemink, van den Hout, & Kindt, 2007b). Such generalisation seems more likely to occur when the emotional concerns tapped in training and test overlap in their content; for example, training with socially threatening descriptions can generalise to the interpretation of test items concerned with academic success (Salemink, van den Hout, & Kindt, 2010a). Such findings presumably reflect the extent to which the domains sampled in training and test phases are related, or are based on the same fundamental emotional concern. One promising area for future research is to explore this possibility more systematically, and perhaps use the extent of generalisation across domains to investigate the taxonomy of emotional concerns. That is, if modifying interpretations within one domain (e.g., social encounters) causes changes in how another (academic success) is interpreted, then we can infer that the two domains share at least some common basis.

Most experiments showing successful transfer to emotional reactivity effects have used training items and stress tests drawn from the same general domain of emotional concern. For example, Mackintosh et al. (2006) used ambiguously threatening physical descriptions (concerning crime, injury, etc.) in training and found significant amelioration of anxiety in the positive trained group when viewing videos of accidents 24 hours later. The negative meanings of English homographs are mostly physically threatening (e.g., batter, growth, sink) and training with homographs has similarly produced congruent emotional changes when later viewing accident videos (Hoppitt et al., 2010b; Wilson et al., 2006). However, such emotional effects have not always been found in the absence of a close match between the content of processing elicited in training and a subsequent stress challenge. For example, Salemink, van den Hout, and Kindt (2007a) reported that having participants practise making positive inferences about social situations influenced later social interpretations but failed to reduce the anxiety elicited by the later experience of test failure. A similar absence of congruent emotional effects of

social training on giving a speech was reported by Standage, Ashwin, and Fox (2009). In an unpublished series of experiments, we (Mackintosh, Mathews, Hoppitt, & Eckstein, 2010) also found that training with either positive social or test outcomes (e.g., you have to give a difficult presentation but it eventually goes well) actually tended to worsen the deleterious emotional consequences of later failure on difficult cognitive tasks. However, when the training material was changed so as to promote benign interpretations of test *failure* (e.g., others might also fail, the test content was inappropriate or irrelevant, etc.) training did successfully decrease the negative emotional response to actual failure. These findings suggest that successfully enhancing emotional resilience to setbacks depends on correctly anticipating the type of processing likely to promote adaptive interpretation of subsequent challenging experiences and tailoring training appropriately.

A more perplexing issue is the variability in generalisation from one type of interpretation task to another. The transfer-appropriate processing framework might suggest that the processes practiced in training would be more likely to be recapitulated when tests are similar in form. Consistent with this expectation, generalisation from one type of training task to another at test often occurs when there are clear similarities between the two, as when training with word-fragment completion or relatedness judgements between homographs and their associates transfers to a primed lexical decision test (Grey & Mathews, 2000; Hoppitt et al., 2010b; Wilson et al., 2006). However, generalisation sometimes fails even with apparently related tasks: For example, Saleminck et al. (2010a) reported that interpretation training with social scenarios failed to generalise to a test requiring participants to report freely on their impressions of either descriptions or videos of ambiguous social encounters between others. The training method developed by Mathews and Mackintosh (2000), and adopted by Salemink et al. (2010a), involves imagining oneself in the situations described, so one possibility is that training with self-imagery does not generalise to reported interpretations about others. On the other hand, training with homographs (without any imagery instructions) does seem to influence the emotional content of reported images elicited by new homograph cues (Hertel, Mathews, Peterson, & Kintner, 2003) or ambiguous descriptions (Hoppitt et al., 2010a).

Furthermore, as noted previously, the fact that practice in the interpretation of homographs can influence emotional reactions to viewing a video seems surprising, given the obvious differences between training and test. Retention of the transfer-appropriate processing explanatory framework would require that future research must establish whether and when the trained interpretative style is recapitulated in test situations, to allow the transfer hypothesis to be adequately tested. In the meantime, it remains somewhat unclear when generalisation from training to a different test task will occur or otherwise.

INTERACTIONS WITH OTHER EMOTIONAL PROCESSING BIASES

The focus in the present paper has been on biases in interpretation, but as most readers will be aware, there is a large parallel research literature documenting that attentional bias is associated with anxiety (and depression) and showing that modifying attention to threat cues causes corresponding changes in emotional vulnerability (MacLeod et al., 2002; See, MacLeod, & Bridle, 2009). It is tempting to speculate that the same fundamental processes underlie both attention to external threat cues and the tendency to interpret ambiguous information in a threatening manner, because both presumably reflect the allocation of processing priority to threatening representations, whether externally cued or internally generated (and indeed we have made this theoretical assumption in the past; see Mathews & Mackintosh, 1998). Hirsch, Clark, and Mathews (2006) further proposed that in real life various cognitive biases serve to reinforce one another and act additively to maintain anxiety. If so, one might expect at least some effects of modifying interpretation on attention, and vice versa, although little evidence is as yet available regarding this issue.

One attempt in this direction was reported by Amir, Bomyea, and Beard (2010), who allocated socially anxious participants to a single session of either positive interpretation training or a control condition. Participants saw single positive or negative words (e.g., "funny" or "embarrassing") followed by ambiguous sentences (e.g., "People laugh at something you said") and were required to decide if the word and sentence were related. The positive trained group was always given "correct" feedback when they endorsed a positive word and "incorrect" when they endorsed a negative word, encouraging them to generate positive interpretations of the ambiguous sentences. Thus, in the example above, positive trained participants learn that the reason people laughed was because the thing said was amusing, rather than embarrassing (for more details of this method, see Beard & Amir, 2008). All participants were then tested using a modified Posner attentional search task, in which neutral targets sometimes appear in the prior location of threatening or nonthreatening cues, and sometimes in an alternative location. Results showed that positive interpretative training, but not the control condition, led to participants becoming faster to detect targets in the alternative location following a threatening word cue, implying that they found it easier to disengage attention from threat (a pattern resembling that differentiating nonanxious from anxious individuals; Fox, Russo, Bowles, & Dutton, 2001; Yiend & Mathews, 2001). In other words, it does seem that change in one form of bias (interpretation) can lead to congruent change in another (attention). Although no significant differences in state anxiety were observed in this study, in view of the therapeutic benefits previously reported for this training method by Beard and Amir (2008); see later), it may be that rather than direct transfer of procedural learning, attentional change may have been due to the words used in the attention task being perceived as less threatening. Clearly, further research into this issue is warranted, but whatever the exact mechanism, it seems likely that training aimed at one bias can have effects on others.

Another example of such an interaction is provided by work reported by Hertel and her colleagues on the interaction between interpretation and memory biases (see Hertel & Brozovitch, 2010, for a summary). Negative memory biases in depression are well established, although less so in anxiety states (see Mathews & MacLeod, 2005). In one experiment described by Hertel and Brozovitch (2010), participants varying in social anxiety were asked to read emotionally ambiguous social descriptions, and then to interpret them by providing their own endings for each. Not surprisingly, these interpretations tended to reflect the participant's anxiety status and were more negative in those with elevated social anxiety. Later, participants were required to recall the original scenarios (and separately, to recall their idiosyncratic endings). Aspects of their interpretations often found their way into memories of the original scenario. The same misremembering of interpretations as being part of the original event was found in another experiment with nonanxious participants who were trained to disambiguate scenarios in a positive or negative direction. Those trained to make negative interpretations not only provided more negative endings but also confounded these interpretations with the original scenarios that they remembered as having more negative content. In other words, it may sometimes be impossible to disentangle biases of interpretation and memory, since interpretations can be confused in memory for real events, and memories for such events are presumably subject in turn to biases of interpretation. Future research is likely to reveal other instances in which emotional processing biases that have been studied independently will turn out to be related or additive in their effects.

APPLICATIONS TO EMOTIONALLY VULNERABLE GROUPS

Given the finding of an association between interpretative bias and both anxiety and depression, together with the development of methods for modifying such biases, it is not surprising that there has been considerable interest in applying these methods to emotionally vulnerable groups. In one such study, we (Mathews, Ridgeway, Cook, & Yiend, 2007) selected participants with elevated scores on a questionnaire measure of trait anxiety (Spielberger, Gorsuch, Lushene, Vagg, & Jacobs, 1983) and provided half of them with four sessions of training in disambiguating social and physical threat scenarios in a benign manner over a 2 week period. Because in pilot work some anxious participants reported feeling that the more extreme positive outcomes were not realistic or applicable to themselves, the resolutions used were graded so that on first presentation they were only nonnegative (see Alden & Wallace, 1995), but become progressively more positive in subsequent presentations. On readministration of the trait anxiety measure 1 week after training was complete, trait anxiety scores were significantly reduced in positive-trained participants relative to an untrained control group

(for a replication see Salemink, van den Hout, & Kindt, 2009).

Building on an earlier finding with unselected volunteers that interpretation training influenced anticipated anxiety about a stressful social situation (Hirsch, Mathews, & Clark, 2007), Murphy, Hirsch, Mathews, Smith, and Clark (2007) tested the effects of an adapted form of this training with selected participants reporting high levels of social anxiety. Anxious groups trained either to make positive or nonnegative (benign) resolutions of ambiguously stressful social situations reported less anxiety when anticipating meeting two strangers than did those in a control group who had been exposed to irrelevant resolutions of the same descriptions. This reduced anxiety contrasts with the failure reported by Salemink et al. (2009) to find decreased anxiety during a social and performance stress task after similar training. Possible reasons include differences in the participant populations (those with elevated social anxiety versus unselected students), and the stress being an anticipated meeting with strangers rather than involving an actual stress task.

Beard and Amir (2008) reported on the effects of another variation of interpretation training (described earlier) in which socially anxious participants saw single positive (e.g., funny) or negative words (e.g., embarrassing) followed by an ambiguous sentence (e.g., "People laugh at something you said") and decided if the word and sentence were related. A positive trained group was always given "correct" feedback when they endorsed a positive word and "incorrect" when they endorsed a negative word, whereas a control group was given noncontingent feedback. Greater decreases in scores on a questionnaire assessing social anxiety occurred following eight sessions of positive training than in the control group. Mediation analyses showed that reductions in social anxiety were partially mediated by the extent to which endorsement of positive word/ sentence pairs had increased (rather than decreases in negative endorsements) in noncontingent test of interpretation bias. Related studies have found that similar methods can be effective even with 10- to 11-year-old children (Vassilopoulos, Banerjee, & Pratzaloue, 2009).

Other experiments have shown that, in addition to social anxiety, interpretation training can have beneficial effects on excessive worry. Hirsch et al. (2009) reported that a single session of practice in selecting the benign meaning of emotionally ambiguous words and worry-related descriptions was sufficient to reduce later negative thought intrusions while participants attempted to focus their attention elsewhere, in contrast to control participants who accessed benign and threatening meanings equally often. This reduction in worry was accompanied by improvements on a simultaneous working memory task, suggesting that the observed changes did not depend on increased effort, but were due to less preemption of attentional resources by worrying thoughts. In a related clinical study, the same training was successful in reducing negative thought intrusions in patients suffering from Generalised Anxiety Disorder (Hayes et al., 2010).

Interpretation training may also be helpful in ameliorating or preventing depression. Holmes, Lang, and Shah (2009) compared training in making positive interpretations with or without self-imagery, and found that imagery-based training was more effective in reducing negative mood (see also Blackwell & Holmes, 2010).

Although it is too early to know whether such methods will develop into "stand-alone" therapies, they differ from existing cognitive-behavioural treatments in potentially interesting and useful ways: For example, they allow easy computer (and Internet) implementation (e.g., See et al., 2009), and, rather than depending on conscious and deliberate efforts to change, are intended to modify more habitual cognitive styles that are likely to persist even when attentional control resources are depleted (Hirsch et al., 2009).

GENERAL IMPLICATIONS FOR UNDERSTANDING THE RELATIONSHIP BETWEEN COGNITION AND EMOTION

Beyond the application to clinical problems, the approach outlined here has implications for improving our understanding of the causal links between cognition and emotion. There has been a long-running debate about the role of cognitive processing in emotions, with positions varying from the extreme view that all emotions depend on cognitive appraisal, to the opposing position that emotions are largely independent of (at least conscious) cognitive processes (Williams, Watts, MacLeod, & Mathews, 1997). The methods discussed here suggest a more nuanced approach: that of systematically investigating *when* particular ways of cognitive processing play a causal role in producing *what* specific types of emotion reaction.

To illustrate this point, a widely held theory suggests that depressive reactions to a negative event depend critically on attributions made about its cause (Abramson, Metalsky, & Alloy, 1989). Specifically, people who attribute negative personal events (such as failing a test) to internal and stable causes (e.g., I am incompetent) are supposedly more prone to persisting depressive reactions than are those who attribute such events to external or unstable causes (e.g., the test was unfair). Although attributional style does predict risk of later depression, directly testing the causal role of attributions in emotion has proved difficult to achieve. However, it is possible to investigate this issue experimentally by directly manipulating the attributions made about (imagined) events and then testing the emotional consequences of a subsequent real event. In one such experiment (Peters, Constans, & Mathews, 2011), students read about and imagined themselves in both negative and positive situations, with one group induced to make stable internal attributions for negative outcomes and unstable external attributions for positive outcomes, and vice versa for another group. Subsequently, all participants performed a cognitive task that appeared easy, but was in fact extremely difficult. As predicted, type of prior training influenced the attributions reported for poor test performance, and, more critically, led to greater reported depression in those who had practised stable internal attributions for negative events. Related results of reappraisal training on reactions to videos were reported by Schartau, Dalgleish, and Dunn, 2009).

Although these experiments address relatively limited issues, a similar approach can be applied to many other questions about the causal relationship between cognitive processing of affective information and emotion reactivity. Related methods could be used to investigate the taxonomy of emotions and emotional concerns: To take only some examples, questions can be asked about whether different emotions are influenced by distinct types of cognitive processing, whether training with one type of affective content influences reactions only to events tapping that specific concern, or generalises to other emotional concerns. In general, a better understanding of the critical links between cognitive processing style and emotions, both positive and negative, may ultimately offer even greater potential for the prevention (as well as treatment) of emotional disorders.

CONCLUSIONS (AND AN APPRECIATION)

The present paper describes a research journey that had its origins in a very productive collaboration with Michael Eysenck, from which emerged our first papers together documenting systematic differences in the interpretation of emotional information (and attention to threatening cues) in anxious versus nonanxious populations. The ideas and results arising in this research led directly to the later development of experimental procedures adapted so as to modify interpretation biases, and the demonstration that such modification can cause subsequent changes in emotional vulnerability. The original finding that anxiety-disordered individuals tend to interpret ambiguity in a relatively threatening manner has thus led us to a method for helping them reverse this tendency. However, the fact that these procedures have been shown to lead to improvements in emotional vulnerability does not in any way reduce the need for more research into the processes involved, and how to maximise the durability and generality of change. More fundamentally, emotional bias modification provides a general research tool that can be used to better understand how and when particular types of cognitive process influence different affective states, whether in the treatment of emotional disorders or, more generally, in the promotion of emotional well-being.

REFERENCES

Abramson, L. Y., Metalsky, G. I., & Alloy, L. B. (1989). Hopelessness depression: A theory-based subtype of depression. *Psychological Review, 96,* 358–372.

Alden, L. E., & Wallace, S. T. (1995). Social phobia and social appraisal in successful and unsuccessful social interactions. *Behaviour Research and Therapy, 33,* 497–505.

Amir, N., Bomyea, J., & Beard, C. (2010). The effect of single-session interpretation modification on attention bias in socially anxious individuals. *Journal of Anxiety Disorders, 24,* 178–182.

Beard, C., & Amir, N. (2008). A multi-session interpretation modification program: Changes in interpretation and social anxiety symptoms. *Behaviour Research and Therapy, 46,* 1135–1141.

Bisson, S., & Sears, C. (2006). The effect of depressed mood on the interpretation of ambiguity, with and without negative mood induction. *Cognition and Emotion, 21,* 614–645.

Blackwell, S., & Holmes, E. (2010). Modifying interpretation and imagination in clinical depression: A single case series using cognitive bias modification. *Applied Cognitive Psychology, 24,* 338–350.

Blaxton, T. (1989). Investigating dissociations among memory measures: Support for a transfer appropriate processing framework. *Journal of Experimental Psychology: Learning, Memory, and Cognition, 15,* 657–668.

Calvo, M., Eysenck, M., & Castillo, M. (1997). Interpretation bias in test anxiety: The time course of predictive inferences. *Cognition and Emotion, 11,* 43–63.

Eysenck, M., Mogg, K., May, J., Richards, A., & Mathews, A. (1991). Bias in interpretation of ambiguous sentences related to threat in anxiety. *Journal of Abnormal Psychology, 100,* 144–150.

Fox, E., Russo, R., Bowles, R., & Dutton, K. (2001). Do threatening stimuli draw or hold visual attention in subclinical anxiety? *Journal of Experimental Psychology: General, 130,* 681–700.

Grey, S., & Mathews, A. (2000). Effects of training on interpretation of emotional ambiguity. *Quarterly Journal of Experimental Psychology, 53,* 1143–1162.

Grey, S., & Mathews, A. (2009). Cognitive bias modification—Priming with an ambiguous homograph is necessary to detect an interpretation training effect. *Behavior Therapy and Experimental Psychiatry, 40,* 338–343.

Halberstadt, J. B., Niedenthal, P. M., & Kushner, J. (1995). Resolution of lexical ambiguity by emotional state. *Psychological Science, 6,* 278–282.

Hayes, S., Hirsch, C., Krebs, G., & Mathews, A. (2010). The effects of modifying interpretation bias on worry in Generalized Anxiety Disorder. *Behaviour Research and Therapy, 148,* 171–178.

Hertel, P., & Brozovitch, F. (2010). Cognitive habits and memory distortions in anxiety and depression. *Current Directions in Psychological Science, 19,* 155–160.

Hertel, P., Mathews, A., Peterson, S., & Kintner, K. (2003). Transfer of training emotionally biased interpretations. *Applied Cognitive Psychology, 17,* 775–784.

Hirsch, C., Hayes, S., & Mathews, A. (2009). Looking on the bright side: Accessing benign meanings reduces worry. *Journal of Abnormal Psychology, 118,* 44–54.

Hirsch, C., & Mathews, A. (1997). Interpretative inferences when reading about emotional events. *Behaviour Research and Therapy, 12,* 1123–1132.

Hirsch, C., & Mathews, A. (2000). Impaired positive inferential bias in social phobia. *Journal of Abnormal Psychology, 109*, 705–712.

Hirsch, C. R., Clark, D. M., & Mathews, A. (2006). Imagery and interpretation in social phobia: Support for the combined cognitive biases hypothesis. *Behavior Therapy, 37*, 223–236.

Hirsch, C.R., Mathews, A., & Clark, D.M. (2007). Inducing an interpretation bias changes self-imagery: A preliminary investigation. *Behaviour Reserach & Therapy, 45*, 2173–2181.

Holmes, E. A., Lang, T. J., & Shah, D. M. (2009). Developing interpretation bias modification as a "cognitive vaccine" for depressed mood—Imagining positive events makes you feel better than thinking about them verbally. *Journal of Abnormal Psychology, 118*, 76–88.

Hoppitt, L., Mathews, A., Yiend, J., & Mackintosh, B. (2010a). Cognitive bias modification: The critical role of active training in modifying emotional response. *Behavior Therapy, 41*, 73–81.

Hoppitt, L., Mathews, A., Yiend, J., & Mackintosh, B. (2010b). Cognitive mechanisms underlying the emotional effects of bias modification. *Applied Cognitive Psychology, 24*, 312–325.

Lange, G., Salemink, E., Windey, I., Keijsers, G., Krans, J., Becker, E., & Rinck, M. (2010). Does modified interpretation bias influence automatic avoidance behaviour? *Applied Cognitive Psychology, 24*, 326–337.

Lawson, C., & MacLeod, C. (1999). Depression and the interpretation of ambiguity. *Behaviour Research and Therapy, 37*, 463–474.

Lawson, C., MacLeod, C., & Hammond, G. (2002). Interpretation revealed in the blink of an eye: Depressive bias in the resolution of ambiguity. *Journal of Abnormal Psychology, 111*, 321–328.

Mackintosh, B., Mathews, A., Hoppitt, L., & Eckstein, D. (2010). *Specificity effects in the modification of interpretation bias.* Unpublished manuscript.

Mackintosh, B., Mathews, A., Yiend, J., Ridgeway, V., & Cook, E. (2006). Induced biases in emotional interpretation influence stress vulnerability and endure despite changes in context. *Behavior Therapy, 37*, 209–222.

MacLeod, C., & Cohen, I. L. (1993). Anxiety and the interpretation of ambiguity: A text comprehension study. *Journal of Abnormal Psychology, 102*, 238–247.

MacLeod, C., Rutherford, E., Campbell, L., Ebsworth, G., & Holker, L. (2002). Selective attention and emotional vulnerability: Assessing the causal basis of their association through the experimental manipulation of attentional bias. *Journal of Abnormal Psychology, 111*, 107–123.

Mathews, A., & Mackintosh, B. (1998). A cognitive model of selective processing in anxiety. *Cognitive Therapy and Research, 22*, 539–560.

Mathews, A., & Mackintosh, B. (2000). Induced emotional interpretation bias and anxiety. *Journal of Abnormal Psychology, 109*, 602–615.

Mathews, A., & MacLeod, C. (2005). Cognitive vulnerability to emotional disorders. *Annual Review of Clinical Psychology, 1*, 167–195.

Mathews, A., Ridgeway, V., Cook, E., & Yiend, J. (2007). Inducing a positive interpretation bias reduces trait anxiety. *Journal of Behavior Therapy and Experimental Psychiatry, 38*, 225–236.

Mogg, K., Bradbury, K., & Bradley, B. (2006). Interpretation of ambiguous information in clinical depression. *Behaviour Research and Therapy, 44*, 1411–1419.

Moors, A., & de Houwer, J. (2006). Automaticity: A theoretical and conceptual analysis. *Psychological Bulletin, 132*, 297–326.

Murphy, R., Hirsch, C., Mathews, A., Smith, K., & Clark, D. M. (2007). Facilitating a benign interpretation bias in a high socially anxious population. *Behaviour Research and Therapy, 45*, 1517–1529.

Ouimet, A., Gawronski, B., & Dozois, D. (2009). Cognitive vulnerability to anxiety: A review and integrative model. *Clinical Psychology Review, 29*, 459–470.

Peters, K., Constans, J., & Mathews, A. (2011). Experimental modification of attribution processes. *Journal of Abnormal Psychology, 120*, 168–173.

Richards, A. (2004). Anxiety and the resolution of ambiguity. In J. Yiend (Ed.), *Cognition, emotion and psychopathology* (pp. 130–148). Cambridge, UK: Cambridge University Press.

Richards, A., & French, C. C. (1992). An anxiety-related bias in semantic activation when processing threat/neutral homographs. *Quarterly Journal of Experimental Psychology, 45*, 503–525.

Rude, S., Vladez, C., Odom, S., & Ebrahimi, A. (2003). Negative cognitive biases predict subsequent depression. *Cognitive Therapy and Research, 27*, 415–429.

Salemink, E., van den Hout, M. A., & Kindt, M. (2007a). Trained interpretive bias and anxiety. *Behaviour Research and Therapy, 45*, 329–340.

Salemink, E., van den Hout, M. A., & Kindt, M. (2007b). Trained interpretive bias: Validity and effects on anxiety. *Journal of Behavior Therapy and Experimental Psychiatry, 38*, 212–224.

Salemink, E., van den Hout, M. A., & Kindt, M. (2009). Effects of positive interpretive bias modification in highly anxious individuals. *Journal of Anxiety Disorders, 23*, 676–683.

Salemink, E., van den Hout, M. A., & Kindt, M. (2010a). Generalization of modified interpretive bias across tasks and domains. *Cognition and Emotion, 24*, 453–464.

Salemink, E., van den Hout, M. A., & Kindt, M. (2010b). Trained interpretative bias survives mood change. *Journal of Behaviour Therapy and Experimental Psychiatry, 41*, 310–315.

Schartau, P., Dalgleish, T., & Dunn, B. (2009). Seeing the bigger picture: Training in perspective broadening reduces self-reported affect and psychophysiological response to distressing films and autobiographical memories. *Journal of Abnormal Psychology, 118*, 15–27.

See, J., MacLeod, C., & Bridle, R. (2009). The reduction of anxiety vulnerability through the modification of attentional bias: A real-world study using a home-based cognitive bias modification procedure. *Journal of Abnormal Psychology, 118,* 65–75.

Spielberger, C., Gorsuch, R., Lushene, R., Vagg, P., & Jacobs, G. (1983). *Manual for the State–Trait Anxiety Inventory.* Palo Alto, CA: Consulting Psychologists Press.

Standage, H., Ashwin, C., & Fox, E. (2009). Comparing visual and auditory presentation for the modification of interpretation bias. *Journal of Behavior Therapy and Experimental Psychiatry, 40,* 558–570.

Standage, H., Ashwin, C., & Fox, E. (2010). Is manipulation of mood a critical component of cognitive bias modification procedures? *Behaviour Research and Therapy, 48,* 4–10.

Teachman, B. A., & Addison, L. M. (2008). Training non-threatening interpretations in spider fear. *Cognitive Therapy and Research, 32,* 448–459.

Vassilopoulos, S., Banerjee, R., & Pratzalou, C. (2009). Experimental modification of interpretation bias in socially anxious children: Changes in interpretation, anticipated interpersonal anxiety, and social anxiety symptoms. *Behaviour Research and Therapy, 47,* 1085–1089.

Williams, M., Watts, F., MacLeod, C., & Mathews, A. (1997). *Cognitive psychology and emotional disorders* (2nd ed). Chichester, UK: Wiley.

Wilson, E., MacLeod, C., Mathews, A., & Rutherford, E. (2006). The causal role of interpretative bias in anxiety reactivity. *Journal of Abnormal Psychology, 115,* 103–111.

Yiend, J., & Mathews, A. (2001). Anxiety and attention to threatening pictures. *Quarterly Journal of Experimental Psychology, 54,* 665–681.

Variation on the serotonin transporter gene and bias in the interpretation of ambiguity

Elaine Fox and Helen Standage

Department of Psychology & Centre for Brain Science, University of Essex, Colchester, UK

Previous studies have established that carriers of the low expression form of the serotonin transporter gene have an early attentional bias towards threatening relative to benign or positive information, in contrast to those with a high expression form of this gene. In the present study we extend this finding of a link between variation on the serotonin transporter gene and attentional bias to biases in the interpretation of emotional ambiguity. Specifically, a series of homophones were verbally presented (e.g., PAIN/PANE) and in line with research on attentional bias, participants with a low expression form of the serotonin transporter were more likely to select the threatening meaning more than those with a high expression form of the gene. This is the first evidence that variation on the serotonin transporter gene is correlated with interpretative bias and further strengthens the proposal that genetic variation, like processing bias, may play a role in the development and maintenance of emotional disorders.

Keywords: Cognitive bias; Interpretation bias; Serotonin transporter gene.

Cognitive models of emotional disorders have implicated biases in attention, interpretation, and memory as playing a central role in the maintenance as well as the development of anxiety and depression (e.g., Eysenck, 1992; Mathews & Mackintosh, 1998; Williams, Watts, MacLeod, & Mathews, 1997). Michael Eysenck was among the first to argue that a cognitive approach was valuable when attempting to understand individual differences in anxiety among both normal and clinical populations (Eysenck, 1992) and he laid much of the groundwork for integrating cognitive theories with both theories of emotion and dimensional models of personality traits (Eysenck, 1997). A key notion is that the selective processing of negative, as opposed to positive or benign information, is a key characteristic of anxiety states. Much of the empirical base has focused on biased attention and demonstrates that levels of self-reported trait-anxiety correlate with an enhanced vigilance for threat-related information (e.g., Mathews & MacLeod, 1985) as well as a delay in disengaging attention from threat-related material (Fox, Russo, Bowles, & Dutton, 2001). Anxiety-related attentional biases for threat have been reported in a wide variety of experimental paradigms in both normal and clinically anxious populations (see Bar-Haim, Lamy, Pergamin, Bakermans-Kranenburg, & van Ijzendooen, 2007; Mathews & MacLeod, 2005, for reviews) and have now been shown to play a *causal* role in the development of anxious states

Correspondence should be addressed to Elaine Fox, Department of Psychology, University of Essex, Wivenhoe Park, Colchester CO4 3SQ, UK. E-mail: efox@essex.ac.uk

The authors are grateful to Konstantina Zougkou, Rachel Martin, Andrea Devigili, and Sarah MacKinnon for help with collection of DNA samples. We are also grateful to Peter Issacs of The John Innes Genome Centre, Norwich, who conducted the genotyping analysis. The study was supported by a Research Promotion Fund grant from the University of Essex to EF.

(see Bar-Haim, 2010; Browning, Holmes, & Harmer, 2010; MacLeod, Koster, & Fox, 2009, for reviews).

Another class of experimental paradigms widely used within cognitive psychopathology index biases in *interpretation*, which can be considered as a form of attentional bias to *meaning*. This is illustrated in real-life settings by, for example, entering a room, seeing someone smile, and then interpreting that smile negatively (e.g., as a *smirk*) or positively (e.g., a warm greeting). Such fundamental biases in how we interpret ambiguous social signals can have a profound impact on our social interactions and levels of social anxiety. Once again, Michael Eysenck pioneered a series of early studies to assess anxiety-related biases in the *interpretation* of ambiguity. Pointing out that a lack of warmth from a friend may signify either rejection or a temporary preoccupation, he and his colleagues proposed that anxious individuals systematically attend to the more threatening or negative personal meaning of such ambiguous events (Eysenck, MacLeod, & Mathews, 1987; Mathews, Richards, & Eysenck, 1989).

To test this hypothesis, Eysenck and his colleagues initially developed a series of homophones that had different spellings (e.g., Guilt/Gilt; Pane/Pain) for both a threatening and a neutral meaning (Eysenck et al., 1987). These homophones were read aloud among unambiguous neutral and unambiguous threat-related words and it was found that people reporting high levels of trait anxiety were more likely to select the *threatening* version of the ambiguous homophones to write down relative to less anxious individuals (Eysenck et al., 1987). The ambiguity of homographs—words with the same spelling but different meanings, such as "BEAT"—have also been exploited to test for interpretation bias in anxious individuals. For instance, Richards and French (1992) used homographs with threatening and nonthreatening meaning as primes in a *lexical decision task* in which targets were associated with either the benign or threatening meaning. High anxious participants were faster to endorse the word targets related to the threatening rather than nonthreatening meaning of the priming homograph, relative to nonanxious controls. In a similar vein, Eysenck, Mogg, May, Richards, and Mathews (1991) presented ambiguous sentences such as "The doctor examined little Emily's growth". Participants then had to read a second sentence

that was similar in meaning to the first. The second sentence was either a positive or negative disambiguation of the original sentence e.g., "the doctor measured little Emily's height" or "the doctor measured little Emily's cancer". Eysenck et al. (1991) reported that participants with generalised anxiety disorder (GAD) endorsed more negative sentences as being similar in meaning to the original sentences compared to the control group. Conversely, the nonanxious controls were biased to favouring nonthreatening meaning.

More recent studies of biased interpretation have used descriptions of social situations in which participants have to imagine themselves as the central character. Set points in the social descriptions are left ambiguous and anxious participants are more likely to make negative rather than positive inferences as indicated by their lexical decision times (Hirsch & Mathews, 1997). As with attentional biases, a growing body of evidence indicates that such biases in how everyday events are interpreted play a causal role in the development of anxiety states. Thus, Mathews and Mackintosh (2000) developed a *cognitive bias modification* (CBM) procedure utilising a series of short vignettes designed to induce interpretative biases. They presented 100 scenarios of three lines in length, each followed by a word-stem completion task and comprehension question. Participants were asked to read a series of scenarios such as the following: "Your partner asks you to go to an anniversary dinner that their company is holding. You have not met any of their work colleagues before. Getting ready to go, you think that the new people you will meet will find you?" The options then given were either "bo-ing" (boring) or "fri–dly" (friendly) depending on experimental condition and participants had to fill in the missing letters (Mathews & Mackintosh, 2000). The valence of the word-stem completion task forms the crux of the manipulation. The assumption is that repetitive generation of valenced resolutions to initially ambiguous social scenarios creates a generalised and underlying shift in participants' interpretation bias. Several studies have shown that these procedures are successful in inducing a biased interpretation of ambiguous scenarios that is congruent with the valence of their induction (e.g., Hirsch, Mathews, & Clark, 2007; Holmes, Lang, & Shah, 2009; Mathews & Mackintosh, 2000) and visual and auditory presentations of the scenarios appear to be equally effective (Standage, Ashwin, & Fox, 2009).

The ability to induce selective processing biases in interpretation and attention is a powerful experimental tool to assess the nature of the relationship between cognitive biases and emotional vulnerability (MacLeod et al., 2009). With regard to interpretative bias, several CBM studies have now attempted to establish whether such induced negative or positive biases have a *causal* impact on emotional vulnerability or resilience. A typical interpretative CBM study uses a stress task, such as giving a speech into a camera and then measuring participants' affective responses to the stressor (e.g., Amir, Weber, Beard, Bomyea, & Taylor, 2008). The results show that those participants exposed to *positive* CBM scenarios do direct their processing resources away from the threatening meaning and towards the more benign or positive information present. Those exposed to *negative* CBM conditions show a shift in bias in the opposite—more negative—direction. The most important findings are that these shifts in interpretation bias are associated with differences in emotional vulnerability as measured by responses to stressful situations. For example, Mackintosh, Mathews, Yiend, Ridgeway, and Cook (2006) using a scenario-based form of bias modification reported that positive CBM reduced stress reactivity in participants viewing distressing video clips. Similar findings have been reported by Wilson, MacLeod, Mathews, and Rutherford (2006) using a homograph-based method of induction. Importantly, such reductions in emotional vulnerability induced by positive CBM interventions have been reported to last for up to 4 months (Schmidt, Richey, Buckner, & Timoano, 2009).

In summary, a growing body of empirical evidence indicates that selective processing biases in both interpretation and in attention can maintain as well as induce anxious mood states, which may develop into clinical conditions. Therefore, it is important to try to uncover the factors that lead to the development of such potentially toxic cognitive biases in the first place. There are likely to be several pathways to bias, but one may relate to the balance of neurotransmitters, such as serotonin, in the brain.

The aim of the present study is to combine the investigation of cognitive biases in the interpretation of ambiguity with recent developments in molecular genetics to try and elucidate the neurobiological underpinnings of selective processing biases in more detail. It has been shown that the *serotonin transporter gene* (5-HTT gene) plays an important role in the modulation of mood states in humans and primates and has been associated with increased self-reported levels of neuroticism or trait-anxiety (Lesch et al., 1996). A length polymorphism in the promotor region of this gene results in differences in how efficiently serotonin is cleared from the synaptic cleft. There are two alleles of this gene, the long (L) and the short (S) variant, with each individual carrying two alleles, one from each parent. An individual can therefore be homozygous for the short (S/S) or long (L/L) allele or heterozygous (S/L). Two new variants of the L allele have also been identified—L_G and L_A—and studies have shown that the neurobiological effects of the L_G variant are equivalent to the S allele (Hu et al., 2005). The job of the serotonin transporter is to clear excess serotonin from the synaptic cleft between neurons and the S allele and its equivalents (i.e., S/S, L_G/L_G, or S/L_G) seem to be a low expression form of the gene. In other words, those with this genotype are *less* efficient in clearing excess serotonin leading to higher levels of brain serotonin when compared with those with an intermediate expression genotype (i.e., S/L_A or L_A/L_G). Those with the high expression form of this gene (L_A/L_A) are the most efficient in clearing excess brain serotonin.

In one of the first Gene × Environment interaction studies in psychopathology, it was shown that carriers of the short allele of the serotonin transporter gene were at higher risk of developing clinical depression, but *only* if they were exposed to environmental adversity (Caspi et al., 2003). The link between variation on this gene and reaction to adversity has been controversial and some meta-analyses report no Gene × Environment (GXE) effects (Risch et al., 2009). However, it seems that when studies with detailed and thorough outcome measures of depression are assessed the link is statistically significant (Caspi, Hariri, Holmes, Uher, & Moffitt, 2010) and a more recent meta-analysis including several new studies found strong evidence for GXE effects (Karg, Burmeister, Shedden, & Sen, 2011). Thus, although the low expression form of the serotonin transporter gene does not confer greater risk of emotional disorders per se, it does increase risk when people are exposed to nonsupportive and adverse conditions.

An emerging body of experimental evidence shows that carriers of at least one short form of the 5-HTT gene exhibit enhanced amygdala activation to threatening facial expressions (see Munafò, Brown, & Hariri, 2008, for a meta-analysis) relative to carriers of two long alleles. This suggests that the increased risk of emotional vulnerability may be mediated by an enhanced neural reaction to threat in those with the low expression form of this gene. Furthermore Dannlowski et al. (2010) and Heinz et al. (2005) confirmed that enhanced amygdala activation in short allele carriers is specific to negative stimuli rather than emotionally salient stimuli in general. There is also growing evidence that variation on this gene is associated with attentional biases. The first study sampled a group of psychiatric inpatients and found biased attention on a Stroop task for anxiety-related words in short allele carriers relative to those homozygous for the long allele (Beevers, Gibb, McGeary, & Miller, 2007). In a healthy sample, attentional bias towards fear-relevant stimuli (spiders) was found in short, but not long, allele carriers (Osinsky et al., 2008). Following up on this work but including positive as well as negative stimuli, it was reported that carriers of the S allele selectively allocated attention towards negative pictorial scenes and *avoided* more positive scenes. In marked contrast, carriers of two long alleles showed a propensity to allocate attention towards positive scenes while they avoided the negative material (Fox, Ridgewell, & Ashwin, 2009). Fox et al. (2009) did not distinguish between the L_G and the L_A categories, but in a subsequent study (Pérez-Edgar et al., 2010) it was found that people with a low expression form of the gene (S/S, L_G/L_G, or S/L_G) showed a stronger bias towards angry facial expressions relative to those with an intermediate expression form (S/L_A or L_A/L_G), who in turn showed a stronger allocation of attention to angry faces than those with a high expression form of the gene (L_A/L_A). Finally, a recent study has replicated the Fox et al. (2009) finding that those homozygous for the long allele (L_A/L_A) demonstrate a significant bias *away* from negative material, words in this case (Kwang, Wells, McGeary, Swann, & Beevers, 2010).

Chris Beevers and his colleagues have also found an interesting pattern in that those with the low expression form of the gene were more likely to turn their eye gaze towards *positive*, relative to negative emotional scenes after a long time period (i.e., more than 5 s) had elapsed (Beevers, Ellis, Wells, & McGeary, 2010; Beevers et al., 2011), and one study found that this group took

longer to disengage their attention from both negative and positive stimuli (Beevers, Wells, Ellis, & McGeary, 2009). Thus, normal variation on the serotonin transporter gene is associated with biases in attention in both positive and negative directions. The general pattern of findings can be summarised by the assumption that carriers of the short expression form of the serotonin transporter are characterised by an initial vigilance for threat, and avoidance of positive stimuli, and they may go on to gaze towards positive material at a later time point. This later bias towards positive material may be an attempt to regulate potential negative emotional reactions in low expression carriers (Beevers et al, 2011).

The ability to dynamically allocate attention to emotional cues in the environment is a crucial means of regulating emotion, which is why biased processing of emotional information is a plausible and important potential endophenotype for major depression (Hasler, Drevets, Manji, & Charney, 2004) and for anxiety disorders (Fox, Cahill, & Zougkou, 2010; Mathews & MacLeod, 2005). As we have seen, the propensity to interpret ambiguous information in either a threatening or benign way is also an important mechanism of emotion regulation. However, to the best of our knowledge no study has yet examined variation on the serotonin transporter gene and biases in the interpretation of ambiguity. It seems likely that normal variation on the serotonin transporter gene may lead to different patterns of bias in interpretation as it does in attention (Beevers et al., 2007; Fox et al., 2009). Specifically, we propose that the low expression form of the 5-HTT gene predisposes people to developing a negative interpretation bias for ambiguous emotional material—given the appropriate environmental conditions—which in turn predisposes people to different degrees of anxiety vulnerability. The current study is a preliminary attempt to establish, in a healthy population, whether those with the low expression form of the serotonin transporter gene show a more negative interpretation bias than those with the high expression genotype.

METHOD

Participants

Participants were selected from a larger ongoing study of genotyping and cognitive processing in which samples of DNA in the form of three eyebrow hairs were taken from each participant and assessed for the serotonin polymorphism at the John Innes Genome Centre in Norwich, UK. The selection criteria of the larger study included young adults (18–35) of Caucasian origin and participants were excluded if they had had a previous or current psychiatric diagnosis. Twenty participants who carried the *low* expression version of the gene (S/S, L_G/L_G, S/L_G) and 20 who carried the *high* expression version of the gene (L_A/L_A) were randomly selected from this sample for the current study. All were fluent speakers of English, although not all were native speakers, and the majority was studying at the University of Essex. All participants were paid £2 for their participation in the study.

Materials

A list of 56 words taken from Mathews et al. (1989) was used. This consisted of 28 unambiguous neutral words (e.g., Month, Spade, Willow), 14 unambiguous threat-related words (e.g., Disease, Infirm, Hearse), and 14 homophones having both a threat-related and a neutral meaning (e.g., Die/Dye, Weak/Week). Each threat-related interpretation of the homophone was matched with an unambiguous threat-related word and the neutral interpretation was matched to an unambiguous neutral word in terms of threat ratings. In addition, the homophones, unambiguous threat-related, and neutral words were all matched for word frequency (see Mathews et al., 1989).

These words were presented in a female voice in one of four fixed random orders by means of computer sound files. In addition to the 56 critical words, a list of 10 practice words was presented as in the previous research (Mathews et al., 1989). Each trial began with an alerting tone followed by the pronunciation of a word, a 2 s gap, and then the repeated pronunciation of the same word again. There then followed a 10 s silent period during which participants wrote down each word in an answer book.

Procedure

All testing took place in groups of about 10 participants. Participants were seated at individual tables well apart from each other and the

nature of the study was explained to them. Each participant was then asked to sign an informed consent form and complete the trait and state version of the Spielberger Trait-State Anxiety Inventory (STAI; Spielberger, Gorsuh, Lushene, Vagg, & Jacobs, 1993) and the Beck Depression Inventory (BDI; Beck, Steer, & Brown, 1996). Each participant then completed a series of visual perception tasks that were unrelated to the present study. This consisted of rating a number of artistic images for how "uncomfortable" they were and this phase took about 10 min. Following this, one of the prerecorded lists was then presented. The nature of the task was explained and began with the presentation of 10 practice trials. Upon completion of the practice trials, the full list of 56 critical words was presented. As in the Mathews et al. (1989) study, participants were given the following (slightly modified) instructions:

> In this experiment you are going to hear a series of words. A warning beep will be sounded followed a word. This word will then be repeated. Following the second presentation of the word a tone will sound. When you hear the tone please write down the word you heard on your answer sheets. A second tone will then be sounded which indicates that the trial is over and you should stop writing. There will then be a few seconds break before you hear the next word. Please make sure that you write each word on the appropriate line numbered 1 to 56.

RESULTS

The low expression and high expression groups did not differ on trait-anxiety, state-anxiety, or self-reported depression. There were also equal numbers of male and female participants in each group (see Table 1).

Our participants were relatively accurate in spelling the unambiguous threat-related words (80.2%) and neutral words (81.3%) and ambiguous homophones (77.5%), with no difference in accuracy across the three types of words, $F(2, 78) < 1$, $MSE = 214.3$. The percentage of correct spellings that corresponded to the more threatening of the two meanings for homophones was then calculated and these are shown in Figure 1 for each of the genotyping groups.

TABLE 1

Mean demographic information (means and standard deviations) for the low expression (S/S, L_G/L_G, or S/L_G) and high expression (L_A/L_A) genotyping groups; there were no between-group differences

	Low expression (n = 20)	High expression (n = 20)	t(38)	χ^2(1)
Trait anxiety	44.1 (7.5)	40.7 (10.4)	1.2*	—
Depression	7.8 (3.0)	6.7 (4.0)	0.9*	—
State anxiety	38.5 (10.5)	38.3 (12.3)	0.05*	—
Male/female	5/15	4/16	—	.143*

* = nonsignificant difference (α = .05).

As can be seen in Figure 1, all means were above 50%, indicating that the threatening meaning was dominant for both genotype groups. Our a priori prediction that the low expression group would select significantly more threatening spellings (68.9%) than the high expression group (60.1) was confirmed by an independent samples t-test, $t(38) = 2.0$, $p < .03$, one-tailed. Because of the known association between trait-anxiety and biased interpretation, we conducted two partial correlations. We found that trait-anxiety did not correlate with a negative interpretation bias when controlling for genotype group, $r = .09$, whereas there was a trend for genotype to correlate with a negative interpretation bias while controlling for trait-anxiety, $r = -.29$, $p < .08$.

DISCUSSION

We hypothesised that carriers of the low expression form of the serotonin transporter gene might predispose people to developing a negative inter-

pretation bias for ambiguous emotional material. In a standard homophone interpretation task (Eysenck et al., 1987; Mathews et al., 1989), we found evidence that this was indeed the case. Those with the low expression form of the serotonin transporter gene presented more negative interpretations of ambiguous homophones than did those with the high expression form of the gene. Thus, normal variation on the serotonin transporter gene was related to significant differences in the interpretation of ambiguity.

These results are consistent with the growing evidence for associations between variants of the serotonin transporter polymorphism and attentional bias towards emotional stimuli (e.g., Beevers et al., 2007, 2009, Beevers et al., 2011; Fox et al., 2009; Kwang et al., 2010). Individuals with a low expression form of the serotonin transporter gene were more likely to interpret ambiguous homophones in a negative way when compared with those who had the high expression form, even though these samples did not differ in terms of self-reported anxiety or depression. Our sample size was not large enough to fully examine the possible additive and/or interactive effects of self-reported anxiety and genetic variation. Nevertheless, partial correlations indicated that genotype was driving the interpretation bias rather than self-reported trait-anxiety, consistent with previous evidence that cognitive biases provide better indicators of emotional vulnerability than self-report measures (Fox et al., 2010). The increased propensity to interpret ambiguity in a negative way shown by short allele carriers is of interest and suggests that this polymorphism may be an important factor to consider in models of vulnerability to psychopathology. This preliminary

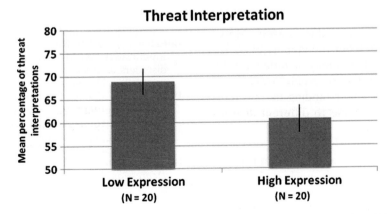

Figure 1. Mean percentage of threat interpretations for the low expression (S/S, L_G/L_G, or S/L_G) and high expression (L_A/L_A) genotyping groups.

observation suggests that genotype might make a unique contribution to interpretation bias independent of the recognised relationship between trait anxiety and interpretation style established by previous research (e.g., Eysenck et al., 1991).

There are a number of limitations of this study. First, as noted previously, our sample size was small ($n = 40$), with just 20 in each genotyping group. It is important to replicate these effects with larger sample sizes before concluding that the serotonin transporter gene is associated with different patterns of interpretation bias. Low statistical power has been a problem in this field of research (see Munafo et al., 2008) and it is unfortunate that we were unable to test a larger sample. Munafo et al. (2008) suggest a sample size of at least 70 in candidate gene studies and therefore we cannot draw definitive conclusions until larger studies are conducted. Nevertheless, the present results provide preliminary evidence that different alleles of this gene may be related to interpretation bias, which adds to previous findings showing a relationship between these alleles and attention bias. A second limitation of this study is the fact that only negative homophones were included so that valence and arousal were confounded. Hence, no conclusions regarding bias towards positive interpretations can be drawn from these data. A further limitation relates to the fact that we examined just one gene, when several genes are likely to be involved in the development of cognitive biases and enhanced vulnerability to emotional disorders. In spite of this limitation, however, several studies that utilise sensitive outcome measures like attention biases or measures of brain activity have consistently shown that the serotonin transporter gene plays an important role in determining reactivity to emotional events (Caspi et al., 2010). Given the growing evidence that negative biases in interpretation can induce anxiety (Mathews & MacLeod, 2002), our preliminary evidence that biases in interpretation may be influenced by normal variation on the serotonin transporter may be important in understanding the mechanisms that predispose people to different degrees of anxiety vulnerability.

The mechanism underlying the association between variation on the serotonin transporter gene and cognitive biases is unclear. The low expression form of the gene (S/S, L_G/L_G, or S/L_G) leads to higher levels of brain serotonin since excess levels are not efficiently cleared away from the synaptic cleft. This excess serotonin may render people more sensitive to environmental contingencies (Belsky & Pleuss, 2009; Caspi et al., 2010), and this enhanced sensitivity may be an important part of the mechanism that leads to potentially toxic biases in attention and interpretation.

To conclude, there is now a substantial body of evidence that cognitive biases are important factors in determining emotional vulnerability and resilience. A tendency to orient attention towards threat and to interpret ambiguous social situations in a negative manner can lead to a highly negative encoding of environmental events, which in turn can set people on a course of developing serious problems with anxiety and depression. We suggest that incorporating a genetic level of analysis in these cognitive studies may be very informative and should facilitate the development of more comprehensive and integrated models of why some people thrive and some struggle under fairly similar circumstances. In particular, examining whether variation on the serotonin transporter gene moderates the effect of psychological interventions such as cognitive behaviour therapy (CBT) or cognitive bias modification (CBM) procedures is an important focus for future research. Integrating cognitive psychology and molecular genetics in this way may help to identify those individuals most likely to benefit from therapeutic interventions.

REFERENCES

Amir, N., Weber, J. G., Beard, C., Bomyea, J., & Taylor, C. (2008). The effect of a single session attention modification program on response to a public speaking challenge in socially anxious individuals. *Journal of Abnormal Psychology*, 117(4), 860–868.

Bar-Haim, Y. (2010). Research review: Attention Bias Modification (ABM): A novel treatment for anxiety disorders. *Journal of Child Psychology and Psychiatry*, 51(8), 859–870.

Bar-Haim, Y., Lamy, D., Pergamin, L., Bakermans-Kranenburg, M. J., & van Ijzendoorn, M. H. (2007). Threat-related attentional bias in anxious and nonanxious individuals: A meta-analytic study. *Psychological Bulletin*, 133(1), 1–24.

Beck, A. T., Steer, R. A., & Brown, G. K. (1996). *Beck Depression Inventory–manual* (2nd ed). San Antonio, TX: Psychological Corporation.

Beevers, C. G., Ellis, A. J., Wells, T. T., & McGeary, J. E. (2010). Serotonin transporter gene promotor region polymorphism and selective processing of emotional images. *Biological Psychology*, 83, 260–265.

Beevers, C. G., Gibb, B., McGreary, J. E., & Miller, I. W. (2007). Serotonin transporter genetic variation and biased attention for emotional word stimuli among psychiatric inpatients. *Journal of Abnormal Psychology, 116*, 208–212.

Beevers, C. G., Marti, C. N., Lee, H. J., Stote, D. L., Ferrell, R. E., Hariri, A. R., & Telch, M. J. (2011). Associations between serotonin transporter gene promotor region (5-HTTLPR) polymorphism and gaze bias for emotional information. *Journal of Abnormal Psychology, 120*, 187–197.

Beevers, C. G., Wells, T. T., Ellis, A. J., & McGeary, J. E. (2009). Association of the serotonin transporter gene promoter region (5-HTTLPR) polymorphism with biased attention for emotional stimuli. *Journal of Abnormal Psychology, 118*(3), 670–681.

Belsky, J., & Pleuss, M. (2009). Beyond diathesis stress: Differential susceptibility to environmental influences. *Psychological Bulletin, 135*, 885–908.

Browning, M., Holmes, E. A., & Harmer, C. (2010). The modification of attentional bias to emotional information: A review of techniques, mechanisms and relevance to emotional disorders. *Cognitive, Affective and Behavioral Neuroscience, 10*, 8–20.

Caspi, A., Hariri, A. R., Holmes, A., Uher, R., & Moffitt, T. E. (2010). Genetic sensitivity to the environment: The case of the serotonin transporter gene and its implications for studying complex diseases and traits. *American Journal of Psychiatry, 167*(5), 509–527.

Caspi, A., Sugden, K., Moffitt, T. E., Taylor, A., Craig, I. W., Harrington, H., et al. (2003). Influence of life stress on depression: Moderation by a polymorphism in the 5-HTT gene. *Science, 301*(5631), 386–389.

Dannlowski, U., Konrad, C., Kugel, H., Zwitserlood, P., Domschke, K., Schöning, S., et al. (2010). Emotion specific modulation of automatic amygdala responses by 5-HTTLPR genotype. *NeuroImage, 53*(3), 893–898.

Eysenck, M. W. (1992). *Anxiety: The cognitive perspective.* Hove, UK: Lawrence Erlbaum Associates Ltd.

Eysenck, M. W. (1997). *Anxiety and cognition: A unified theory.* Hove, UK: Psychology Press.

Eysenck, M. W., MacLeod, C., & Mathews, A. (1987). Cognitive functioning and anxiety. *Psychological Research, 49*, 189–195.

Eysenck, M. W., Mogg, K., May, J., Richards, A., & Mathews, A. (1991). Bias in interpretation of ambiguous sentences related to threat in anxiety. *Journal of Abnormal Psychology, 100*(2), 144–150.

Fox, E., Cahill, S., & Zougkou, K. (2010). Preconscious processing biases predict emotional reactivity to stress. *Biological Psychiatry, 67*, 371–377.

Fox, E., Ridgewell, A., & Ashwin, C. (2009). Looking on the bright side: Biased attention and the human serotonin transporter gene. *Proceedings of the Royal Society: Biological Sciences, 276*, 1747–1751.

Fox, E., Russo, R., Bowles, R., & Dutton, K. (2001). Do threatening stimuli draw or hold visual attention in subclinical anxiety? *Journal of Experimental Psychology: General, 130*(4), 681–700.

Hasler, G., Drevets, W. C., Manji, H. K., & Charney, D. S. (2004). Discovering endophenotypes for major depression. *Neuropsychopharmacology: Official Publication of the American College of Neuropsychopharmacology, 29*(10), 1765–1781.

Heinz, A., Braus, D. F., Smolka, M. N., Wrase, J., Puls, I., Hermann, D., et al. (2005). Amygdala-prefrontal coupling depends on a genetic variation of the serotonin transporter. *Nature Neuroscience, 8*(1), 20–21.

Hirsch, C. R., & Mathews, A. (1997). Interpretative inferences when reading about emotional events. *Behaviour Research and Therapy, 35*(12), 1123–1132.

Hirsch, C. R., Mathews, A., & Clark, D. M. (2007). Inducing an interpretation bias changes self-imagery: A preliminary investigation. *Behaviour Research and Therapy, 45*, 2173–2181.

Holmes, E. A., Lang, T. J., & Shah, D. M. (2009). Developing interpretation bias modification as a "cognitive vaccine" for depressed mood—Imagining positive events makes you feel better than thinking about them verbally. *Journal of Abnormal Psychology, 118*(1), 76–88.

Hu, X., Oroszi, G., Chun, J., Smith, T. L., Goldman, D., & Schuckit, M. A. (2005). An expanded evaluation of the relationship of four alleles to the level of response to alchohol and the alchoholism risk. *Alchoholism: Clinical and Experimental Research, 29*, 8–16.

Karg, K., Burmeister, M., Shedden, K., & Sen, S. (2011). The serotonin transporter promotor variant (5-HTTLPR), stress, and depression meta-analysis revisited: Evidence of genetic moderation. *Archives of General Psychiatry, 68*, 444–454.

Kwang, T., Wells, T. T., McGeary, J. E., Swann, W. B., & Beevers, C. G. (2010). Association of the serotonin transporter promoter region polymorphism with biased attention for negative word stimuli. *Depression and Anxiety, 27*(8), 746–751.

Lesch, K. P., Bengel, D., Heils, A., Sabol, S. Z., Greenberg, B. D., Petri, S., et al. (1996). Association of anxiety-related traits with a polymorphism in the serotonin transporter gene regulatory region. *Science, 274*, 1527–1531.

Mackintosh, B., Mathews, A., Yiend, J., Ridgeway, V., & Cook, E. (2006). Induced biases in emotional interpretation influence stress vulnerability and endure despite changes in context. *Behaviour Therapy, 37*, 209–222.

MacLeod, C., Koster, E. H. W., & Fox, E. (2009). Whither cognitive bias modification research? Commentary on the special section articles. *Journal of Abnormal Psychology, 118*(1), 89–99.

Mathews, A., & Mackintosh, B. (1998). A cognitive model of selective processing in anxiety. *Cognitive Therapy and Research, 22*(6), 539–560.

Mathews, A., & Mackintosh, B. (2000). Induced emotional interpretation bias and anxiety. *Journal of Abnormal Psychology, 109*(4), 602–615.

Mathews, A., & MacLeod, C. (1985). Selective processing of threat cues in anxiety states. *Behaviour Research and Therapy, 23*, 563–569.

Mathews, A., & MacLeod, C. (2002). Induced processing biases have causal effects on anxiety. *Cognition and Emotion, 16*(3), 331–354.

Mathews, A., & MacLeod, C. (2005). Cognitive vulnerability to emotional disorders. *Annual Review of Clinical Psychology, 1,* 167–195.

Mathews, A., Richards, A., & Eysenck, M. W. (1989). The interpretation of homophones related to threat in anxiety states. *Journal of Abnormal Psychology, 98,* 31–34.

Munafo, M. R., Brown, S. M., & Hariri, A. R. (2008). Serotonin transporter (5-HTTLPR) genotype and amygdala activation: A meta-analysis. *Biological Psychiatry, 63,* 852–857.

Osinsky, R., Reuter, M., Kupper, Y., Schmitz, A., Kozyra, E., Alexander, N., & Hennig, J. (2008). Variation in the serotonin transporter gene modulates selective attention to threat. *Emotion, 8,* 584–588.

Pérez-Edgar, K., Bar-Haim, Y., McDermott, J. M., Gorodetsky, E., Hodgkinson, C. A., Goldman, D., et al. (2010). Variations in the serotonin-transporter gene are associated with attention bias patterns to positive and negative emotion faces. *Biological Psychology, 83*(3), 269–271.

Richards, A., & French, C. C. (1992). An anxiety-related bias in semantic activation when processing threat/neutral homographs. *Quarterly Journal of Experimental Psychology, 45A*(3), 503–525.

Risch, N., Herrell, R., Lehner, T., Liang, K.-Y., Eaves, L., Hoh, J., et al. (2009). Interaction between the serotonin transporter gene (5-HTTLPR), stressful life events, and risk of depression. *Journal of the American Medical Association, 301*(23), 2462–2471.

Schmidt, N. B., Richey, J. A., Buckner, J. D., & Timoano, K. R. (2009). Attention training for generalised social anxiety disorder. *Journal of Abnormal Psychology, 118*(1), 5–14.

Spielberger, C. D., Gorsuh, R. L., Lushene, R. E., Vagg, P. R., & Jacobs, G. A. (1983). *Manual for the State-Trait Anxiety Inventory.* Palo Alto: CA: Consulting Psychologists Press.

Standage, H., Ashwin, C., & Fox, E. (2009). Comparing visual and auditory presentation for the modification of interpretation bias. *Journal of Behavior Therapy and Experimental Psychiatry, 40,* 558–570.

Williams, J. M. G., Watts, F. N., MacLeod, C., & Mathews, A. (1997). *Cognitive psychology and emotional disorders.* Chichester, UK: Wiley.

Wilson, E., MacLeod, C., Mathews, A., & Rutherford, E. (2006). The causal role of interpretative bias in anxiety reactivity. *Journal of Abnormal Psychology, 115*(1), 103–111.